In No Time

Linux

In No Time

Linux

Ute Hertzog

Prentice
Hall

AN IMPRINT OF PEARSON EDUCATION

PEARSON EDUCATION LIMITED

Head Office:
Edinburgh Gate
Harlow CM20 2JE
Tel: +44 (0)1279 623623
Fax: +44 (0)1279 431059

London Office:
128 Long Acre
London WC2E 9AN
Tel: +44 (0)20 7447 2000
Fax: +44 (0)20 7240 5771

First published in Germany in 1997

© Pearson Education Limited 2001

ISBN 0130-31976-7

First published in 1997 as *Linux*
by Markt & Technik Buch und Software-Verlag GmbH
Martin-Kollar-Straße 10–12
D-81829 Munich
Germany

This edition published 2001 by Pearson Education

British Library Cataloguing in Publication Data

A CIP catalogue record for this book can be obtained from the British Library.

10   9   8   7   6   5   4   3   2   1

Translated and typeset by Cybertechnics, Sheffield.
Printed and bound in Great Britain by Henry Ling Ltd, at The Dorset Press, Dorchester, Dorset.

The publishers' policy is to use paper manufactured from sustainable forests.

Contents

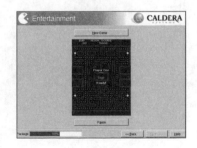

5 Working with files, directories 174

6 KDE applications and utilities 232

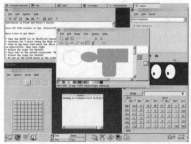

7 Managing the system 290

Dear Reader,

A year ago no one would have believed that Linux for beginners would be 'easy'. Yet with the increasingly simple installation, and thanks to the award-winning KDE graphic interface, the system has become much more user-friendly.

In Linux you will find everything you need for everyday work – professional office programs as well as high-quality internet software. And it won't cost you a penny.

In this book twelve detailed illustrated workshops guide you step-by-step through the installation of Caldera OpenLinux, while the basics and first steps give a practical insight into working with the operating system and the KDE graphic user interface. You will be introduced to system and data administration, and shown how to install software, how to work with the StarOffice package, how to use the internet or set up a network. There is also a troubleshooting section and a small glossary.

It doesn't really matter whether you work through individual chapters or the entire book – you will find Linux is open and friendly, yet highly professional. In fact, discover Linux and discover your possibilities!

Have fun with Linux and with this book!

Ute Hertzog

The keyboard

The following three pages show the structure of your computer keyboard. Most of the keys operate exactly as keys on a typewriter, however, there are a few additional keys, designed especially for computer work. See for yourself.

Typewriter keys

Use these keys exactly as you do on a typewriter.
The Enter key is also used to send commands to your computer.

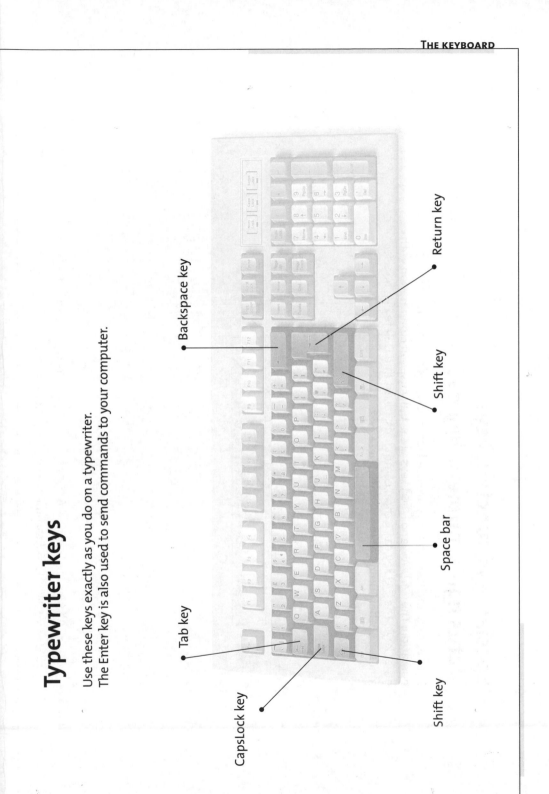

Tab key

CapsLock key

Backspace key

Return key

Shift key

Space bar

Shift key

Special keys, function keys, status lights, numeric key pad

Special keys and function keys are used for special tasks in computer operation. The Ctrl, Alt and AltGr keys are usually used in combination with other keys. The Esc key can cancel commands. Insert and Delete can be used, amongst other things, to insert and delete text.

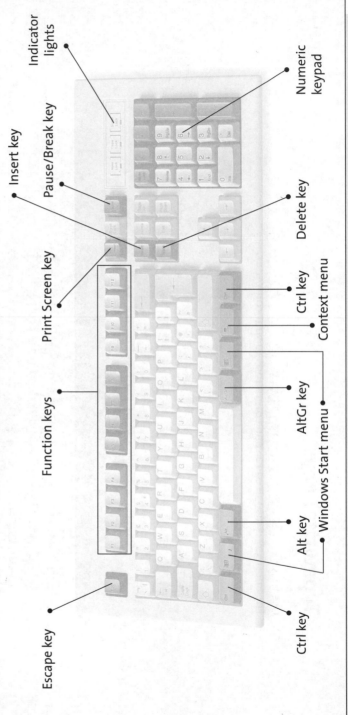

Escape key

Function keys

Print Screen key

Insert key

Pause/Break key

Indicator lights

Numeric keypad

Delete key

Ctrl key

Context menu

AltGr key

Windows Start menu

Alt key

Ctrl key

Navigation keys

These keys are used to move around the screen.

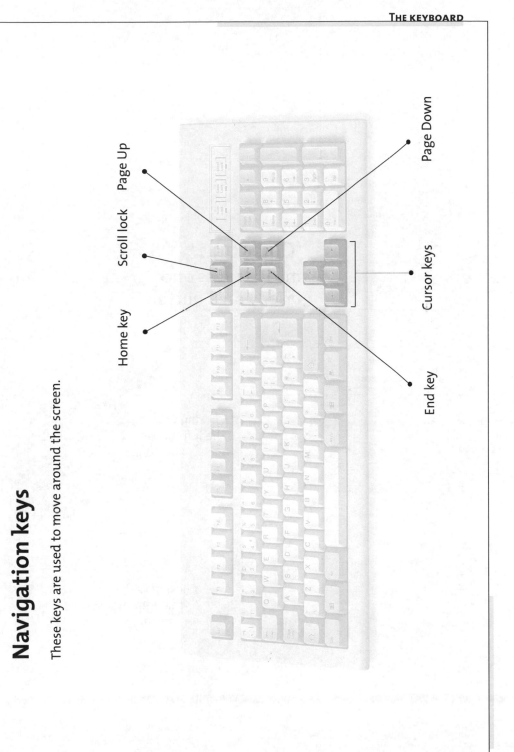

Scroll lock Page Up

Home key

Page Down

Cursor keys

End key

'Click on...'

means press once
briefly on a button.

Clicking with
the left mouse
button...

Clicking with
the right mouse
button...

'Double-click on...'

means press the left button
twice briefly in quick
succession.

Double-clicking

'Drag...'

means click on an object with the left
mouse button, keep the button
pressed, move the mouse and drag the
item to another position.

Drag

What's in this chapter:

This chapter explains the installation of Linux. When you have read this chapter, you will be able to set up OpenLinux 2.4 by Caldera Systems on your PC. You will learn how to select a language and a mouse, and how to define the type of installation and the hard drive. You will also understand what a Linux partition is and how to format it. You will be able to specify the extent of the installation, and determine keyboard, graphics card, monitor and video mode type. You will also be able to define the Superuser password and create other users. You will learn about address network definition and how to select select a time zone. By the end of the chapter, you will have completed the installation and will have a fully functional Linux system.

You are going to learn about:

Installation requirements

The graphic installation interface of OpenLinux 2.4 means it almost installs itself. Even if yours is an older computer, for example a 80486 processor, 16MB RAM will be sufficient. So that you can install and use the many programs supplied with the operating system, your hard drive should be at least 500MB. Of course, your PC will also require floppy and  CD-ROM drives. These are minimum requirements for a modern computer.

As a beginner it is recommended that you install Linux on a separate hard drive. This chapter assumes that you install Linux on the entire hard drive.

> **TIP**
>
> If you have no experience of working with a mouse and graphic user interface at all, you should first read chapter 2, 'Basics and first steps'. Alternatively you could read through the appropriate steps as you work through the installation process.

Partitioning before installation

You may already have Windows 95 or 98 installed on your system and may not want to remove it until you have tried Linux or you may wish to work with both systems. To keep both systems, you will have to divide the hard disk between the systems. This is called partitioning.

There are three ways of installing Linux on a hard drive.

➡ The first scenario is when setting up Linux on a separate hard disk. In this case the system can be installed as described below.

➡ The second only occurs when there is a large hard disk on which another operating system such as Microsoft Windows 95 is already installed. Sometimes, the first operating system is installed but there is still enough space on the hard drive. This means it was assigned a partition which did not take up the entire hard disk. You could also install Linux directly. The installation system recognises free space and recommends that Linux be installed there. The free hard drive space will then be used for the Linux partition.

➡ The third situation is if your current operating system is using the entire hard drive. A special program such as *Partition Magic* from PowerQuest is required to reduce the partition of the first operating system. The hard drive space created during this process can then be used to install Linux.

This program has additional manuals, and the instructions in the manual should be followed to the letter in order to avoid damaging or destroying your operating system. Furthermore, a backup of important data of the current operating system is required!

If you have the full version of Caldera OpenLinux you will find a scaled-down version of Partition Magic on the CD-ROM labelled 'Commercial Packages' in the \col\winsetup\pm CD-ROM directory path. Open the *readme.txt* file in Microsoft Internet Explorer and follow the instructions exactly.

11

Modifying partitions with the *fips* tool

Alternatively, you could use the *FIPS* tool supplied with Caldera OpenLinux 2.4 to reduce an existing DOS or Windows partition. This tool is located in the \co1\tools\fips directory on the installation CD-ROM. Use the following procedure:

System (C:) Properties

General | Tools | Sharing

Label: **SYSTEM**

Type: Local Disk
File system: FAT32

■ Used space: 1,219,338,240 bytes 1.13GB
□ Free space: 4,379,316,224 bytes 4.07GB

Capacity: 5,598,654,464 bytes 5.21GB

Drive C   Disk Cleanup...

OK   Cancel   Apply

1. Check in DOS or Windows to see the size to which you need to modify the available memory space of the partition. Note the required value. For example, if you have 4GB available in Windows 98, this can be reduced to 2GB, which can then be used for the installation of Linux.

You can check the amount of hard drive space available by opening Microsoft Windows Explorer.

1 Click on the drive letter for the hard disk.

TIP The occupied and free memory space give the total capacity of the hard drive.

2 The free and occupied space on the hard drive is displayed in the General tab.

2. Run the *SCANDISK* and *DEFRAG* tools on the Windows or DOS partition to be reduced. Data will then be written at the start of the partition, and memory space will be available at the end.

These tools can be started by opening Microsoft Windows Explorer.

1 Click on the drive letter for the hard disk.

2 Then click on the *Extras* tab.

3 First click on the *Check Now* button.

4 Then click on the *Optimise Now* button.

3. Create a bootable DOS disk in DOS or in the Windows DOS box using the command 'format a: /s'. Copy the *FIPS.EXE, RESTORRB.EXE* and *ERRORS.TXT* files from the CD-ROM directory specified above onto this disk.

4. Reboot your machine and call up the *FIPS* program. The program asks you which partitions you wish to modify if there are several partitions.

5. You should answer *Y(es)* when asked if you wish to make a backup copy on disk of your existing partition table.

CAUTION

If the partition modification is unsuccessful, the original hard drive settings can easily be restored. Insert the disk and click on the *RESTORRB* command. The partition table is restored to its original settings almost immediately. This should be executed only if the partition table modification is unsuccessful.

6. *FIPS* then prompts you to modify the partition to suit you. Use the cursor keys and confirm your alteration by pressing ⏎.

7. Remove the disk when the program has finished. Restart Windows in DOS mode and check to see if the system still works. Then check the available memory space on-it should be as you specified.

Consult documentation of the *FIPS* tool if any problems arise. This is located in the same directory as the program itself on the CD-ROM in the extensive *FIPS.DOC* file.

An irremediable message can arise with FIPS as the tool is still in its embryonic stages. All that remains for you to do is work out the partition table and acquire a commercial tool such as *Partition Magic*.

Creating a boot disk

Installation can usually be started using a bootable installation CD-ROM. If this is not possible using your CD-ROM device, you can easily create your own boot disk.

A Caldera OpenLinux 2.4 boot disk contains the following files:

A README.txt file is also located on the
installation CD-ROM in the *\col\launch\floppy*
directory with advice on how to create an
installation disk.

An installation disk is created as follows:

1 Insert an empty disk in the
floppy drive.

2 Insert the installation
CD-ROM.

3 If the CD does not automatically start
with a menu display, open Microsoft
Windows Explorer.

4 Click on the
winsetup.exe file in the
winsetup directory.

5 Select *Create Install Disk*,
then *Install Lizard*.

6 Wait until the disk has
finished, then click on *done*.

7 Close the Setup
window.

8 Label the disk *Caldera
OpenLinux 2.4 boot disk*.

Starting the installation

Before you start the installation of Linux, have the manuals for your PC, monitor, keyboard, printer and network card (if necessary) ready. Then you can give any information which may be required by the installation program.

TIP

An arrow is shown in one corner of the disk. Insert the disk so the arrow points towards the drive and slide it into the drive carefully.

1 Now we can begin: place the OpenLinux boot disk in the floppy drive, marked 'OpenLinux 2.4 Boot/ Install Disk'.

WHAT'S THIS?

A boot disk is a disk containing a small part of the operating system. This disk can start a PC on which there is no operating system installed. The program with which to install the operating system is also located on the boot disk, Linux in this case.

Every computer requires an **operating system** before you can begin to work with it. The operating system is the medium between the PC hardware and the actual applications, for example a word processing system. If for example you use the *Print* function in a text editor, the operating system receives the command to print the file. It passes on this command to the hardware, in this case the printer, and the print process is carried out.

2 Now turn on your PC and monitor.

3 As soon as the PC starts you can open the CD-ROM drive. Press the rectangular button on the CD-ROM drive which has a small symbol with an upward facing arrow. Place the disc marked 'OpenLinux Installation CD 2.4 – CD 1' in the drive and close it again. Close the drive by pressing the same button again as above.

CAUTION
A mini operating system is created to start installation. Do not interrupt this under any circumstances. Wait for the prompt to appear.

TIP
If you have a soundcard and speakers installed on your PC, you will hear a loud tone as soon as the soundcard is recognised.

A? Select Language   CALDERA

Language Selection

Please select your language.

Bitte wählen Sie die gewünschte Sprache aus.

Sélectionnez votre langage.

Scegliete la sua lingua.

  • English
  ○ Deutsch
  ○ Francais
  ○ Italiano

LIZARD Version: 20000223-1   Next>>   Help

4 After a few seconds you will see the first window of the installation program. The entire installation is carried out using graphic windows.

You can return to the previous window at any point during installation using the *Back* button. Move to the button using the arrow keys and press *Enter* ⏎.

> **TIP**
>
> If your mouse pointer does not yet react to movements of the mouse, you will have to move in the window using the keyboard. Simply use the cursor keys to move through the selection menu. Move up with the up arrow ⏶ key, down with the down arrow ⏷ key, left with the left arrow ⬅ key, and right with the right arrow ➔ key.

As soon as the mouse is activated, you can also press buttons by clicking with the left mouse button.

5 ◉ English

Once you have decided on the language to be used, move to your selection using the ⏷ key. If the round button before the language of your choice is marked with a black dot, then press Enter ⏎ to confirm your selection. If the language of your choice has not been activated, move using the cursor keys until the correct selection is activated.

TIP
The help function is always located in the lower right-hand corner of the window during installation. Activate help by moving to the *Help* button using the cursor keys and then press ⏎.

6 You can call the help function at any time. This provides the appropriate guidance for each window.

As soon as the mouse is active, you can also press the help button with the left mouse button.

In the following pages you will find detailed installation help displayed in the right-hand side of the window.

A new window appears immediately after language selection – if you have chosen English, then the installation continues in English. Move to the required choice using the cursor keys.

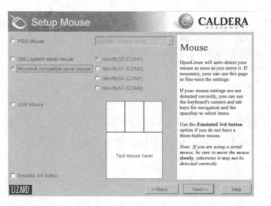

Now the mouse has to be adjusted. Simply move the mouse around on the desk. You should see a mouse pointer in the form of a small arrow on the screen.

Check the settings in the window containing your mouse details. If you are unsure as to which type of mouse you are using, use the mouse handbook provided. Read through the information on your mouse and compare the settings.

If the settings are not correct, modify them accordingly. The mouse is selected when the round button in front is marked with a dot, as in the *Language Selection* window. For example:

⊙ PS/2 Mouse

If you are using a PS/2 mouse with a wheel, then use the selection list on the right next to the *PS/2 mouse* display. Click on the small black arrow next to the list field with the left mouse button.

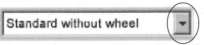

Then click on the appropriate selection with the left mouse button. It will be displayed in the selection window.

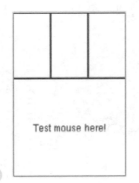

3 If the settings correspond to your type of mouse, you can test it again. Move the mouse to the dark grey test field marked *Test mouse here!* Click once on each of the mouse buttons. The buttons pressed by you will immediately be indicated as black on the mouse shown on the left of the test field.

Your mouse is now ready and can be used for further installation! If you experience installation difficulties in activating the mouse, read the chapter in Troubleshooting entitled *Installation problems*.

Next >>

4 If you are satisfied with the installation of the mouse, click on the *Next* button.

Now you should determine which type of keyboard you are using.

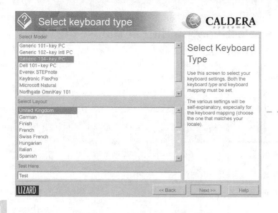

1 In the window now displayed you will be asked to enter the type of keyboard. If you have a special type of keyboard, select the *Generic 104-key PC* and *British English* as the language.

2 Click on the appropriate selection.

3 In the lower part of the window you can test to see whether your selection is correct: press any key.

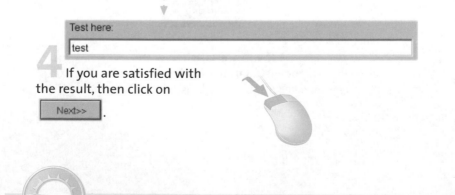

4 If you are satisfied with the result, then click on

Next>> .

Modifying graphics settings

This section is somewhat harder to follow if you are not familiar with your hardware. It is easier if you use the manual provided.

The **graphics card** is the interface between your screen (or monitor) and the computer itself. It passes on data from the computer to the screen and ensures it is displayed correctly. Your monitor plug will be connected to a corresponding 'socket' on your graphics card.

Your graphics card should usually be recognised by the system and correctly identified in this window. Check the details using the manual if necessary.

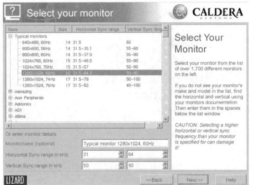

1 Now you must select your type of monitor. The installation program contains a long list of monitor manufacturers at this point. You can search for the manufacturer of your monitor using the scroll bar on the right-hand side of the selection window

Monitor is just another name for the display screen. The name of the manufacturer and/or type of monitor is indicated somewhere at the edge of the screen. Otherwise you should consult your monitor manual.

A scrollbar is located on the left-hand side of the selection window.

This means that not all the selection options can be displayed in one window. The list contains more entries than you can currently see. You should modify the window view using the scrollbar.

2 Click on the grey scrollbar button with the left mouse button.

3 Keep the mouse button pressed and drag the grey button downwards.

Now search for the name of your monitor manufacturer.

4 Click on the plus sign before the name of the manufacturer with the left mouse button, for example:

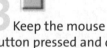

This means that there are more details underneath the entry. When clicked, the plus sign becomes a minus sign, and a sub-menu of different selection options for this manufacturer name is displayed.

5 Click on the appropriate monitor type.

Alternatively, and more tediously, you could type in your selection manually in the fields in the lower window area:

Or enter monitor details:		
Monitorname (optional)	Typical monitor 1280x1024, 60Hz	
Horizontal Sync range in kHz	31	64
Vertical Sync range in kHz	50	90

CAUTION

If you type in the details (for example, if your monitor type is not listed), then consult your manual for advice first. Incorrect entries can damage your monitor or graphics card in extreme cases.

6 Click in the entry field.

Use the ⌫ key to delete the existing settings. Type in your own details.

7 Then click on Next>>

Select Video Mode

CALDERA
systems

Resolution	Refresh	Depth	Availability	Horiz. Sync	Mode Clock
1280*1024	87 Hz interl.	8 bpp	Ok	51 kHz	80 MHz
1152*864	84 Hz	8–16 bpp	Ok	76 kHz	135 MHz
1152*864	78 Hz	8–16 bpp	Ok	70.8 kHz	110 MHz
1152*864	70 Hz	8–16 bpp	Ok	62.4 kHz	92 MHz
1152*864	60 Hz	8–16 bpp	Ok	53.5 kHz	88.9 MHz
1152*864	89 Hz interl.	8–16 bpp	Ok	44 kHz	65 MHz
1024*768	85 Hz	8–16 bpp	Ok	70.24 kHz	98.9 MHz
1024*768	76 Hz	8–16 bpp	Ok	62.5 kHz	85 MHz
1024*768	70 Hz	8–16 bpp	Ok	56.5 kHz	75 MHz
1024*768	60 Hz	8–16 bpp	Ok	48.4 kHz	65 MHz
1024*768	87 Hz interl.	8–16 bpp	Ok	35.5 kHz	44.9 MHz
800*600	100 Hz	8–32 bpp	Ok	64.02 kHz	69.65 MHz
800*600	85 Hz	8–32 bpp	Ok	55.84 kHz	60.75 MHz
800*600	72 Hz	8–32 bpp	Ok	48 kHz	50 MHz
800*600	60 Hz	8–32 bpp	Ok	37.8 kHz	40 MHz

Millions colors (24bpp)

no virtual desktop

☐ show all modes

Test this mode

LIZARD   << Back   Next >>   Help

Select Your Video Mode

The video mode (think of them as screen resolutions if that is more comfortable) that are listed by default are those that the installation program determined would work with your video card and monitor combination. You can optionally elect to also show unsupported video modes.

CAUTION: Selecting unsupported video modes could cause serious damage to your hardware!

After you have selected a video mode to try, click the

8 A final window for monitor settings now appears. Select the graphics mode and number of colours here.

WHAT'S THIS?

The **screen resolution** is set using the **graphics mode**. If you have a new 17" monitor, you can use a higher screen resolution than with an older, smaller screen (15"). More can be displayed on the screen with a higher resolution. The default value for 15" monitors is 800x600, and 1024x768 for 17" monitors in 8-24 bpp respectively.

TIP

You should also consult your monitor manual for the correct settings for your monitor. Incorrect settings can lead to your screen no longer being displayed.

9 Click on the scroll box in the scrollbar with the left mouse button.

In this way you will see all settings options.

11 Open the colour depth selection menu using the black arrow on the edge of the field.

10 Select the desired resolution.

> Millions colors (24bpp) ▼

12 Click on the desired number of colours.

These settings options are located in the lower half of the screen.

The monitor manual even gives corresponding information on setting the colour depth. If you cannot find anything, select the *Thousand* setting.

By all means test the setting by clicking on the *Test mode* button. If the settings are correct, the Linux graphic desktop interface will be displayed for ten seconds. If this does not happen, then your settings should be re-edited and re-tested.

Selecting installation type and hard drive

Once the mouse has been installed correctly, you need to install OpenLinux. In the following section you will learn how to apply the operating system to the entire hard drive. However, if you wish to use several operating systems on your hard drive, then refer back to the *Partitioning before installation* section in this chapter first.

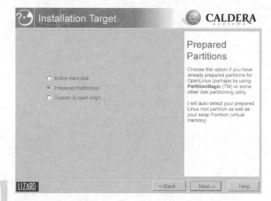

WHAT'S THIS?

The **hard drive** is the hardware component of your PC on which stored data is located. All programs, the operating system and application programs (e.g. StarOffice from Stardivision) and your own files (e.g. letters or other documents) are stored on the hard drive.

1 You will see a window offering several options. You can either install Linux on the complete hard drive or on a partition prepared in advance.

2 ● Prepared Partition(s)

In this case you only wish to install OpenLinux on your hard drive. Select this option with the mouse.

3 Click on the button

Next>>

.

You can now see the available **partitions** on your PC.

Partition	Start	End	Size	System	Boot	Mount-P
/dev/hdb	1	1244	9758MB			
/dev/hdb1	2	1027	8048MB	Win95 Extended (LBA)		/mnt/hdb1
/dev/hdb5	2	97	753MB	DOS / Windows		/mnt/hdb5
/dev/hdb6	98	361	2070MB	Linux		
/dev/hdb7	362	364	23MB	Linux	*	
/dev/hdb8	365	381	133MB	Swap		
/dev/hdb9	382	764	3004MB	Linux		
/dev/hdb2				Not used		
/dev/hdb3				Not used		
/dev/hdb4				Not used		
/dev/hda	1	1027	8056MB			
/dev/hda1	256	510	2000MB	Hidden HPFS/NTFS		
/dev/hda2	1	255	2000MB	Win95 FAT32	*	/mnt/hda2
/dev/hda3				Not used		
/dev/hda4				Not used		

Edit
Delete
Add logical

LIZARD   <<Back   Next >>   Help

4 🖳 /dev/hda3 Root–Partition   2010MB

This may look rather confusing to Linux beginners. However, it is not that difficult: select the root partition on */dev/hda1:*

Your details may differ slightly – just follow the */dev/hda1* text.

> The labels *hda1, hda2* and so on apply to IDE/EIDE hard drives. If you have SCSI hard drives installed in your system, the corresponding labels *sda1, sda2* apply. Linux usually recognises the type of hard drive automatically and suggests this in the selection list.

5 Use the left mouse button again for selection.

6 Once you have made your selection, simply click on ⬚ Next>> .

> **Hard drives** are divided into **partitions** in Linux. These partitions have a label. The first partition on the first hard drive is always called */dev/hda1*, the second partition on the first hard drive */dev/hda2*, and so on. If there are two or more hard drives, then the first partition on the second hard drive is always called */dev/hdb1*, the second */dev/hdb2*, and so on. The first partition on the third hard drive in the PC will therefore be called */dev/hdc1*.
>
> Set up the **root partition** generously. This means you should divide your disk into areas of at least 1GB. In this way a large number of programs can be installed and used together with the operating system. If you use the entire hard drive for installation, the memory space should be sufficient. Otherwise you must set the partition size correspondingly.

7 Linux always requires at least two partitions to operate. The root partition contains the entire operating system and all programs, i.e. all stored data. The second partition contains the **virtual memory**, also called the **swap partition**.

The **virtual memory** is an area of memory on the hard drive which Linux uses if the main or working memory is too small. The programs no longer used which are located in the main memory are extracted to the virtual memory temporarily.

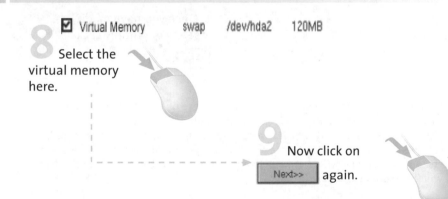

8 Select the virtual memory here.

9 Now click on Next>> again.

The selected partitions now need to be **formatted**. This means that the hard drives are prepared for the installation of OpenLinux. All existing data on the hard drive will be deleted during this process.

Have you already installed another **operating system** on the hard drive? You should decide whether you really want to delete all data from the hard drive before formatting. You can easily cancel at this stage of the installation.

Formatting lasts only a few seconds. The hard drive now contains no data and has no operating system. If you wish to cancel installation, then your PC must be started with the boot disk, as it no longer has an operating system.

10 Click on the *Format selected partition* button.

11 If you are satisfied with the settings, click on Next>> .

Otherwise go back to what you wish to alter by clicking on <<Back .

You can return to the previous window at any stage of the installation by clicking on *Back*.

Defining the extent of the installation

With an empty hard drive, you begin with nothing. So you can decide whether you wish to install everything on the hard drive. This mainly depends on the memory space available.

Minimal installation requires only 160MB, and consists of only the operating system. **Standard installation** requires 580MB. Apart from OpenLinux, this contains graphics tools, word processing applications and other useful programs. If you also wish to install the **commercial**

software, for example WordPerfect for Linux, you will need at least 800MB of free memory. The individual additional packages are selected by clicking the corresponding options: *Business, Development, Home, Netserver* and *Webserver*. **Complete installation** (all packages) requires about 1.4GB and also contains software development tools. Standard installation is recommended.

1 If you have sufficient memory space, then install *all packages*. A new PC will in all probability have enough space available.

2 Now click on the selection option.

○ [All Packages]

3 Now click on

Next>>

The system begins to load in the background while you enter a few more hardware details. The installation progress is constantly indicated in the *Packages* display.

Creating passwords and users

It gets slightly easier now – you have to think of a **username** and **password**.

You have the option of working with different access rights in Linux. You can also set up several users on your system, such as your wife, husband or children – even with their own name and settings. Depending on what type of user you are, you may delete or modify anything; or create, delete and modify selected files only. The **root** user has the highest authority level. This user has unrestricted authority.

1 The **root** user is automatically created by the system. You will need to enter a password for root twice.

The **root** user has unrestricted system authority. However, there is a danger of deleting or modifying files involuntarily. For this reason you should only log on as the ROOT user when making alterations to the operating system. Otherwise log on as a 'normal' user.

The second entry is merely a means of verification, as you cannot see what you have typed (stars appear instead of letters). Password entry is always concealed.

2 Click in the first entry field and type in the password. Then click in the second field and repeat the entry.

3 As you should not always work as the *root* user, create one or more system users in the window displayed.

Real Name:

4 First click in the *Real name* field and type in the selected username, such as your first or last name.

Login Name:

5 Click in the *Next* and type in a logon name in the *Login Name* field.

TIP Only the username and password are required by Linux. The full name serves only to give a fuller description of the user.

This is the name by which all created users will log on to the system in future. This can only be the first or last name, or a combination of both. A popular combination is the initial of the first name and the complete surname.

Password: [_____]

6 Click in the next field: a password now has to be entered for this user.

The password should now be confirmed by retyping it.

Retype Password: [_____]

Once you have entered all the necessary details, the *Add User* button becomes active. Before this it is marked as light grey.

7 Click on *Add User*.

The recently created user is marked in the list below.

If you wish to create more users, repeat the above steps. Every successfully created user will be displayed in the list.

8 If you do not wish to create any more users, click on [Next>>].

Completing the installation

There are just a few last details to enter before the installation can be completed.

1 You will now be asked for different network settings. You can set up a network only if you have at least two computers.

If you have two or more computers, both with network cards and connected via a network cable, you can install a network. A network has the advantage of being able to exchange files and printers between these two computers. Further information can be found in chapter 11.

2 Simply select the *No Network* option with the mouse.

Your computer must be given a name. In a network, **host name** is a clear title.

Hostname. | Linux Machine

TIP

This name is only a label for your computer. You could enter any name at all.

3 Click on the *Hostname* field with the left mouse button and type in the desired name

4 Now click on *Next*.

TIP

If you have only one PC, you can skip the chapter on *network installation* later. To operate a network, at least two computers with network cards and a network cable are required. If you have several network computers, take care with the **host name** you assign to each of them. You should not assign the same name to more than one computer or the network will not be able to distinguish between them.

TIP

You will learn how to establish an internet connection with Linux later in the book.

The next installation window prompts you to set up an internet service provider (ISP). If you have your ISP details to hand, these can be entered at this point. The following steps are only valid for this case.

Internet Provider Setup — CALDERA

☑ Use Dial-Up Network

Provider
- User-defined
- ⊞ France
- ⊞ Germany
- ⊞ Netherlands
- ⊞ Switzerland
- ⊞ USA

Details...

☑ Save logon data

Logon: `00011127899907121556789O#0001`

Password: `********`

Note: By saving the logon data all users get access to a Dial-Up connection!

ISP Setup

You can configure OpenLinux so that it is established from this place on the Dial-Up Network connection to your ISP (Internet Service Provider). Should the ISP not be put on this list, choose the entry **user-defined** and then click on **Details...**, to open your account. You will receive further information about the configuration of your account by choosing **Help**.

Please take into account: If particular numbers

Package [35%]   <<Back   Next >>   Help

1 Click on the *Use dial-up networking* option.

2 Click on the *Save logon data* option.

3 Click on the *logon* entry field and enter your registration number

4 Click in the *Password* entry field and enter your logon password to connect to the internet.

5 Then click on *Next*.

If Linux is not the only operating system installed on your hard drive, you can now select where the *Linux Loaders* (also called *LILO*) should be installed. LILO is used to start Linux and other operating systems if necessary.

1 Linux is usually installed either in the *Master Boot Record* or the target partition.

2 Select the *Master Boot Record* option if you wish to install Linux on a second hard drive.

Different operating systems can be started on your hard drive using a boot manager. If there is no boot manager installed or you wish to replace your existing boot manager, activate the option as outlined above. Otherwise leave this option deactivated.

TIP

The *Master Boot Record* contains information on which partitions are located on the hard drive and which operating system will be started. This functions well if only one operating system is installed (such as Linux or Windows 95).

If several operating systems are available, the *Master Boot Record* has to start another program (a boot manager, such as the OS/2 boot manager, or BootMagic by Partition Magic) which asks which of the available operating systems should be started.

If a boot manager is already installed, select the *Target Partition* option and leave the Linux partition behind in the boot manager (see the boot manager manual). Otherwise install LILO in the *Master Boot Record* so this functions as the boot manager. So that LILO knows which partitions are available on the hard drive, click the bootable partitions listed with a check mark in the upper area of the window. LILO announces itself briefly at startup and waits for an entry. You need to enter the label of the respective partition (if you do not know the label, click on ⬚ to display a full list).

3 Select *Target Partition* if Linux is to be installed on the first hard drive.

If your system has a soundcard and speakers, these will usually be recognised automatically by OpenLinux.

1 Set the *Volume* by dragging the slide rule.

2 Set the *Balance* by dragging the slide rule.

3 Click on the *Test digital sound* button to test the settings.

You will only hear sounds or noises.

4 Then click on *Next*.

The following window gives details of the soundcard recognised. The same settings can be tested here as in the previous window.

5 When you are satisfied, click on *Next*.

41

If you have not yet connected a printer, you can do so at any time by following the instructions in one of the later chapters in the book.

If you have not yet connected a printer to your system, you can do so now.

Printer Setup

CALDERA

Name: Brother1

Model: Brother MFC-6550MC

Variant:

Port: /dev/lp0 (LPT1)

Paper: A4   Test

Add   Remove   Standard

Name	Model	Port/Destinsation	Standard

Printer setup

Lizard recognizes most printers. However, should your printer not have been recognized, you can configure it.

To setup your printer manually, you must provide it with a name and then select the corresponding model in the menu.

If you print with a remote printer, you must indicate a destination.

Select a standard printer. This printer is used for all print jobs

Package   58%   <<Back   Next >>   Help

1 Click in the *Name* entry field and enter a name for your printer.

2 Click on the black arrow on the right-hand side of the *Model* selection field, and select your printer model from the list.

3 Now select another port from the *Port* selection list if your printer is not connected to the first parallel port of the computer.

4 Only modify paper size if your printer supports various formats.

5 Then click on *Add*.

The printer is now displayed in a list of printers connected to your PC. Several printers can now be installed in the same way if required.

6 Then click on *Next*.

The last required setting is to select a **time zone**.

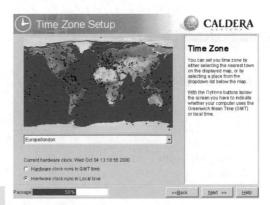

1 Here you should select *Europe/ London* (assuming you live in this time zone), as well as the format in which the hardware clock should be displayed.

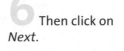

2 Click on the small black arrow to the right of the selection field.

3 Click on *Europe/London* in the selection menu.

You can find out from your PC manual if the computer runs on GMT or local time. Select the corresponding option. If in doubt, select *Local time*.

4 Select the time format for the hardware clock.

The white circular button now contains a black dot before your selection, for example:

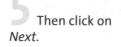

Finished! Are you happy with your settings?

5 Then click on *Next*.

You will see the last installation display running in the background. This can take **up to an hour**. You can play Tetris while you are waiting.

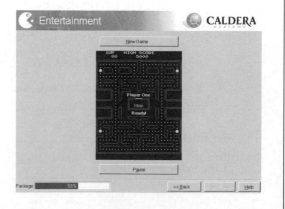

1 Start the game by pressing

| New Game |

Immediately after installation you can create an emergency boot disk. This can be used to boot the system in an emergency.

1 Insert a blank disk in the floppy drive.

2 Then click on *Write*.

Once the installation is complete (as soon as the entire package is installed) you will see the OpenLinux **initialisation screen**. The core operating system will first be loaded and then started. Your hardware will be checked and OpenLinux started. You will receive a graphically prepared screen immediately, and can log on to the system with one of the usernames created.

Don't forget to remove the **installation disk** from the drive and place it back in your Linux package!

3 Click on *End* when the installation is complete.

The *End* button is activated. The system then processes several maintenance operations before displaying a graphic login window.

What's in this chapter:

This chapter explains the basics of working with Caldera OpenLinux. You will be able to start and close OpenLinux. You will also learn the most important elements of the KDE graphic interface. You will be able to use the mouse and get to know the basic functions such as pointing, dragging and clicking. You can work with windows, i.e. opening, closing, reducing, enlarging and moving them. You will also learn how to activate the Linux help function.

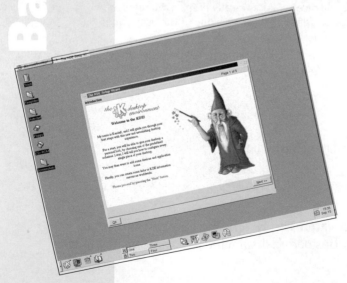

You already know about:

You are going to learn about:

Starting OpenLinux

Linux is only started automatically after installation.

Before you can use OpenLinux, you need to start your computer.

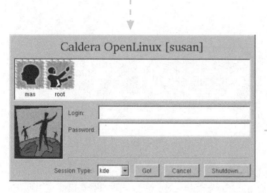

1 Turn on the PC and monitor – ensure there is no disk in the floppy drive.

2 After about two minutes the OpenLinux **logon window** appears. Type in your username and password.

3 Click in the corresponding fields with the mouse and type in both.

If an icon is already displayed for the name under which you log on, you can click on this button. You do not need to type the username as it is entered automatically. The password must always be entered manually.

4 Select the **KDE** graphic interface, usually already installed.

CAUTION

Note that this book explains all settings with KDE. If you select another graphic interface, there may be a difference in explanation between the book and your screen display!

Should you prefer another interface, you can open the selection list of graphic interfaces by clicking the black arrow on the right-hand side of the list. Then click on the desired interface.

5 Then click on GO!

TIP

If you make an error whilst typing the username and/or password, the logon window remains open. The error message *Logon not permitted* appears in the lower left-hand corner of the screen. Just try again: check and correct your username if necessary and type in your password carefully. Make sure the Caps Lock function on your keyboard is turned off.

CAUTION

Log on as a 'normal' user and not as the root user if you do not wish to carry out system maintenance. This prevents important data from inadvertently being deleted or the operating system from being damaged.

If you are logging on with KDE for the first time, the **KDE Configuration Wizard** is started. First place the window in the background as described below. The KDE Configuration Wizard is explained in more detail in chapter 4.

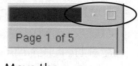

Page 1 of 5

6 Move the mouse to the upper right-hand corner of the window.

You will see two small buttons, which will be explained in more detail in this chapter.

The small mouse pointer must point to the button with the dot in the middle:

7 Now click on the left mouse button.

The window is now placed in the background. If windows other than the KDE Configuration Wizard are opened, place these in the background

What is a desktop?

As soon as you have logged on, Linux appears with the following picture.

You will see the Linux work area, also called the **user interface** or **(virtual) desktop**. You will find different tools on this interface exactly as you would on a normal desktop, such as the *Recycle Bin* or *Filing Folder*.

The desktop of the graphic

A *user interface* describes the way a computer accepts information from the user, and in turn makes information available. KDE is a Linux graphic user interface, which works with icons and windows.

If your *desktop* looks different, for example if it contains fewer icons or more windows, or if everything is displayed in a different language, don't panic! Every user can modify the desktop as they wish. You will learn how to do so in this chapter.

KDE interface is subdivided into three sections:

➡ The **Program Bar** on the lower margin:

this contains programs to be started.

➡ The **Taskbar** on the upper margin:

this contains programs already running.

➡ The **Desktop**:

the area in which other program icons can be placed.

51

Different **icons** and opened windows are located on the **desktop.** The icons represent executable programs or actions.

A brief explanation of what the individual symbols mean now follows. You will learn how to work with these in detail in the next chapter.

 Should you no longer require files (for example, a letter), then simply 'throw' the document in the Recycle Bin, called Trash. You will learn exactly how this works in the next chapter.

You can see whether the recycle bin is empty or not from the type of icon displayed.

 Copies, also known as **templates**, are hidden behind this icon. These can be very useful if you wish to leave links behind on the desktop for websites or addresses of important FTP servers. You will learn how this works in the next chapter.

The Autostart folder has the following function: the KDE automatically starts programs entered as soon as you log on.

These three icons are available by default after installation. You can increase the number of icons to suit you.

The program bar on the lower margin contains all the programs installed in Linux:

The icons with the small black arrow above contain **sub-menus**, as does the button with the letter 'K'.

Sometimes the program bar takes up too much space and prevents you from working with other programs. There is a solution:

1 You can 'slide' the program bar across by clicking on either the left or right-hand side of the program bar.

Only this part of the program bar now remains visible.

The program bar icons are called buttons. These are rectangular KDE items activated by clicking a corresponding function with the left mouse button.

2 'Slide' the program bar back out by using the mouse.

If you move the mouse over one of the buttons, a small yellow mini help (also known as QuickInfo) appears on the respective button. This briefly explains what is hidden behind the option.

A short summary of all the icons of the program bar now follows. The program options will be described in detail in the next chapter.

The most important button on the program bar is the main menu, which contains all installed programs.

The icon can also be called an **Application Starter**. Installed programs can be started from here. All other programs in the program bar can also be found in the main menu. When the main menu is activated using the left mouse button, all available programs on your computer are listed.

 If you click on this icon with the left mouse button, you can modify the settings in the **KDE control centre**, for example the background and screensaver.

 This icon offers extensive documentation on different areas, also on Linux installation, for example.

You can log off using this icon. Simply click on it with the left mouse button. A window then appears with which you can end your KDE session.

 If you click on the padlock with the left mouse button, your screen is blocked to unauthorised users. Your password must be re-entered to access your work.

You can switch between four **virtual desktops** using these four buttons. Other virtual desktops can also be added or

One	Three
Two	Four

renamed. Every virtual desktop can be set up individually with your own icons and windows. For example, a desktop can contain all text programs, another one all graphic programs, and so on.

This icon opens a view of your own work directory – your documents, text and graphics. You can see the content of your directory using the file manager, with which you will become more familiar in chapter 5.

This icon stands for Netscape Communicator. It contains a **Browser**, a program with which to 'surf' the internet.

A **browser** is a program which displays homepages or websites on the internet in graphic form. You cannot surf the internet without a browser. The two best known browsers are Netscape Communicator and Microsoft Internet Explorer.

KDE help is used when you have a query on the use of the graphic interface. This will be explained in detail later in the chapter.

A terminal emulation is a graphic interface program which simulates the behaviour of a simple non-graphic terminal. Such terminals were once used to control computers. Individual commands which control the computer can be entered. But most commands are contained in the KDE.

Clicking this symbol opens a terminal window, also known as 'kvt' under Linux. This **terminal emulation** enables commands to be entered directly.

This button is used when you wish to compose **electronic post**, or **e-mails**. However, the 'Kmail' program must be set up on the KDE interface beforehand. How this is done will be explained in the next chapter.

This part of the program button is not a button, merely the current date and time display. The date is set at a different point in the system, yet to be explained.

15:36
Sep 15

(file:/root/Desktop/... | ● (The KDE Setup W... | ● kshapshot

The third part of the desktop is the **taskbar** on the upper margin which displays all currently opened windows.

These are (in this order) a terminal window, the KDE Configuration Wizard (also called Setup Wizard), the file manager and another program. How to move between the windows will be explained later in this chapter.

Working with the mouse

A mouse looks like this, or similar. Sometimes there are only two buttons, other times three. The mouse can be moved over the desktop surface, and the mouse buttons can be pressed.

Pressing a mouse button is also known as **'clicking'.** You will already have used this function on installation to place the KDE Configuration Wizard window in the background. With Linux, the left mouse button is used the most, to activate, tick or select an item. The right mouse button usually opens a context-sensitive menu, from which something else can be selected with the left mouse button. If a middle mouse button is available, a function can be applied, following the instruction in the appropriate manual. This mouse button usually combines functions of both the left and right buttons. You will become more familiar with working with the mouse and use of the left and right buttons in the following few pages.

1 Move the mouse on the mouse mat so that you can see the mouse pointer move on the desktop in the form of a small arrow. This arrow is also called a **mouse pointer**.

2 Move the mouse until the mouse pointer is over the *Trash* icon.

The term 'POINT WITH THE MOUSE TO...' is not linguistically correct. The mouse remains on the desktop, while you move the mouse pointer across the screen by moving the mouse.

The yellow QuickInfo appears immediately with the message *Contains removed files*.

Note that the appearance of the mouse pointer can differ. Move the mouse over the desktop, and the mouse pointer appears as a black cross. Point the mouse at an icon, and the mouse pointer changes to an arrow. Move the mouse into a window in which text can be entered, and it changes to an italic '*I*'. Drag the mouse into a window similar to a browser and point it at a hyperlink, and the pointer appears as a hand with an outstretched finger. Hyperlinks are addressed in more detail in this chapter.

3 Now point to the *Main Menu* option in the program bar.

Pointing with the mouse is very easy. Apart from pointing, you can also **click** with the mouse. This is done as follows:

1 Drag the mouse over the *Trash* icon.

2 Press the left mouse button, then release it again.

This process is known as **clicking.**

Clicking with the left mouse button selects and opens an icon at the same time. You will now see a window with the title *Trash*.

Place it in the background as you did the **KDE Configuration Wizard.**

3 Click on the small button with the dot in the upper right-hand corner of the window.

4 Now click on the *Main Menu* button in the program bar.

Development ▸
Documentation ▸
Editors ▸
Games ▸
Graphics ▸
Internet ▸
Multimedia ▸
Office ▸
Toys ▸
Utilities ▸

Settings ▸
System ▸

KDE Help
Home Directory
KDE Control Centre

Disk Navigator ▸
Panel ▸
Lock Screen
Logout

5 If you move the mouse over the **Selection Menu** of the *Main Menu*, the entry where the mouse pointer is located becomes highlighted.

It will be marked in blue where the mouse pointer is located.

X Editor
GVim
KEdit Texteditor
KWrite: Advanced Editor

6 Press the left mouse button again, and either an application or another **sub-menu** opens.

A further sub-menu is called every time the menu entry is provided with a small black arrow on the right. For example, the Applications, Games and Graphics options have a respective sub-menu.

The sub-menu opens automatically when the mouse pointer is placed over the subordinate menu entry or when clicked on, for example on *Editors*. The upper entry of the sub-menu will appear as highlighted.

7 Now move the mouse pointer over the sub-menu.

8 A function can then be opened by clicking with the left mouse button.

TIP

If you wish to close a menu again, simply click on a free area of the desktop, or press the Esc key.

WHAT'S THIS?

A **menu** is a small window containing different selection options – similar to a restaurant menu. An option can be selected from the menu using the mouse. The KDE main menu, the Application Starter, contains various programs and functions.

TIP

If you have already used Microsoft Windows, you will probably know the term **double-click**. This means that the left mouse button is pressed twice in quick succession. Windows or files are opened in this way in Microsoft Windows, but a single click is (almost always) sufficient with Linux.

TIP

If you have a mouse with three buttons, the middle button is usually assigned a special function. On the desktop, the middle button may be used to call a menu, for example, or to switch between virtual desktops. On the other hand, the left mouse button can be used to mark text in an editor or terminal window, and then clicked with the middle button. The marked text is then copied and inserted at the cursor. Further functions can be assigned using the KDE control centre in the 'Window/Mouse' menu.

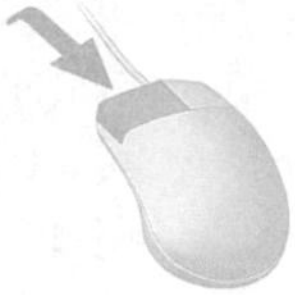

Working with windows

Programs and functions are executed in windows with the KDE graphic interface. Different information is displayed in these windows. In order to cope with windows techniques, the most important windows topics will be addressed in this section. You will learn how to open, close and enlarge or reduce such windows.

The appearance of a window differs to a normal user and the root superuser. Are you logged on as a normal user, as recommended? Then you should first use the following procedure so as to avoid confusion in explanations given later.

1 Open the *KDE control centre* program using the symbol in the program bar.

The entry page offers general information, and a menu on the left-hand side. The KDE control centre is explained in detail in chapter 4. At this point only the function for the layout of the window title bar is used.

2 Click on the plus symbol before the *Windows* menu entry.

The plus symbol immediately changes to a minus symbol, and a sub-menu appears.

3 Click on the *buttons* menu entry (window icon).

Editing options for the layout of the window title bar are now offered on the right-hand side. At this point you determine in which corners the five following window icons appear, if at all. You will see that the *Sticky* and *Close* icons are set to *Off* with normal users. This should be altered.

4 Click on the *Left* setting with the *Sticky* option.

You will immediately see how the title line of a window is set up in the preview.

5 Apply the settings by clicking on *OK*.

6 Place the KDE control centre window in the background by clicking on the corresponding button in the title bar.

You will learn how to close windows in the following sections. First we will familiarise ourselves further with the setup of windows.

1 Open the File Manager window using the icon in the program bar.

63

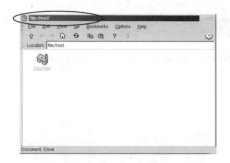

Window setup is largely the same with KDE. For this reason, the majority of commands can be explained with the file manager window. The **title bar** is always located in the upper margin. The name of the window is displayed here.

With most windows, a **menu bar** with the options FILE, EDIT, VIEW and so on can be seen underneath the title bar. This menu bar contains the functions available in this program.

With most windows an icon bar is also displayed. Frequently used functions can be summoned directly via the **icon bar** without having to take the conventional route through the menus.

A **status bar** in which additional information is displayed is frequently found in the lower margin. For example, a report on the language.gif file is displayed here.

For the next steps only the icons of the three small buttons in the upper right-hand corner of the title bar are required.

A window can be closed or its size altered using these buttons. Most windows have at least one or two of these buttons.

2 If you point the mouse at the middle button of the opened window, this button will be highlighted.

The button maximises the window. This means that the size of the window changes to occupy the entire screen.

3 Now click on the middle button with the left mouse button.

The window increases in size until it occupies the entire screen, apart from the buttons on the program bar and taskbar.

If the window is already maximised, another click on this icon reduces the window to its original size.

4 Then click on the left of the three icons with the left mouse button.

We have already used this function once to place the **KDE Configuration Wizard** in the background.

| 🖥 kvt | 🗁 file:/home/jonathan/ |

The window disappears from the desktop interface. However, it is either minimised or moved into the background. This is as before, and can be seen in the taskbar.

| 🖥 kvt | 🗁 file:/home/Jonathan/ |

5 If you wish to re-open the window, simply click on the corresponding button in the taskbar.

This example addresses the *file:/home/Jonathan* application.

This is the file manager with the working directory of the user Jonathan.

> The KDE shows the icons of the windows and programs opened in the taskbar. If you click on one of these buttons, the accompanying window is retrieved from the desktop foreground. If the window can already be seen in the foreground, a mouse click reduces the window to an icon on the button in the taskbar again. The window button in the foreground is always represented as 'pressed in'. A switch to another program window is possible at any time by clicking on the corresponding button.

Alternatively, you could switch to the desired window using the keyboard.

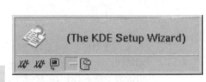

2 Every time ⇤ is pressed you jump from one window to another. The window currently open is displayed in the upper part of the window.

1 Press the Esc key and hold it depressed whilst holding down the ⇤ (Tab) key. A small window appears in the middle of the screen.

3 As soon as the desired window has been found, simply release both keys. This window is then opened in the foreground of the desktop.

The last symbol in the far right-hand side of the title bar enables an opened window to be completely closed.

1 Click on the button with the large *X* in the upper right-hand corner.

The window is then completely closed, and the icon disappears from the taskbar.

Alternatively, you can close a window with the small icon in the upper left-hand corner of the title bar.

1 Click twice in succession on the small button in the upper left-hand corner in which the icon for this type of window is displayed.

In the file manager the icon appears as a small filing cabinet with an opened drawer.

Location: file:/root

Desktop/

Document: Done

Most windows also have this button. Click on it once and a window menu opens which can be used as an alternative to the window.

Modifying window sizes

In the previous section you enlarged a window to full screen size or reduced it to an icon using the buttons in the upper right-hand corner of the window. However, it is often more advantageous to set a window directly to a certain size. This is also easily done.

Open the file manager again.

1 Click on the file manager button in the program bar.

2 Move the mouse to the right edge of the window. Point to the lower margin in the corner. At this point the appearance of the mouse pointer changes.

As soon as the mouse has been correctly positioned on the respective window edge on a corner, the **mouse pointer** appears as a thin arrow leading to a line. Move the mouse around near the desired margin until this arrow appears. The left, right, upper and lower window margins can all be used in this way.

3 Move the mouse to the lower left-hand corner of the window.

The appearance of the mouse pointer changes again:

4 If the mouse pointer appears in the form of the arrow described above, then drag the corner in the desired direction while holding the left mouse button down.

The window is widened with the left or right margin, and the height altered using the upper and lower margin. Alter the window size proportionally using the corners.

According to the setting, the new window size will already be displayed or will be represented by a grey line.

The size of any window can be altered in this way. Move the frame outwards with the mouse, and the window becomes larger. Move the frame inwards, and the window becomes smaller.

5 When the window reaches the desired size, simply release the mouse button.

69

Moving windows

One of the advantages of a graphic user interface such as KDE is that you can work with several programs or windows at the same time. We will try this in this section.

1 You have already opened the *File Manager* window by right-clicking on the icon in the program bar.

2 Now open the *Trash* window on the desktop in the same way.

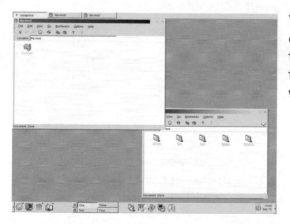

You will now see two overlapping windows on the desktop. The content of the background window will be partly hidden.

Now you could close one of the windows or reduce it to icon size. However, you may wish to see the contents of both windows.

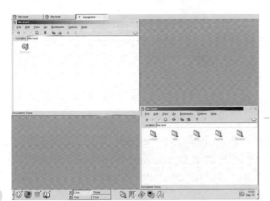

3 Reduce both windows by moving the mouse so that the window width now occupies about half the width of the screen.

4 Now point to the window title bar with the mouse. Now click in the **title bar** with the left mouse button.

5 Hold the left mouse button depressed and drag the window to the desired position. Move the mouse in the corresponding direction.

6 As soon as the window is in the desired position, release the left mouse button.

The window is now located in a new position on the desktop. With correspondingly selected window sizes you can now see the content of both windows on the screen at the same time.

Scrolling in windows

Sometimes the content of a window is far too extensive to display entirely in the current window size. You then have to scroll through the window if need be in order to access the desired content.

1 You have already opened the *File Manager* window with the right mouse button by clicking the icon in the program bar.

2 Now reduce the window until part of the content is no longer displayed.

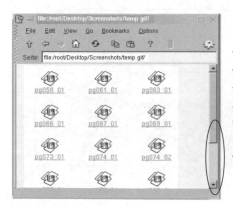

Here you will see the *File Manager* window reduced. As soon as the window can no longer display all information, the window contains a **scrollbar** on the right-hand margin. With some programs, such as Netscape Browser, a scrollbar can also be displayed on the lower margin.

This scrollbar enables you to select the window content you wish to view. It is like moving a piece of paper up or down.

In order to scroll content in a window, use the following procedure:

1 Point to the grey rectangular button in the scrollbar with the mouse.

This button is also called the scroll box.

2 Now click on this button and hold the left mouse button depressed. Move the scroll box up or down.

Other sections of content will then be displayed in the window. You can home in exactly on the contents you wish to be displayed by moving the **scroll box**.

The image shows only a vertical SCROLLBAR. But windows can also have a horizontal scrollbar, or both. The window content can then be moved both up and down, and left and right.

The buttons ▲ and ▼ can be found at the end of the scrollbar. You can then scroll gradually in the window by clicking with the left mouse button on the arrow in the desired direction. Gradual browsing means by line with vertical scrollbars, and by character with horizontal scrollbars.

There is also a third way of scrolling in windows with the mouse. Click in the free space between the arrow buttons and the scroll box with the left mouse button. Windows can be scrolled by page in this way.

Where is help?

There will usually be questions left unanswered after reading a Linux manual. These can probably be answered with the help functions available with KDE.

Help can be summoned in three different ways in KDE.

The first option is to call the KDE help via the main menu.

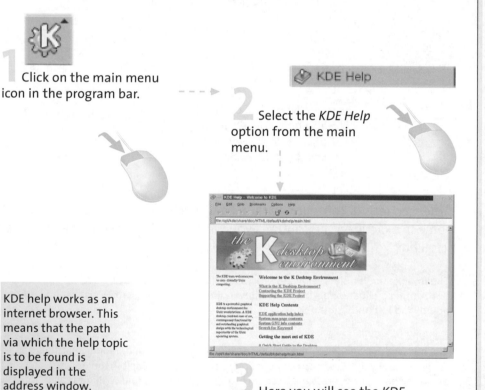

1 Click on the main menu icon in the program bar.

2 Select the *KDE Help* option from the main menu.

KDE help works as an internet browser. This means that the path via which the help topic is to be found is displayed in the address window.

3 Here you will see the *KDE Help* opening window with a first overview of the help functions.

Such a path for the opening window could for example be constructed as follows:

```
file:/opt/kde/share/doc/HTML/default/kdehelp/main.html
```

WHAT'S THIS?

A **path** contains the exact details of directories and sub-directories in which a file is located. The file containing the document *main.html* is located here, for example in the *opt*, *kde* or *share* directories. The term **directory** will be explained in more detail in the next chapter.

An **internet browser** is the window of a program which can graphically display websites or homepages on the internet. Such a window consists of a title bar, status bar, menu lines and icon bars, as already explained with the *File Manager* window. An internet browser window also has an entry field in which a known internet address or the path to a file (as in the above example) can be displayed.

Move in the *KDE Help* window exactly as you would in an internet browser. You can move through menus using **hyperlinks** by clicking with the left mouse button.

WHAT'S THIS?

A **hyperlink** is the address of another page, meaning another internet page or another file. It is usually displayed in a different colour from the rest of the text, and is usually underlined. The mouse pointer also assumes a different form as soon as the mouse points ☝.

The opening window of the help function is subdivided into three parts:

▭► General information on KDE and the KDE project.

▭► KDE help directory contents.

▭► KDE tips.

4 Click on the *What is the K Desktop Environment?* hyperlink in the KDE help window.

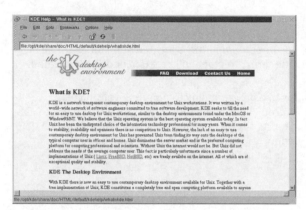

Different window content is now displayed. An explanation of KDE now follows. The content of the address field is also altered.

If you wish to return to the main window, use the button on the far left-hand side in the icon bar.

 Click on this icon.

Clicking on this button takes you one step backwards at a time, until you return to the original page.

The icon bar contains a few extra buttons with the following functions:

 The button with the arrow pointing right means that you can also move forward a step. The button is active only if you have already gone back one or more steps. Otherwise the button is marked grey, and is inactive.

You can return to the previous level by clicking this icon. Its opposite, which is inactive in the above image, takes you a step ahead to the next level – provided this option is available.

This arrow takes you one level up.

 This icon takes you to the highest level.

This icon takes you back to the help function entry page with the content directory.

This icon is typical for an internet browser: the page displayed can be updated by reloading (meaning it can be called again). This is sometimes required on internet pages.

The last icon shows a red traffic light to indicate that the program is currently working. You can interrupt this process by clicking on this button. The program is then prevented from executing the task. This can be very useful if the execution takes too long. The red symbol is coloured grey as soon as the task is executed. The icon is used on the internet if loading a page takes too long.

You have now returned to the help function opening page. The previously selected hyperlink *What is the K Desktop Environment?* has now assumed another colour as it has already been used.

1 Now click on the first option: *KDE Applications Index.*

A window with the title *KDE Application Index* appears. This is a type of main menu for KDE help and contains help text on most KDE applications. You can select the desired help topic by clicking on the corresponding hyperlink. The pages which follow usually contain further hyperlinks, or sub-pages.

Are you familiar enough with KDE help yet?

2 Return to the main window using the arrow icon.

3 Now click on the *System main pages contents* hyperlink.

This window contains the *Manual Pages*. This contains the original Linux help. First select the *Section 1* hyperlink and then any command from the following list to display a **manual page.**

Previously, Linux had no graphic interface like KDE. Everything was executed on a character-oriented terminal interface: commands entered, text registered and so on. The MANUAL PAGES, meaning the original Linux help, are purely text-oriented. All commands, devices, system files and so on available in Linux are explained in the style of Linux help.

If you wish to close the *Manual Pages* display, simply return to the main window. Use this icon:

4 Click once on the icon.

5 Now click on the *System GNU info contents* hyperlink in the main window.

The window contains hyperlinks with help text on different **GNU Utilities**. If you wish, follow a hyperlink and view one of the help texts.

Utilities are help programs. These can be commands, such as the Copy command, or programming languages such as Assembler, or word processing programs, and so on. Utilities are also often called tools.

GNU stands for 'GNU is not Unix'. The **GNU project** is based on the commendable idea that software should be free and computer systems accessible for everyone. So programs, or utilities distributed to the public in connection with the GNU project, are free of charge to the user.

79

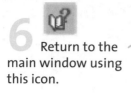

6 Return to the main window using this icon.

7 Select the last hyperlink to the KDE help directory: *Search for Keyword*.

The following window is a typical search window, meaning you can enter a string for which you wish to retrieve information. Here, for example, help texts containing the keyword 'printer' are searched for.

The system can require anything from a few seconds to a few minutes to search. However, you can tell from the red light whether your query has been processed or not. You will receive a list with 'hits', which are hyperlinks to pages containing your search string.

8 Select the hits which interest you by clicking them.

You can access other KDE help functions via the menu bar. The functions of the icon bar buttons are partly the same, but there are also new options.

1 First open the *File* menu and click on the desired function.

New Help Window	Ctrl+N
Open file...	Ctrl+O
Reload	
Search	
Print...	Ctrl+P
Close	Ctrl+W
Quit	Ctrl+Q

Here you can start a second *New Help Window*, *Open* a file or help function whose path you know, *Reload* the display (using the ↻ icon), *Print* the displayed help text, or *Close* the displayed help file, which corresponds to *Quitting* the window.

The *Edit* menu only offers three functions: you can mark and *Copy* a text (the exact process will be explained in a later chapter), *Find* a keyword on the current page or continue the search after a hit (*Find Next*).

Copy	Ctrl+C
Find...	Ctrl+F
Find Next	F3

Back
Forward
Contents
Top
Up
Previous
Next

The *Goto* menu repeats several functions of the icon bar: you can go a step backwards (*Back*) or forwards (*Forward*), go back to the KDE content directory (*Contents*), also known as the homepage, as well as to the *Top* of the page, the *Previous* and the *Next* page.

Bookmarks enable you to return quickly to an interesting or frequently required position later on.

Pages you wish to access directly later can be marked under *Bookmarks* without having to browse via different hyperlinks. Just click on *Add Bookmark* when you come to such a page, and it will be placed in the menu. Three **bookmarks** are listed here. This is also a typical browser function.

Add Bookmark

man page(1)
Online Manual
KDE Applications Index

General Preferences...
✓ Show Toolbar
✓ Show Location
✓ Show Status Bar
Save Options

Different settings can be modified in the *Options* menu. You can specify exactly what is displayed by clicking on the desired display option, such as *Show Address*. An active display option is marked with a check mark, as here in the example.

The settings can be permanently saved by clicking on *Save Options*. Each option either displays or removes a line in the window.

2 If you click on the *General Preferences* sub-menu, another window appears.

You will see a display with two **tabs,** previously known as scripts. The font size, standard font and fixed font can be modified here. This means that you will be modifying the appearance of the help text. Enlarge or reduce the font and/or select a different font.

KDE Help options

| Fonts | Colours |

Font Size
⦿ Small   ◯ Medium   ◯ Large

Standard Font   times

Fixed Font   courier

| OK | Apply | Cancel |

If the KDE functions are to be subdivided in a function window, they will appear as **tabs**. As in a real filing cabinet, the tabs appear behind each other. A tab can be placed in the foreground by clicking the title with the left mouse button.

3 Click on the desired size to select the font size.

You can either enter the corresponding word or click the circular icon before it, so it is marked with a black dot.

Font Size		
⦿ Small	○ Medium	○ Large

Standard Font	times ▾

4 If you wish to change the font, click on the small black arrow on the right of the selection field.

A selection list is 'rolled out', and the desired font can be selected with the mouse.

5 Now click on the second tab, Colours.

KDE Help Options

Fonts | Colours

Backgroung Colour:

Text Colour:

URL Link Colour:

Followed Link Colour:

☑ Underline Links

☐ Always use my Colours

OK | Apply | Cancel

Background colour, text colour and hyperlink colour can be modified here. Colour settings are explained in detail in one of the following chapters.

6 Click on OK to close the Options window.

If you click on *Apply*, you can store the settings already made without closing the window, unlike clicking on *OK*. The *Cancel* button closes the window without saving the settings as they have not yet been applied.

You now know the most important functions of KDE help, and how to use them. A second option for calling KDE help is activating it in a window directly.

1 Click on the Help menu entry.

Contents   F1
About kdehelp...
About KDE...

This menu entry can be found in almost all KDE windows. There are three options.

2 Select the *Contents* option.

This window gives general information on the KDE help system, in great detail. You can also navigate using hyperlinks here. If you activate the *Help* menu entry in another window, you receive help on this window according to the topic.

KDE Help - KDE Help System User Manual

File Edit Goto Bookmarks Options Help

file:/opt/kde/share/doc/HTML/default/kdehelp/index.html

KDE Help System

The KDE help system is designed to make accessing the common UNIX help systems (man and info) simple, as well as the native KDE documentation (HTML).

Invoking KDE Help

The help system may be started using a URL to display a file, e.g.

kdehelp file:/usr/local/src/qt/html/index.html

URL's have been added for info and man, e.g.

kdehelp info:"(gcc)G++ and GCC"

kdehelp man:strcpy

If no command line parameter is supplied, an index is displayed (currently just has links to info and man directories, but may have links to installed **KDE** application's help in the future). Alternatively, a file or URL may be opened using menus or dragged from the **KDE** file manager — **kfm**.

Navigating in Help

Navigation in the help system is achieved by clicking on links within the documents and by using the options in the *Goto* menu and the toolbar.

Contents

If the help system is started with general information on the KDE system documentation are divid

file:/opt/kde/share/doc/HTML/default/kdehelp/index.html

3 Close this help window by clicking on the *X* icon in the upper right-hand corner.

4 Open the Help menu item again. Now click on *About KDE help*.

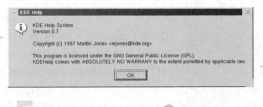

KDE Help

KDE Help System
Version 0.7

Copyright (c) 1997 Martin Jones <mjones@kde.org>

This program is licensed under the GNU General Public License (GPL).
KDEHelp comes with ABSOLUTELY NO WARRANV to the extent permitted by applicable law.

OK

5 Click on *OK* to close the *Options* window.

6 Open the *Help* menu item one last time to activate the *About KDE* option.

About KDE

ⓘ The KDE Desktop Environment was written by the KDE Team, a world-wide network of software engineers committed to free software development.

Visit http://www.kde.org for more information on the KDE Project. Please consider joining and supporting KDE.

Please report bugs at http://bugs.kde.org.

OK

TIP
Only the first option in the *Help* menu genuinely helps with queries. The other two menu items serve only as general information.

7 This window also contains brief information on KDE. Click on *OK* to close.

The third and final KDE help option concerns context-sensitive help.

1 This is activated by right-clicking over the position where you require help, such as on the desktop.

New ▶
Bookmarks ▶
Help on desktop
Execute Command
Display Properties
Refresh Desktop
Unclutter Windows
Cascade Windows
Arrange Icons
Lock Screen
Logout

The context-sensitive menu offers several desktop functions which will be addressed in more detail in a later chapter. The important menu item here is *Help on desktop*. Left-click on this to open a well-known help window – the KDE help entry window. This function corresponds to the KDE help menu item in the main menu of the program bar.

Closing Linux

Linux can be closed very easily. However, you must decide between closing the KDE graphic interface and shutting down the operating system.

You will now learn how to log off from the KDE interface.

1 Click on the small Logoff icon in the program bar with the left mouse button.

If applications containing unsaved data are still open, this will be reported. You must then decide whether you wish to leave KDE with or without saving.

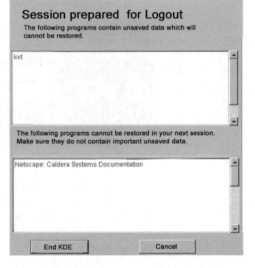

Session prepared for Logout

The following programs contain unsaved data which will cannot be restored.

> kvt

The following programs cannot be restored in your next session. Make sure they do not contain important unsaved data.

> Netscape: Caldera Systems Documentation

| End KDE | Cancel |

2 Click on *Cancel* if you do not wish to log off, or click on *End*.

Note that data can go missing if you end KDE despite the above displayed warning message. If in doubt you should cancel the logoff process and close your applications individually by closing the corresponding windows. Then you will not receive a message when logging off.

Logging off means that you are ending your graphic session as a user. A session exists as long as you are logged into the system with your username and password. You work with KDE during a session while the Linux operating system runs in the background and helps by passing your commands to the hardware. If you wish to stop working and end your session, then log off from the graphic interface. Now another user has the option to log on to the system and use Linux.

Caldera OpenLinux [susan]

mas   root

Login:

Password:

Session Type: kde   Go!   Cancel   Shutdown...

3 After KDE has ended, the Caldera OpenLinux login window appears again. At this point you or someone else can log on with a username and password registered under the graphic interface.

If you work with a Linux system which was not installed as described in chapter 1, you may not receive a new login window. Instead, only a character-based screen is displayed on which the word *Login*: appears. You can log on here in the same way as in the graphic login window. First enter the username, confirm with the ⏎ key, and then type in your password. Confirm this with the ⏎ key. You are now logged on to the character-based interface.

If you wish to turn off the Linux computer completely, there is just one step left. You will see a *Shutdown* button in the lower right-hand corner of the login window

4 Now click on this button with the left mouse button.

Another window appears, which asks: *Shutdown or restart?* If you wish to close down the computer completely, check to see if the *Shutdown* option is also marked with a black dot.

TIP

A system shutdown means that all operations currently running are ended correctly. The computer should only be switched off in this way, or the operating system may become damaged. System processes continue to run once you have logged out of KDE, as these can only be ended correctly by shutting down.

5 If this is not the case then click on this option, then *OK*.

The screen is now black and several messages are displayed. These messages mean that system processes are stopped and are closed properly. As soon as you can see the message **System halted** on the screen, you can switch off the computer.

WHAT'S THIS?

System processes are programs which the operating system keeps hidden in the background. These include programs which operate the graphic user interface or printing, etc.

The last selection list after clicking *Shutdown* gives the option of restarting the system immediately after shutting it down (*Shutdown or restart*). This can be useful if you have problems and hope to solve them by rebooting. This is recommended for certain problems with the operating system, as system processes can be ended properly and started again in the correct way.

This process is called a *reboot*. **Booting** means starting up the system, and rebooting means **restarting** it.

If you receive a character-based **Login** prompt after logging off but you want to shut down the system completely, then you first have to log in as described above (by entering your username and password). If after this login only a character-based screen is displayed, then type in the command **halt**. Your system will now shut down as described. Switch off the computer when the message **System halted** appears on the screen.

It may sometimes suddenly happen when working with KDE that you can no longer make any entries or move the mouse pointer. **Even in this case you should not switch off the computer**. Instead, press the Ctrl+Esc+⇐ keys (Ctrl+Alt+Backspace). This allows you to leave KDE and log on again.

What's in this chapter:

When you open a window in Linux, print something out or write a document, a program is always executed. In this chapter you will learn how to start programs from the main menu in the program bar or using the desktop icons. You will also be shown how to use the different virtual desktops and how to switch between these and several programs.

You already know about:

You are going to learn about:

What is the main menu?

You have already familiarised yourself with the main menu in the second chapter.

Development	▶
Documentation	▶
Editors	▶
Games	▶
Graphics	▶
Internet	▶
Multimedia	▶
Office	▶
Toys	▶
Utilities	▶
Settings	▶
System	▶
COAS	▶
Applications	▶
KDE Help	
Home Directory	
KDE Control Centre	
Disk Navigator	▶
Control Panal	▶
Lock Screen	
Logout	

1 Click on the button on the far left-hand side of the program bar in the lower margin:

2 You will now see the main menu.

The number of entries may differ in your menu, depending on how you installed Linux on your computer. This was explained in chapter 1.

TIP

A KDE or Linux program is hidden behind each entry with which you can execute different functions, open sub-menus or start programs. This has already been used several times in chapter 2, to call *KDE Help* for example.

KDE opens a window with many different icons and names. This window is called the **main menu**, from which you can now select an entry. Click your entry with the left mouse button.

Starting a program

You have actually already started programs. For example, you listed the contents of your work directory by clicking the *File Manager* icon. You have also started *KDE Help* from the main menu. Programs were started in both cases. There are of course other KDE programs which can usually be called from the **main menu**. We will now look at a few examples.

1 Open the **main menu** in the program bar by clicking on the corresponding icon.

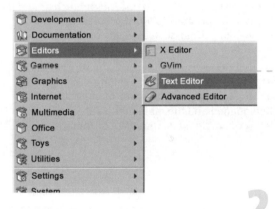

2 Click on the *Editors* entry in the **main menu.**

Another window is opened, also called the **sub-menu.**

3 Click on the *Text Editor* option in the upper part of the **sub-menu**.

```
Text Editor                              · □ ×
File  Edit  Options  Help
  🗋 📂 💾  📋 📑 ✂  🖨 ✉  ?



                              INS  Line: 1 Col: 1
```

A window is opened, called **Text Editor.** Working with an editor will be explained in more detail in one of the following chapters.

Every program which has an icon in the main menu can be started in this way. Further examples can be found later in the book.

In the previous step, a program from the applications sub-menu was called. In the following example you will call a program from a different position on the menu. This time you will open the *File Manager*, which shows the contents of the work directory.

1 Open the *Main Menu* in the program bar by clicking on the corresponding symbol.

2 Now click on the *Disk Navigator* entry.

3 Click on the *Home/* icon in the sub-menu.

Development ▸	Open Folder
Documentation ▸	Desktop/ ▸
Editors ▸	1–1.gif
Games ▸	1–2.gif
Graphics ▸	1–3.gif
Internet ▸	1–4.gif
Multimedia ▸	1–5.gif
Office ▸	1–6.gif
Toys ▸	1–7.gif
Utilities ▸	2–1.gif

Settings ▸		lizard01.png
System ▸	Shared:	lizard02.png
COAS ▸	KDE/ ▸	lizard03.png
Applications ▸	Root/ ▸	lizard04.png
KDE Help	Personal:	lizard05.png
Home Directory	Desktop/ ▸	lizard06.png
KDE Control Centre	Home/ ▸	lizard07.png
Disk Navigator ▸	Recent:	lizard08.png
Control Panal ▸	Shisen-Sho	lizard09.png
Lock Screen	Same Game	lizard10.png
Logout	Option...	lizard11.png
		lizard12.png
		lizard13.png
		lizard14.png
		More... ▸

4 Click on the *Open Folder* entry in the *Home/* sub-menu.

97

The *File Manager* is now started, which displays the contents of your home directory. Further information on the file manager can be found later in the book.

All entries of the main menu or a sub-menu which have another small black arrow ▶ after the entry have one or more sub-menus. Which menus and sub-menus are entered in your main menu depends on the programs installed.

Working with virtual desktops

Another window is required to test switching between desktops and programs. We are currently working exclusively with virtual desktop *One*.

1 Open the *main menu* again in the program bar.

- Development ▶
- Documentation ▶
  - Non KDE Applications ▶
- Editors ▶
  - Refresh Desktop
- Games ▶
  - Archive
- Graphics ▶
  - Cut & Paste History (Klipper)
- Internet ▶
  - Find Files
- Multimedia ▶
  - GV
- Office ▶
  - Hex Editor
- Toys ▶
  - KJobs
- Utilities ▶
  - KNotes
- Settings ▶
  - Konsole
- System ▶
  - Kpilot
- COAS
  - KpilotDaemon
- Applications ▶
  - Menu Editor
- KDE Help
  - Trashcan
- Home Directory
  - Calculator
- KDE Control Centre
  - Terminal
- Disk Navigator ▶
  - Tree Browser
- Control Panal ▶
- Lock Screen
- Logout

2 Now click on the *Utilities* menu entry.

Several KDE help programs are located here, which will be explained in more detail later in the book.

3 Click on the Calculator icon in the Utilities sub-menu.

A third window opens displaying a calculator. This can be used exactly like a normal calculator. Either use the mouse to click the buttons on screen, or type in the numbers using the keyboard.

Since you have opened all the other windows, these will presumably now be partly hidden.

The desktop contains three overlapping windows belonging to the programs started. You can now use the calculator whilst writing a letter or viewing files without having to close the program you last used.

99

You can see which programs are currently open by looking at the taskbar in the upper margin:

🖩 Calculator	● ksnapshot	✍ Text Editor	🗐 file:/root/

The **taskbar** contains the **icons** of the **programs** loaded. The buttons of the active window appear 'pressed in'. You can **switch** to another program window by clicking the desired button at any time. **Double-clicking** the button of an opened window places it in the background.

4 Now click on the File Manager icon in the taskbar (marked file:/root/ in this case).

The selected window is immediately placed in the foreground and partly covers any other windows.

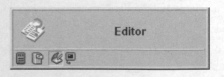

You can also switch windows using the keyboard. Hold down the [Esc] key and press [⇆] (Tab) at the same time. A small window will appear in the centre of the screen containing the icons of all loaded programs:

Every time you press [⇆] another program window is marked, where the window currently active is displayed in the upper window part. Release the key and the window last selected 'returns' to the foreground of your desktop.

Until now we have only addressed virtual desktop *One*. We will now switch virtual desktops.

1 Click on virtual desktop *Two*.

A second desktop appears on which no windows are opened. Desktop *Two* is otherwise identical to desktop *One* as it has the same icons, taskbar and program bar. Now click on desktops *Three* and *Four*, and you get the same picture.

In the program bar the corresponding button for the active desktop appears 'pressed in'.

WHAT'S THIS?

Virtual desktops are simply different work surfaces with the same standard equipment. Basic functions are identical on all virtual desktops, but you can specify the type and number of opened windows per virtual desktop. Working with virtual desktops avoids the need for too many windows on a single desktop. It also makes sense to assign similar windows to the same desktop, for example desktop one for general, desktop two for accounting programs, and so on.

2 If you wish to return to virtual desktop *One*, click on button number one.

101

You return to the user
interface with the opened
windows.

An opened program window is therefore always assigned to a
single desktop. However, this can be changed.

A small pin can be seen next to the icon
for the file manager itself in the upper
left-hand corner of the *file manager*.

Click on this icon
once with the left mouse
button.

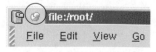

The symbol changes – the pin now
looks like it has been pinned in.

2 Now switch to the other virtual desktops using the mouse.

The file manager window is now located on each virtual desktop – as if firmly attached to the desktop with a pin.

If you wish to undo a function with the pin, simply click on the corresponding icon. It will immediately be changed to a 'loose' pin. From now on the window is visible only on the desktop on which the function was raised.

If you wish to open the context menu of a window in the taskbar with the right mouse button, you can move a window to the current desktop using the MOVE TO CURRENT DESKTOP option. This is especially useful after rebooting if all programs are located on the first desktop. They can then be redistributed quickly using this function.

Closing a program

You have learned how to close a window in chapter 2. Programs can also be closed in this way.
Bring the window with the calculator back to the foreground.

1 Click on the corresponding button in the taskbar.

ksnapshot   Calculator

Most windows have a *Close* button in the upper right-hand corner.

2 Click on this button to close a window definitively.

The calculator window is closed and the corresponding program ended. In this case, ending a program is exactly the same as closing a window.
However, it depends on the program as to how the window is closed.

1 Bring the *Kedit TextEditor* to the foreground by clicking on the corresponding program icon in the taskbar.

2 Click in the window and enter some text.

3 Click on File in the menu bar, and then on the *Close* command.

Most windows have a *File* menu and a command called *Close* or *End*.

105

If the window still contains
unsaved data (in this case, the
text just entered) you will be
asked before closing if the
content of the window should
be saved. You will then see the
Message dialog box.

4 Click on the No button to end the
program without saving the text entered.

Alternative ways of starting programs

The quickest way of calling a program is by using the main
menu. However, the program must be installed with a main
menu entry. You may also need to open several menus before
the desired program appears as a menu entry. There are
therefore different ways of starting programs.

Is the program icon
displayed on the
desktop?

1 Click on the corresponding program icon.

The program is started immediately. You already familiarised yourself with this function in chapter 2 when opening the *Trash* folder. For example, if there is an Editor icon available on the desktop, a simple click will open the Editor window.

You will learn how to set up a program as an icon on the desktop in chapter 4. In addition to the main menu, the most important programs are also executed directly in the program bar. It would of course be easier to start the program directly from this bar by clicking with the mouse. You will learn how to add further program icons to the program bar in the next chapter.

You can also call a program directly.

1 Click on the terminal icon in the program bar.

A **terminal window** opens in which the command for starting a program can be entered directly.

A **terminal window** imitates the interface and operation of a Linux terminal. Before graphic interfaces such as the KDE were developed, only a text-based terminal was available. This means that previously, commands were only processed if entered manually. You will learn about the terminal window in more detail later in the book.

```
Terminal
[root@noname /root]# kedit
```

2 Type in the *kedit* command to start the Editor.

A command is executed in the terminal window as soon as you press the ⏎ key (Enter) after the command name.

An editor window is opened – the *kedit* program.

1 Press ⟨Alt⟩ and at the same time ⟨F3⟩.

A small window appears in which a command can be entered in the same way as in the terminal window displayed above.

Command: kedit

2 Now press ⏎.

An editor window is opened – the *kedit* program.

The latter two alternatives for calling programs quickly work on the premise that you know the necessary command. If this is not the case, the only remaining options are using the program icon on the desktop (not always applicable), or taking the long route via the main menu.

Modifying KDE 4

What's in this chapter:

The Linux KDE graphic interface can be modified to suit you in many different ways. First modifications can be made using the KDE Configuration Wizard. You will learn how to alter the desktop, place icons on the desktop, activate a screen saver and modify colour settings. Then you can place new icons in the program bar and give the virtual desktops new names. You will also get to know the KDE control centre. You can assign a different language to KDE, create further desktop settings and modify windows' properties.

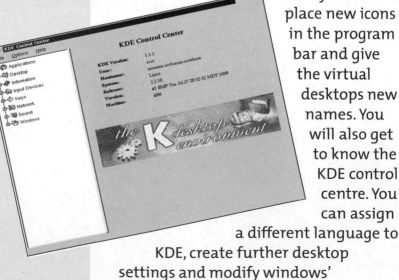

You already know about:

You are going to learn about:

Working with the KDE Configuration Wizard

Is the KDE Configuration Wizard in the background in the taskbar? This was overlooked in chapter 2. We will finally address the **KDE control center Wizard** (this is the same as the **KDE Configuration Wizard** and is also know as the **KDE Setup Wizard**) in this chapter, the windows of which are automatically opened when Linux starts. If you have placed it in the background, you will be able to see the corresponding button (*The KDE control center Wizard*) in the taskbar in the upper margin:

> If you have closed the **KDE Control Center Wizard** in the meantime, then start it again using the *main menu*. Click on the *main menu* button in the program bar and point to the *Utilities* entry with the mouse. Click on the *KDE Configuration Wizard* option in the *Utilities* sub-menu.

1 Click on the KDE Set-up Wizard icon with the left mouse button.

The window is now placed in the foreground. You will learn how to modify desktop settings using this program.

2 However, if you wish to modify some settings using the KDE Configuration Wizard then click on *Next*.

You can end the KDE Configuration Wizard at any time simply by closing the window. Click on the *X* icon in the upper right-hand corner of the title bar. You could also click on *OK* in the lower area of the screen.

You can specify the appearance of your desktop in the second KDE Configuration Wizard window. If you have already worked with an Apple Mac and the MacOS or BeOS, or with a Microsoft Windows computer, and you are familiar with the interface, then you can adjust the desktop accordingly.

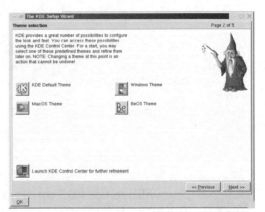

The KDE interface is the default setting. If you wish to apply a different desktop setting, simply click on the corresponding button, for example *Windows Theme*. You could also select *MacOS Theme*.

3 Click on the button of your choice.

If you selected *Windows Theme*, your **desktop interface** will be in the style of Microsoft Windows. Instead of a program bar on the upper margin and taskbar on the lower margin, a single start bar is displayed at the bottom of the screen as in Microsoft Windows.

You will see the **KDE control centre** icon in the lower area of the KDE Configuration Wizard desktop selection window. This is also a component part of the program bar. Further desktop modifications can be made using the KDE control centre. The program will be explained in more detail later in this chapter.

4 If you are satisfied with your settings, click on *Next*.

The third step of the KDE Configuration Wizard gives you the option to place icons for your floppy and CD ROM drives on the desktop.

If you have a floppy drive, it makes sense to use only the icon for the first floppy drive. If you have a CD ROM drive, you should of course set up this icon.

5 Click on the button of the icon to be placed with the left mouse button.

Begin with the *1st Floppy Disc drive* button. This icon is now located on your desktop.

The contents of a floppy disk or CD-ROM can be displayed quickly using this icon simply by clicking on the desired icon on the desktop. This avoids having to use the FILE MANAGER. However, it should be noted that the disk must be in the drive for the content to be displayed. Otherwise an error message will be reported.

An error message will also be reported if you try to display the file contents of a disk not formatted with the Linux FILE SYSTEM. It is therefore not possible to display the contents of DOS disks in this way.

Now set up a corresponding symbol on the desktop for working with the *CD-ROM drive* using the icon of the same name.

6 Click on the icon.

7 Then click on *Next*.

You can place another icon on the desktop at this point: a printer icon. This makes printing files easier.

Note that printing can only be carried out using this icon if a printer is actually installed on your system. The exact process will be explained in more detail later in the book.

8 Click on the printer icon to add it to your desktop.

This last step of the KDE Configuration Wizard addresses placing icons on the desktop. Internet addresses lie behind these icons, meaning you can open an internet browser and homepage with the corresponding address by clicking the appropriate icon on the desktop.

Note that this icon can only be used if an internet connection is already configured. The exact process will be explained in more detail later in the book.

9 Click on the *KDE Homepage* icon.

Now look at your desktop. There are now several more icons than before. We will begin to work with some of these icons in the next chapter.

Configuring the desktop

You have taken the first step towards configuring the desktop using the **KDE Configuration Wizard**: you have placed icons on the desktop. Over the next few pages we will alter the appearance of the desktop itself.

The desktop interface currently has the default colour blue.

1 Click on a free area of the desktop. A context menu appears.

New	▶
Bookmarks	▶
Help on desktop	
Execute command	
Display properties	
Refresh desktop	
Unclutter windows	
Cascade windows	
Arrange icons	
Lock screen	
Logout	

2 Click on the *Display Properties* entry.

There are many options for setting the desktop *background* in this window.

Display settings

Background | Screensaver | Colors | Fonts | Style

Desktop

One
Two
Three
Four

Rename ...

☐ Common Background

Colors

○ One Color

● Two Color

Setup ...

Wallpaper

No wallpaper

Browse...

Arrangement: Tiled

☐ Random   Setup

☑ Dock into the panel   Cache size (kB):

Help | Default | OK | Apply | Cancel

The window has several **tabs** for desktop properties. You can switch between these tabs by clicking on the tab name. The window content of the desired tab immediately moves to the foreground.

There are two options in the upper left-hand corner of the window: the virtual desktop can be renamed and/or assigned a uniform background. If you wish to apply the same background to every desktop, click on *Common Background*. The white box then contains a check mark, and is marked as activated.

The small square fields before a selection option are called **control boxes**. They can be activated by clicking the text or the box itself with the left mouse button. The box is then marked with a check. If already activated, then click again to deactivate, and the check disappears.

Test the different selection options here. Then click on *Apply* and see the result. If you are not satisfied, undo the action.

Now alter the colours.

You will see the *Setup* button for desktop background colours in the lower left-hand corner. You can also select whether the background should have one or two colours.

1 Click on the corresponding selection.

The circular button before your selected option will now contain a dot.

2 Then click on the colour button whose colour you wish to alter.

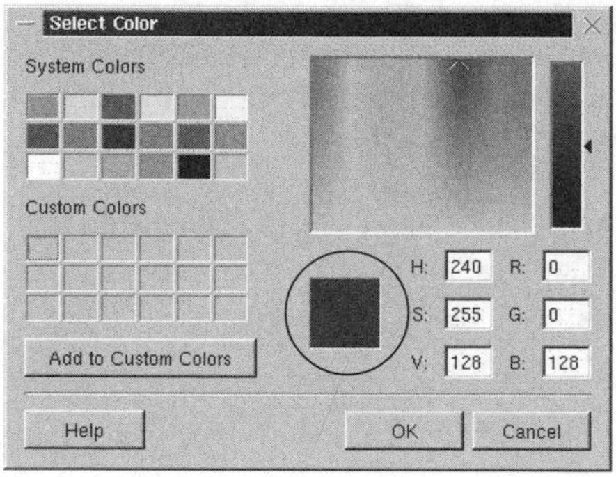

| Select Color |
| System Colors |
| Custom Colors |
| Add to Custom Colors |
| Help | OK | Cancel |

H: 240 R: 0
S: 255 G: 0
V: 128 B: 128

You can alter the background colour in this way. A colour can be selected by clicking in this window. Your selection will be shown in a type of 'preview field', containing the colour grey in this case.

3 Click on *OK* when you are satisfied with your selection.

You can also alter the second colour in the same way if need be.

4 If you are satisfied with your choice, click on *OK*.

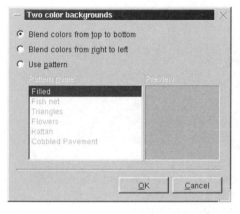

You now have the option of selecting a colour blend either from top to bottom or left to right for your desktop background. Just click on your favourite.

You will be spoilt for choice if you prefer a background pattern to a colour blend.

5 Click with the left mouse button on the *Use pattern* option, and then on a pattern name.

A small preview of the pattern selected appears on the right-hand side. If you are satisfied with the settings, confirm them by clicking on *OK*.

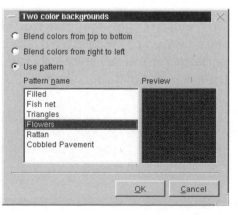

Wallpaper

No wallpaper

Browse...

Arrangement: Tiled

☐ Ra<u>n</u>dom   Setup

1 Click on the small
black arrow on the right-
hand side of the
background image
selection list.

2 Select an arbitrary
background image from the
list with the mouse.

On the upper right-hand side you will
see a preview of the selected desktop
background. You can always change
the image again if you are not
satisfied.

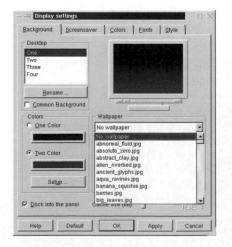

3 Alternatively you could select a background from a specific file. Click on the Browse button. You can now select a file from the file manager using the mouse.

CAUTION

This alternative selection presupposes you have files containing background images available. Such a file must be of a certain file type, meaning it must be saved as a graphic. If you select a file which does not satisfy these criteria, your selection cannot be applied.

You can also set the arrangement as well as the background theme.

4 Click on the small black arrow on the right-hand side of the *Arrangement* field.

5 Select any background image from the list with the mouse. You will see a preview of the selected desktop background in the upper right-hand side.

You can also decide on whether to apply the random effect.

6 Click on the word *Random*.

You have activated the option as shown in the example here. This means that KDE switches between different background images randomly every so often.

This random principle can also be influenced by you.

7 Click on the *Setup* button next to the *Random* option.

You can modify the period of time in seconds after which the next background image will be activated.

8 Click in the entry field containing the number of seconds.

9 Delete the old setting using the ⟸ button, and type in the new time interval.

10 You can also add new images to the list of background images to be displayed by clicking *Add*. When you click on a background image, this becomes highlighted. Click on *Delete* to remove it from the list.

Do you have your own files to use as background images for random selection?

11 Then activate the *Pick files from directory* option.

12 Indicate the corresponding directory by clicking in the field. Delete the old setting with the (⇐) key and type in the new directory.

13 Alternatively, you can activate the desired directory by clicking on *Browse*. A shortened form of the file manager appears, with which you can modify your setting.

Have you finished your settings for background images in random mode?

14 Then click on *OK*

If you wish to cancel your alterations, click on *Cancel*.

> You will learn how to use the **file manager** in more detail later in the book. You can then return to the desktop settings and change the background image again if necessary.
>
> It is best to 'play around' with these settings. This is the best way of discovering which options you have and which background suits you. You should avoid choosing something too brash or you may not be able to recognise the icons on your desktop.

Modifying colours

Further settings can be made in the *Display Properties* window.

1 Click on the *Colors* tab.

The window content changes. Other colour combinations can be assigned to the windows.

2 In the lower left-hand corner you can click and activate a predefined colour scheme. New colour schemes can also be defined. Click on *Add*.

3 Type in a name for a new colour scheme.

4 Click on *OK*.

The new colour scheme is displayed in the lower left-hand area of the window. The predefined schemes can also be removed.

5 Click on the *Remove* button to activate it.

A recently added colour scheme can be modified. Another selection menu is located on the right-hand side of the window.

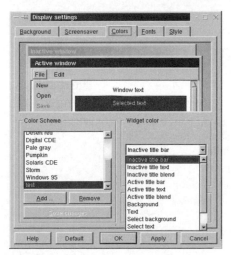

6 Click on the small black arrow on the right-hand side of the *Inactive title bar* selection field. A menu opens from which items can be selected.

Colours can then be edited as explained previously.

7 Now click on *OK*.

Item colours can be edited in this way.

8 Click on *Save changes* to end.

Defining fonts and style

Fonts are used to change the appearance of text. Several fonts look very similar.

The display screen font can also be changed in the *Display Properties* window.

1 Click on the *Fonts* tab with the left mouse button.

A new window appears. Fonts for different desktop items can be defined at this point.

Display settings

Background | Screensaver | Colors | Fonts | Style

General font
Fixed font
Window title font
Panel button font
Panel clock font

Typeface
helvetica

☐ Bold
☐ Italic

Size   Character set
12   default

Sample text

THE QUICK BROWN FOX JUMPS OVER THE LAZY DOG
the quick brown fox jumps over the lazy dog
0 1 2 3 4 5 6 7 8 9 ! " £ $ % ^ & * ( )

Help | Default | OK | Apply | Cancel

2 Select the item to be edited from the list on the left-hand side of the window.

Then select a font.

3 Click on the small arrow on the right-hand side of the *Font* selection list.

charter
helvetica
lucida
lucidabright
new century schoolbook
symbol
times
utopia

Any font can be selected from the menu now displayed. Use the scrollbar on the right-hand side of the menu to browse through all the options.

If you prefer to display the font in bold or italic type, activate the desired option.

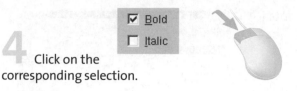

4 Click on the corresponding selection.

The active selection will be marked with a check mark.

Is the font setting too small or too large? Modify this using the *Size* field and the small buttons on the right-hand side of the field. Enlarge the font with the plus sign, and reduce it with the minus sign.

Size

12 ±

5 Click on either the plus or minus sign with the mouse.

6 Click on *Apply*.

You can also change the style of your desktop.

7 Click on the *Style* tab with the left mouse button.

Display settings

Background | Screensaver | Colors | Fonts | Style

☑ Draw widgets in the style of Windows 95

☐ Menubar on top of the screen in the style of MacOS

☑ Apply fonts and colors to non-KDE apps

Help | Default | OK | Apply | Cancel

TIP

The size of the icons in the control bar, the desktop area and so on can be configured in the lower half of the window.

8 Activate or deactivate the desired control box by clicking with the mouse.

You have the option of representing windows in Windows 95 style and/
or the menu bars on the upper margin in MacOS style. You can also
specify that colours and fonts be used with non-KDE applications.

9 Click on *Apply* to end.

Activating a screen saver

A screen saver is activated to prevent a screen view being 'branded' on
the screen. This can happen if the same view is displayed for hours or
even days without the system being used. Many users set the screen
saver so that the screen goes black after the system has not been used
for a certain amount of time. Moving images can also be set up as
screen savers.

1 Click on the Screensaver tab.

If no screen saver is activated,
the preview shows a black
screen. In the example on the
next page, we are going to select
the *Bouboule* screen saver.

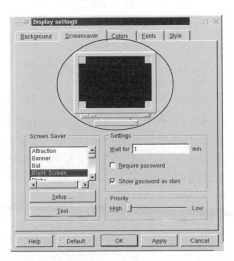

2 Click on the grey scroll box of the *Screensaver* selection menu.

Screen Saver

Blobs
Bouboule
Black Screen of Deat
Flame
Forest

Setup ...

Test

3 Move the scroll box up or down.

As soon as you have made a selection, you will see a screen saver preview in the upper half of the window.

Other settings can also be made to the screen saver.

Screen Saver

Blobs
Bouboule
Black Screen of Deat
Flame
Forest

Setup ...

Test

4 Click on the *Setup* button.

Here you can modify the speed, number of points, point size and colour change frequency of the *Bouboule* screen saver. These options differ according to the type of screen saver, and the settings can easily be modified.

Setup KBouboule

Speed:

Number of points:

Point size:

Color–change frequency:

☐ 3D mode

About   OK   Cancel

5 Click on the slide rule in the desired direction.

The changes made are immediately visible in the preview window on the right-hand side.

You can test the different selection options here. If you are not satisfied with the result, undo it by pressing *Cancel*.

6 Close the window by clicking on *OK*.

Settings

W̲ait for [1]   min.

☐ R̲equire password

☑ Show p̲assword as stars

In the right-hand side of the *Screensaver* window you can specify after how many minutes the screen saver should be activated.

7 Click in the *Wait for* entry field.

8 Delete the number *1* by pressing the ⌫ key, and type in any number.

The amount of time after which the screen saver is activated refers to the amount of time for which the system is unused. As soon as the user touches the keyboard or moves the mouse, the time elapsed will be reset to zero.

Do you wish to reactivate the display using a password?

```
┌ Settings ─────────────────────────────┐
│                                        │
│   Wait for  1                   min.   │
│                                        │
│   □  Require password                  │
│                                        │
│   ☑  Show password as stars            │
│                                        │
└────────────────────────────────────────┘
```

9 Click on the *Require password* option.

Should the password be displayed as stars on entry?

Note that the number of stars corresponds to the number of characters your password contains.

10 If so, activate the *Show password as stars* box.

If the appearance of your desktop suits you, close the window in which the settings are saved.

11 Click on *OK*.

Installing icons on the desktop

We have already installed several icons on the desktop using the KDE Configuration Wizard. However, our selection was relatively limited. In this section you will learn how such an icon is defined and modified.

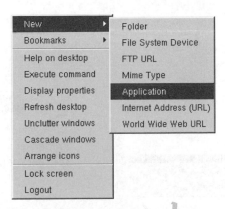

1 Right-click over a free area of the desktop.

A context menu opens.

2 Click on *New*, then on *Application* in the sub-menu.

A window then opens with *Program.kdelnk* written in the entry field.

3 Click on *OK*.

A new icon labelled *Program* is immediately placed on the desktop.

137

4 Click on the new icon.

Open with
Copy
Move to Trash
Delete
Properties

5 Click on *Properties* in the context menu.

kfm   ×

General | Permissions | Execute | Application

File Name

Program.kdelnk

Full Name

/root/Desktop/Program.kdelnk

Size: 605
Last Access: 12:05 26.09.2000
Last Modified: 12:03 26.09.2000

OK   Cancel

7 Delete the word Program using the ⟵ key and type in Texteditor instead (Texteditor.kdelink).

6 Click in the *Filename* entry field.

kfm   ×

General | Permissions | Execute | Application

Execute

kedit   Browse..

⚙

Swallowing on panel

Execute
Window Title

☐ Run in terminal

Terminal Options

OK   Cancel

8 Then click on the *Execute* tab.

9 Click in the *Execute* entry field and type in the command *kedit*.

A little knowledge of the system is of course required to place separate programs as an icon on the desktop. So in this example it had to be known that the *kedit* command opens an editor window. However, separate text files and the like can also be placed on the desktop in this way.

This is the program name for the editor window.

The gear wheel icon is used by default. This can however be changed.

10 Click on the button with the gear wheel icon.

An icon can now be selected from the window displayed. As the selection is fairly extensive you will need to use the scrollbar to alter the window display to view all the icons.

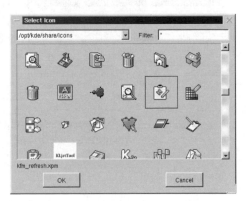

11 First click on the desired icon, then on *OK*.

12 Then close the *kfm* window (icon properties) by clicking *OK*.

The new desktop icon is entitled *Texteditor* and marked with the icon of your choice.

An icon can also easily be removed from the desktop.

1 Right-click over the icon to be deleted.

Open with
Copy
Move to Trash
Delete
Properties

2 Click on *Delete* in the context menu.

KFM Warning

⚠ Do you really want to delete the selected file(s)?
There is no way to restore them.

Yes   No

You will be asked for security reasons whether you really want to delete the icon.

3 If you are sure, click on *Yes*. If not, click on *No*.

The icon will then be deleted or will remain on the desktop, depending on your answer.

Setting up the program bar

The program bar can also be customised.

1 Right-click directly over the program bar.

Configure
Restart

A small context menu appears.

2 Select the *Configure* option from the context menu.

Here you can specify where on the screen the program bar and taskbar should be displayed. The taskbar can also remain hidden.

3 Make your selection with the mouse.

4 Now click on the *Desktops* tab.

Remember: you have already learned how to rename desktops and assign a uniform interface in *Desktop Settings*.

Virtual desktop settings can be modified here.

Desktops can be renamed as well as added here (up to eight in total). You can specify how wide the virtual desktop buttons should be displayed.

5 In order to rename a desktop, click in the entry field of the corresponding desktop.

6 Delete the current name (e.g. *One*) with the ⌫ key and type in a new name.

You can work with more or less than four virtual desktops.

7 Move the small rule on the *View* bar to the left (less than four desktops) or the right (more than four desktops).

TIP

This setting can only be made in 'jumps of two'. This means that you can work with either two, four, six or eight virtual desktops. An odd number is not permitted.

Hold the mouse button depressed until you reach the desired setting.

Do you wish the virtual desktop buttons in the program bar to be displayed smaller or larger? Then drag the small rule on the *Width* bar to the left (reduce) or the right (widen).

8 Hold the mouse button depressed until you reach the desired setting.

Click on *Apply* to see the setting without closing the application.

9 Click on *OK* to close.

The two other program bar setting tabs (*Settings* and *Disk Navigator*) have extra options. However, it is not necessary in the context of this book to explain them in more detail. If you wish to modify your program bar further, simply try out different functions. If you are not satisfied with the result, undo it in the same way!

The Disk Navigator is started from the main menu. It contains a personal menu for the active user.

1 First click on the main menu button in the program bar, and then on the Disk Navigator option.

🖳 Shared:	
🗋 KDE/	▶
🗋 Root/	▶
👤 Personal:	
🖵 Desktop/	▶
🏠 Home/	▶
🖋 Recent:	
🗋 ksnapshot	
🔍 Kfind	
🗐 Options...	

The sub-menu is divided into three sections:

The first area is the *Commonly used*. The *KDE* and *Root* directories and their sub-directories are located here.

The *Personal* section comprises the *Desktop* directory and the *Home* directory of the current user.

The third section contains most recently used directories, files and programs.

You can set the number of most recently used files to be displayed using *Options*.

If you click on one of the selection options regarding a directory, a sub-menu or file manager for this directory opens. Click on a program or file to open it.

If, for example, you click on the *Personal* option, a file manager window opens containing your personal desktop and home directory.

Until now we have only modified general program bar settings. However, it is often more important to add extra buttons to be able to start programs quicker. Or, alternatively, you can remove buttons which you never use. These only take up space in the program bar.

It is very easy to arrange the sequence of buttons differently. As a result the *Documentation* icon is moved. It is currently located in the following position in the program bar:

1 Click on the button of the icon to be moved in the program bar.

Move
Remove
Properties

A context menu for this icon opens. It contains the option of moving, deleting or modifying the settings for the icon.

2 Click on the *Move* option.

The mouse pointer alters: instead of an arrow head you will see a cross with a tiny arrow head on each end.

3 Move the mouse along the program bar without clicking.

The button moves in the direction you drag the mouse. Drag the icon until it is situated in the program bar at the point you wish to insert it.

4 Then click once with the left mouse button.

The icon is inserted at this point.

An insertion can be made at almost any point in the program bar. The only exceptions are where the four virtual desktop buttons, the logout and lock screen buttons are located. If you try to insert here, the icon will be placed on the right-hand side on the program bar.

After moving icons, the program bar may look as follows:

An icon can also be quickly removed from the program bar. Select an icon for a program which you don't really use. This could be the test version of WordPerfect, for example.

1 Click on the button of the icon to be removed in the program bar, for example *Documentation*.

| Move |
| Remove |
| Properties |

The context menu for this icon will appear again.

2 Click on the *Remove* option.

The symbol is immediately removed. You will see the result in the program bar:

| One | Three | | 12:44 |
| Two | Four | | Sep 26 |

Removing an icon from the program bar does not mean that the corresponding program will be deleted. Don't worry if you accidentally delete an icon from the program bar. It can be restored at any time. Use the procedure as described above!

Inserting an icon is slightly different from deleting and moving an icon.

1 Click on the main menu in the program bar.

2 Select the *Control bar* option from the main menu.

A sub-menu appears with which an application, the Disk Navigator or a window list can be added. Furthermore, there are options to configure or restart the program bar and edit the menu.

| Add Application ▶ |
| Add Disk Navigator |
| Add Windowlist |
| Configure |
| Edit Menus |
| Restart |

If you click on *add Disk Navigator*, then a corresponding icon appears in the program bar (according to the entry in the main menu). The same applies to the *window list* which you can use to switch between desktops and active windows. How to configure the program bar was explained earlier in this chapter. *Restart* means that the program bar is recalled – used if modifications are to be activated. *Edit Menu* means deleting or adding applications in the menu structure.

Adding an icon is different from deleting and moving an icon. The *KDE Configuration Wizard* will now be added to the program bar.

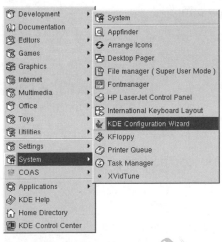

3 Click on *System*, then on the *KDE Configuration Wizard* option.

147

The KDE Configuration Wizard icon is immediately inserted in the program bar. The result looks as follows:

| ⟨K 🖥 🗂 ⚗ | ✂ One ▭ Three
🔒 Two ▭ Four | 🏠 🕮 ✏ 🗐 🎨 | 📖 12:49
Sep 26 |

Do you also wish to add *Documentation*? Just use the following procedure:

1 Click on the main menu in the program bar.

2 Select the *Control bar* option from the main menu.

3 Select the *Add application* option in the sub-menu.

4 Drag the mouse into the next sub-menu to the *Documentation* option.

5 Click on the *WordPerfect* option in this sub-menu.

The *Documentation* icon now appears in the program bar.

1 Right-click in the program bar.

2 Select the *Restart* option in the context menu.

The correct *Documentation* icon now appears in your program bar.

Adding applications to the KDE control centre

WHAT'S THIS?

Modifying an operating system, program or graphic interface is also called CONFIGURATION. Manuals often refer to the modification process as CONFIGURING.

The KDE control centre is a tool for adjusting the graphic interface. You will recognise one of these options from the first part of this chapter.

TIP

The file manager, web browser and console settings will be explained later in the book.

The Login Manager (login window), file manager, web browser, console and program bar (panel) are all applications. You should already have familiarised yourself with the program bar settings in the previous section. You will learn how to modify the *Login Manager* in this section.

CAUTION

You have to log on as the *root* user if you wish to modify the login window settings. This is not permitted to normal users. If you click on the option, an error message will appear.

1 Click on the main menu in the program bar.

2 Click on the *KDE control centre* option in the main menu to open the application.

The KDE control centre opens as shown. It gives information on KDE and Linux kernel versions, the current user, computer name and PC processor.

Modifications can be made to applications, the desktop, input devices, the keyboard, sounds and the appearance of windows. Hardware and network information is also given.

Every KDE control centre menu entry has a sub-menu. These are indicated by plus signs before the entries.

3 Click on the plus symbol.

The plus symbol immediately changes to a minus symbol and the following sub-menu appears:

TIP

The main menu entries have no actual window content. Click on a selection and the most recently opened KDE control centre window remains active. Only when another sub-menu entry is selected is the content of the right half of the window displayed.

CAUTION

Note that the *Login Manager* can only be opened and edited by the *root* superuser. You must log in as *root*.

4 Now click on the *Login Manager*.

Several tabs are available here to modify the login window settings.

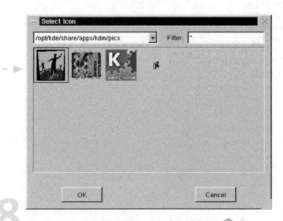

Do you wish to modify the welcome note?

5 Click on the *greetings string* entry field.

6 Delete the current entry with the ⟨⟨=⟩ key and type in the text of your choice.

7 The KDM logo can also be modified by clicking on the logo displayed.

8 You can now choose another logo from this selection window. Select using the left mouse button, then press *OK*.

The graphic interface can also be modified. You can choose between *Motif* and *Windows*.

GUI Style: Windows
Motif
Windows

WHAT'S THIS?

GUI stands for Graphic User Interface. Motif was the standard for Unix system user interfaces for a long time.

9 Click on the black arrow next to the *GUI Style* selection field.

10 Make your selection using the mouse.

The language for the login window is selected in the same way.

C Default language (C)
Breton (br)
Catalan (ca)
Czech (cs)
Danish (da)
German (de)
Greek (el)
English – US (en)
English – UK (en_UK)
Esperanto (eo)

11 Click on English.

12 Confirm by clicking *Apply*.

Use the next tab to alter the font of the login window.

152

1 Now click on the *Fonts* tab.

In the *select font* field you should choose whether the greeting font, error message font or normal text font should be modified.

2 Open the selection menu by clicking the black arrow next to the *select font* field.

3 Click on the option to be modified.

Have you decided on which texts you wish to modify?

4 Then click on the *change font* button.

153

Select a font from this window by clicking in the various selection fields on the black arrow pointing to the right, and then selecting an option from the menu. The settings are executed and a preview is shown in the lower half of the window.

5 Close the settings by clicking on *OK*.

6 Confirm your modifications by clicking on *Apply*.

Modify the background of the login window in the same way as you did for the desktop background.

1 Click on the *Background* tab.

The background colour can be changed and a background image defined specifically (stretched, tiled, centred etc.).

2 Click on the desired option for background colour.

The colours themselves can be modified by clicking on the colour buttons in the same way as you modified the desktop background.

3 Select the background image by clicking on the black arrow next to the *Background* selection field.

A preview of the selected background will immediately be displayed and can be altered in the same way at any time. Experienced users can define a background using the *Select* button.

4 Click on the background of your choice.

You can decide whether you wish the background image to be centred or stretched.

You can test the different settings at this point using the preview window. If you are not satisfied with the settings, they can easily be undone.

5 Confirm your settings with *Apply*.

You can select which users should be displayed at login using the next tab. This makes logging in easier as the name of the user can in this case be entered using the mouse instead of having to type it in manually.

1 Click on the *Users* tab.

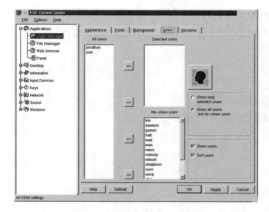

Here you can specify which users should be displayed in the login window. All users created and the root user are displayed in the *All users* section. The *No-show users* displays the users predefined by the system. These are usually only used by the system internally.

To display only *Selected users* at login, use the following procedure.

2 Click on the *Selected users* option.

In this case you also have to fill in the *Selected users* section accordingly.

3 Select the desired users from the *All users* section.

4 First click on the username, and then on the button with the double arrow.

The users selected in this way now appear in the *Selected users* entry field.

5 Confirm your settings using *Apply*.

The last tab contains settings for shutting down the system.

1 Click on the *Sessions* tab.

Here you define who may shut down the system, and with which commands. The settings for the type of session can also be modified.

157

Users other than the root user can shut down the system in the following way:

2 Open the selection field by right-clicking on the black arrow.

```
┌─ Allow to shutdown ─────────────────────────────┐
│                              ┌──────────────────┐│
│                              │ Console Only   ▼ ││
│                              ├──────────────────┤│
├─ Commands ──────────────────┤ None             │┤
│                              │ All              ││
│                              │ Root Only        ││
│ Shutdown  │/sbin/halt        │ Console Only     ││
│                              └──────────────────┘│
└─────────────────────────────────────────────────┘
```

3 Select the *All* entry.

4 Confirm your settings by clicking *Apply*.

Modifying the desktop with the KDE control centre

Most desktop settings found here correspond to the content of the desktop context menu (see the section on Configuring the desktop in this chapter). Only the additional functions are explained here.

The desktop context menu contains the following options:

➡ Background

➡ Screensaver

➡ Colors

➡ Fonts

➡ Style

Click on the plus sign before the *Desktop* option in the *KDE Control Centre*.

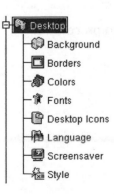

The sub-menu is displayed and the plus becomes a minus symbol.

Now compare the menu with the options on the context menu. There are three additional functions here:

➡ Borders

➡ Desktop icons

➡ Language

2 Click on the *Borders* option.

A single tab opens, as opposed to the desktop context menu. *Active desktop borders* can be modified here.

> If you use the *Active desktop borders*, you can switch between virtual desktops very quickly. You don't have to use the buttons in the program bar any longer – just move the mouse on the respective border to the left, the right, up or down. If for example desktop *One* is active, and you move the mouse to the right, you will switch to desktop *Three*.

If you wish to work with this function, use the following procedure:

1 Click on the A*ctive desktop borders* option.

Should the pointer be in the middle of the desktop after a change?

2 Then select this
option as well.

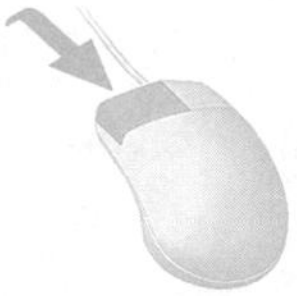

3 Drag the small icon
in the form of a rule on the
Delay desktop switch bar.

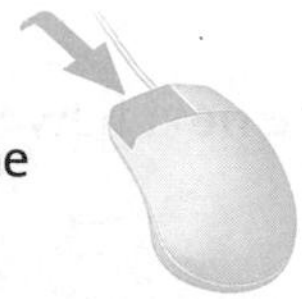

Drag left and the delay time in seconds is reduced (as low as 0), drag
right and it is increased. You will see the delay time in seconds displayed
above the bar.

It does not make sense to set the delay time for a desktop change too high.
Between 0 and 5 seconds is recommended.

A snap zone can be defined in pixels in the magic borders. The edge of the
screen is surrounded by the border snap zone, within which a window snap
zone is located. If you drag the mouse to the border snap zone around the edge
of the screen, you can change desktops.

When you drag a window margin into the screen click zone and drag the
defined window click zone with the mouse, this window will be moved into the
corresponding desktop.

4 Drag the small icon in the form of
a rule to the *Borden Snap Zone* and the
Window Snap Zone bars respectively.

Drag to the left and the zone becomes smaller (as low as 0 pixels). Drag
to the right and it becomes larger. You can see the current setting in
pixels displayed above the respective bar.

The recommended settings are between 10 and 20.

Just play around with the settings to familiarise yourself with them. If in doubt,
reset the settings to *Default*. Click on the corresponding button to do so.

161

Do you wish to end your modifications at this point?

5 Click on *Apply*.

The next new function is the *Desktop Icons* settings.

1 Click on the *Desktop Icons* option in Desktop.

The distance between icons on the desktop can be altered here. You can also specify that hidden files and icon text be displayed. The colour of the icon text can also be modified.

The horizontal and vertical grid spacing of icons is modified by clicking on the plus or minus button next to the values. Clicking on plus increases the distance, clicking on minus reduces it.

A short description is located under every desktop icon. The text colour can also be changed. You must decide if the text should be transparent or be assigned a background.

In this case only the text colour can be modified. The background is now transparent and so it contains no colours. For this reason the background colour is inactive after the option described above.

2 If you prefer the text to appear transparent, click on the corresponding control box.

3 Click on the respective colour buttons to modify the text and background colour if need be.

The *Color selection* window explained earlier in this chapter is now hidden.

There are files in Linux beginning with a full stop, such as the *.profile* file. These files are called hidden files. They usually contain information required by the system or certain programs, and are of no real interest to the user. This is why they are not usually displayed.

Should hidden files also be shown on the desktop?

4 Click on the corresponding control box.

5 To put these settings into effect, click on *Apply*.

In the next option you can modify the appearance of the KDE desktop with a theme of your choice.

1 Select a theme from the list, such as *Style*.

2 Click on the *Content* tab if you only wish to apply one item of the theme.

3 Click on the desired item.

4 Click on *Apply* to save the modifications.

Modifying the appearance of windows

The last desktop settings are located in the *Windows* menu entry of the KDE control centre.

1 Click on the plus sign before the *Windows* option in the KDE control centre.

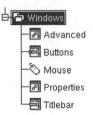

The sub-menu is displayed and the plus sign becomes a minus sign.

The sub-menu has five options. The most important three are described here:

⇨ Advanced

⇨ Buttons

⇨ Titlebar

2 Click on *Advanced* in the *Windows* option.

In this window you can specify how you switch desktops using the (Ctrl), (Alt) and (↹) keys. You can also define the appearance of the window using filters.

If you activate the *Ctrl-Tab walks through desktops* option, you can switch desktops using these keys. There is now no need to use the mouse.

3 Activate the function by clicking on the *Ctrl-Tab walks through desktops* option.

Switch between windows using [Alt] and [⇆]. The most recently selected window is placed in the foreground.

4 Click on the required option if you wish to use keyboard control.

In the additional *Alt-Tab* mode setting option which contains a small selection list, *KDE* and *CDE* should not be modified. Leave the *KDE* setting, then you can switch between all active windows of a desktop. The *CDE* option is awkward to handle.

The *Grab the Right Mouse Button* is activated by default. If this is not so, activate the option.

5 Click on the *Grab the Right Mouse button* option.

To activate a control box you can either click on the text of the option or directly in the corresponding control box.

This option requires a non-KDE application, for example the graphics program **Gimp**. Leave this setting activated.

Additional options can be assigned to windows in the lower area of the window. These include the following options:

```
have tiny decorations
have no decorations
never gain focus
start as Sticky
be excluded from session management
```

1 Open this selection list by clicking on the small black arrow next to the selection field.

2 Click on an option, such as *Start as sticky*.

This means that you can specify that a window should automatically be available after starting on all virtual desktops.

3 Click in the *Title* field and type in KDE control centre.

4 Then click on the activated plus sign on the right-hand side of the entry field.

The entry is displayed in the list here.

```
Filters
Windows will:
have tiny decorations                                     ▼
if they match the following:

Titles                          Classes

KDE Control
```

When you close and restart the KDE control centre, it is available on all virtual desktops. Test it by clicking on the different desktop buttons.

5 Click on *Apply*.

You will now learn about the *Buttons* option.

1 Click on *Buttons* in the *Windows* option.

Here you determine in which corners the five following window icons should appear, or whether they should appear at all:

➡ Minimise

➡ Maximise

➡ Fastened

➡ Close

➡ Menu

The *menu* icon is located by default in the upper left-hand corner, and the *minimise* and *maximise* icons in the upper right-hand corner of a window. *Fastened* and *Close* are placed next to *Out*.

Do you wish to modify this setting?

2 Click on the icon of the desired setting .

Note that no more than two icons can be displayed in the upper left-hand corner, and no more than three in the upper right-hand corner. You may therefore have to place an icon under *Out* from time to time and amend the setting later on. Test the options – you can return to *default* settings at any time.

In the following example the *Minimise* and *Maximise* icons are placed in the upper left-hand corner, and the other icons in the upper right-hand corner.

You will be shown a preview of the window title bar with the modified settings.

3 If you are satisfied with these settings, click on *Apply*.

These settings can now be tested by opening a window. In the following example a terminal window is used.

4 Click on the main menu button in the start bar and select *Utilities*.

5 Click on the *Terminal* option.

The icons of the terminal window are arranged according to your settings.

Finally, click on the *Title bar* option.

1 Click on *Title bar* in the *Windows* option.

Define the appearance of the title bar using this window. You can also define what effect double-clicking with the left mouse button in the title bar has. Finally, set the speed at which the title moves.

In the upper part of the window you can define whether the title appears on the left, centred or on the right.

2 Click on the position of your choice.

You can now modify the colour of the title bar.

3 Select a colour scheme or the *display as a pixmap*.

The *Pixmap* setting is for experienced system users. If activated, there are further setting options on the right-hand side of the window under the name *Pixmap*. This means that prefabricated images can be placed in the title bar.

| (Un)Maximize |
| (Un)Shade |
| Iconify |
| (Un)Sticky |
| Close |

You can also determine whether the active title should have a shaded frame.

Do you wish to perform a certain action by double-clicking in the title bar?

The *Shutters up/down* option is activated by default. This means that the window 'rolls up' to the title bar when double-clicked, just like shutters. Only the title bar is now visible. The window is 'rolled down' again by double-clicking the title bar.

4 First click on *Apply*.

5 Test your settings by double-clicking in the title bar.

The action should now have been executed.

The last setting, *Title movement,* is located at the bottom of the window. Here you can specify how quickly the window title moves in milliseconds.

The title only moves if the window width is not large enough to display everything. The repeat rate of the moving title can be set in milliseconds between 1 and 99. If you set the speed to 0, there is no movement.

6 Click on the slide rule symbol, hold it pressed and drag the button left or right along the bar.

When you let the mouse go, the last selected setting will be kept.

Have you finished making modifications in the KDE control centre?

7 Now click on *Apply* or *OK*.

8 Then close the application by clicking the *Close* icon in the upper right-hand corner.

This of course assumes that you have not modified the position of the icon. If you have, look for the icon marked with an *X*.

> **TIP**
>
> You can see the results on the left-hand side of the bar in the form of a constantly changing number. Drag it left and the speed increases, with the number of milliseconds decreasing. Drag it right and the speed decreases.

What's in this chapter:

In this chapter you will learn what files and directories are, and what types of file are available with Linux. You will also learn how to use the file manager, and how to display, move, copy, delete, rename and create new files and/or directories. You will also learn several ways of modifying the file manager with the KDE Control Centre. You know how the Linux file system and file tree operate. Working with floppy disks, CD-ROMs and the Trash folder will be explained. You will also discover how to find files.

You already know about:

You are going to learn about:

What are files and directories?

The terms **directory** and **file** are common to every operating system. If you are already familiar with these terms, just skip this section.

A file is basically a summary of data. For example, if you write a letter by hand, you have already created a file – it is a document containing data.

If you write a letter with a word processing program, or create an image with a graphics program, data is created in the same way. The only difference is the use of a computer.

You may wish to keep data to be able to use it again. For example, with a report you keep the piece of paper, or at least a copy of it, so you have something to which you can refer again. Keeping data is known as **saving** in computer terminology. Instead of a piece of paper, a *data carrier* is used, which could be a floppy disk or a hard disk.

Data is not just saved on a data carrier, but summarised in a *file*. Just as a report consists of several pieces of paper fastened together, your computer summarises information in an orderly fashion in files. Just as a report is given a title, a file is assigned a **filename**.

It is up to you to assign filenames, so you can find the file later on, using its name.

Rules for filenames in Linux

Linux distinguishes between **upper** and **lower case** letters. This distinction is often referred to as 'case sensitive'. If you create files called REPORT, report and REPort, these are considered to be three different files. This can lead to confusion, so it is recommended that files be assigned different names. You should write all filenames in lower case letters to avoid any confusion.

In principle, any character may be used for a filename. Apart from standard letters, numbers and **special characters** such as + and – may also be used. Certain special characters are used by the system for specific purposes and are therefore best avoided. These include:

^ * ? < > & ; | { } [ ] / \ # $ ( ) ' "

Long filenames may be used in Linux. A filename may contain up to 255 characters. However, it is recommended that files of this length are not used so as to save typing effort. Try to restrict your filenames to around 20 characters.

Dot files (as mentioned in chapter 4) have a special function in Linux. These are usually system files never used by the user. They are therefore not generally displayed, and so are sometimes called **hidden files**.

You may well know the **file extension** with operating systems such as DOS or Microsoft Windows and want to know how Linux handles these. In DOS there are files such as autoexec.bat, report.doc and image.bmp. File extensions after the dot tell the operating system which program this file is connected with.

Linux itself does not recognise these file extensions. If you wish to open a file in Linux, the system checks to see if it is legitimate and legible. If so, the file is opened by the program specified by the user.

KDE refines the Linux system very efficiently. File extensions are not actually required to use a file with a certain program, but a reference to the type of file is given in the file manager using an icon. The following icons refer to certain types of file in the file manager:

Icon	Meaning

Files with the extension *.txt are assigned this icon in the file manager. It denotes that this file is a text file which can be opened and edited with the *Kedit* program.

Files with the extensions *.gif and *.jpg are assigned this graphic icon. This means they contain an image or drawing.

Executable programs (such as the program for opening the *Kedit* editor) are assigned a gear wheel icon.

Internet addresses can also be saved as files, as you did in chapter 4. You have already placed addresses on the desktop. In this chapter you will learn how to place them in your work directory.

Documents created with the StarWriter word processing program with the extension *.sdw are easily recognisable. It will be explained how to work with this program later in the book.

This applies to documents created with the StarCalc spreadsheet program. These have the extension *.sdc. StarCalc will also be explained later in the book.

Images created with the StarDraw graphics program (part of the StarOffice package) have the extension *.sda. StarOffice will be explained in detail later in the book.

Icon	Meaning
	The StarOffice presentation program StarImpress has the extension *.sdd. A presentation program can be used to create transparencies for presentations or lectures, if you use an overhead projector.
	Files created for internet pages have the extension *.htm or *.html. KDE uses a separate icon for these.
	All files with an extension which KDE does not recognise are assigned this icon. The question mark denotes that KDE cannot recognise the file.
	Directories are assigned a folder icon.

There are of course many other file extensions and icons. The ones outlined here are the most important in Linux.

What are directories used for? This can be explained with an example which has nothing to do with a PC. Again, think of a report you have written. Let us assume you write a weekly report. What do you do with the one you need to keep? Place it in a pile of other things? Not usually. Rather, you would store it in a folder created especially for these reports.

When you create documents with the computer, use the following procedure: arrange your documents so you can find them again at any time. You should create folders, also called directories. If your paper-based report folder is called 'Reports 2000', you could do the same on your computer, and then place the corresponding documents in there. How to do so will be explained later in the chapter.

If you look at this image, you can imagine how difficult it is to give a summary of the 9 files in this directory. How would it look if the directory contained 1000 files or more? It would be impossible to find a file quickly.

> This is highly recommended when using a PC. It is much more difficult to find unordered files on a hard drive than in a paper-based environment. You should therefore categorise your files and place them in directories.

Directories should always be created on floppy disks or hard drives for reasons of clarity if the number of files becomes confusing. A directory can contain sub-folders and files, which in turn can contain further sub-folders and files.

Imagine the directory system as placing your 'Reports 2000' folder in a drawer entitled 'Documents 2000', in turn placed in a filing cabinet called 'Department XY 2000'. The 'Department XY 2000' filing cabinet corresponds to the uppermost directory of Linux, the 'Documents 2000' drawer to the first sub-directory, and the 'Reports 2000' folder to a lower sub-directory containing the files 'Report1_2000', 'Report2_2000' and so on.

WHAT'S THIS?

In Linux format the name of the file 'Report22000' consists of the filename specific to that directory. The directory which indicates the file is also known as the **path**. The complete name with path details for 'Report2_2000' would look as follows:

'/Department-XY-2000/Documents2000/Reports2000/Report2_2000'

The individual directories are always separated by slashes in Linux. Also note the slash at the beginning of the path.

TIP

Directories in Linux always have a name, to which the same rules apply as for files. However, a directory never usually has a filename extension.

CAUTION

Files and directories must have a clear name. This means that no two files of the same name may be placed in the same directory (i.e. files which do not differ in upper and lower case letters). Two files of the same name could however be placed in two **different** directories, as the path details will be different.

In Linux, anything saved in any way is a file. A directory is also a file which contains information. There are different types of data in Linux, such as **links**, which will be explained later in this chapter.

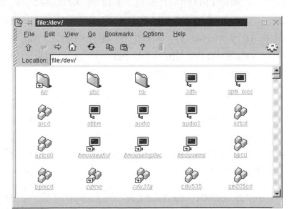

Even the monitor, hard drive, keyboard, floppy drive and so on are seen as files in Linux. They are known as **device files**. They were saved in a file on installation when asked for by the hard drive. This is labelled */dev/hda1*.

181

All **device files** are located in the /dev directory. The operating system responds to the devices via these files. Hard drives are labelled *hd*, with the first system hard drive labelled *had*, and the first partition of the first hard drive *hda1*. The letter *h* is replaced by an *h* with SCSI hard drives.

The Linux file system and the file tree

If you are used to DOS or Microsoft Windows, you will not find drive letters in Linux (abbreviations assigned to hard or disk drives). Hard drives, floppy drives and CD-ROM drives are handled completely differently in Linux.

The Linux file system has a very strong structure – it is regulated precisely as the highest directory. This structure is known as a **hierarchical** structure. The main central directory is called the **root** directory, represented with a slash (/). It is always placed at the top of the directory hierarchy. All other directories stem from this one, which in turn contain further sub-folders, and so on. Branching options in Linux are almost unlimited.

Imagine the Linux file tree as a real tree. The roots and thick trunk are the '/' directory, and the main branches are the directories located directly below the root directory. Further branches stem from these, which in turn contain twigs and leaves. The files can be considered as leaves.

A new directory can be created at any time in Linux. The root superuser can do this at any position on the file tree. As Linux was designed as a **multi-user system**, a normal user may only create new directories and files in his own work directory. If a new user is set up, a work directory is also set up automatically bearing the name of the user.

WHAT'S THIS?

A **multi-user system** means that several users can use the same system at the same time. If every user were allowed to place their files and directories anywhere, the clarity and structure of the file tree would soon be lost. For this reason a normal user may only create files and directories in their own work directory. Work directories are located in every Linux system either under the /home or /export/home directory – the username then follows in the path, for example /home/david or /export/home/david for the user David.

In this image you can see the directories created under the root directory by default after installation. The most important are outlined below.

Directory	Meaning
/bin	Contains the most important Linux commands.
/dev	Contains device files required to operate the monitor, CD-ROM drive, hard drive and so on.
/etc	Contains files with the most important operating system settings, such as data on valid system users.
/home	Contains sub-folders of normal users.
/lib	Abbreviation for 'libraries' used by programs.

183

Directory	Meaning
/opt	Contains additional programs from manufacturers, such as the KDE, Netscape Browser, WordPerfect and StarOffice programs.
/proc	Contains everything currently running on the system, leaving behind a process number. Tasks performed by the Linux system are known as **processes**.
/sbin	Contains commands or programs executable only by the system administrator.
/tmp	Contains temporary files created by certain programs. These files are deleted after use. A normal user can also use this directory, but note that when shutting down or starting the system the contents of this directory will be deleted.
/usr	Contains additional programs for working with Linux.

You can see from the description that very important files are located in most directories. The root superuser can delete these inadvertently, which may damage the system. It is therefore recommended that you use the system as a normal user: then only your own files can be deleted and modified!

The file manager view

You have now learned enough theoretical basics. Let us try to put them into practice. You will now learn to customise the file manager.

1 Open the file manager using the icon in the program bar.

When you open the file manager for the first time, the icons are usually displayed large, as shown here. This view can be modified.

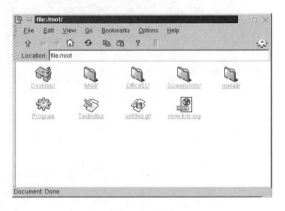

3 A menu opens. Select *Show Tree*.

2 Click on *View* in the menu list.

4 Then select *Short View*.

185

The file manager view changes immediately – it becomes clearer. You will see the 'content directory' in the left-hand side of the window, and the directory currently selected on the right-hand side. This is your work directory.

The address bar shows your exact current location in the file tree. You will see the content of the directory in the right-hand side of the window at the same time. In the above example the address bar looks as follows:

An icon bar is located above the address bar, in which the most important menu commands are repeated:

The icons have the following meaning:

⬆   Up one level.

⬅   One step backwards.

➡   One step forwards (after a step back).

🏠   Back to the work directory of the current user.

🔄   Refreshes the view. It may happen that a recently created file is not immediately visible. Left-click on this icon and the view will be refreshed.

📋   Copies one or more files.

📋   Inserts copied files.

The question mark denotes *Help*, and a *red light* shows that the file manager is busy processing your request.

5 Click on *View* again in the menu list.

6 Click on *Text View*.

Text view displays files and directories without icons. Additional details are also given, such as file rights, file owner and group, and the date last modified. These details will be explained in more detail later in this chapter.

7 Click on *View*, then *Long View*.

Long View displays files and directories as described above (with additional details), with the respective icon.

(File manager window — file:/root/)

Location: file:/root/

Desktop/	drwx------	root root	1024	09:22 28.09.2000
Mail/	drwx------	root root	1024	15:51 15.09.2000
Office51/	drwxr-xr-x	root root	1024	15:36 27.09.2000
Screenshots/	drwx------	root root	1024	11:48 27.09.2000
nsmail/	drwx------	root root	1024	12:51 27.09.2000
Program.kdelnk	-rw-r--r--	root root	521	11:48 27.09.2000
Texteditor	-rw-r--r--	root root	17	11:48 27.09.2000
untitled.gif	-rw-r--r--	root root	2399	15:51 27.09.2000
www.kde.org.kdelnk	-rw-r--r--	root root	118	11:48 27.09.2000

Document: Done

8 Click on *View*, then *Short View*.

Short View displays only files and directories by name and with a small icon.

The display in both halves of the window is always in alphabetical order. However, in the right-hand side of the window the directory is always listed first, followed by the file, both listed alphabetically.

The remaining menu line options will now be described briefly.

9 Click on *Options* in the menu list.

You familiarised yourself with a similar menu in chapter 3. The display of the menu, status, address and toolbars can be activated or deactivated here. New settings can then be saved.

10 Click on *Bookmarks* in the menu list.

You should already know about bookmarks. A new bookmark is created using *Add Bookmark*. The existing bookmarks are visible in the lower part of the menu. Click these to reach the desired position in the file manager quickly.

Edit Bookmarks...

Add Bookmark   Ctrl+B

11 Now click on *Go* in the menu list.

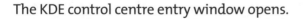

The actions of the icon and toolbars are repeated here. You can move up, backwards, forwards or to the home directory (work directory) using the mouse.

Alternatively you can jump to the last places visited in the file manager. These are listed in the lower half of the menu. This method of browsing in the file tree corresponds to using bookmarks. However, bookmarks remain in place until deleted. The place last visited is overridden when you jump to another page.

Customising the file manager in the KDE control centre

Additional modifications can be made to the file manager in the KDE control centre. The first option concerns text.

1 Click on the *KDE control centre* icon in the program bar.

The KDE control centre entry window opens.

2 Click on the plus sign next to *Applications* and then on *File Manager*.

You will see the first tab for the file manager settings. You can customise font size and type here. You should already know these settings from the desktop in chapter 4.

3 Click on the font size of your choice.

4 Open the *Font Size selection* menu by clicking on the black arrow to the right of the respective field.

5 Click on the desired font setting in the selection menu.

6 Click on *Apply*.

The font and background colours of the file manager can also be modified.

1 Click on the *Color* tab.

Background colour (white by default), text colour and colour of links can be modified. Links are cross-references in the file manager (directories or files) with which you can browse the file tree quicker, or which you can edit. If you have already followed one link, it will be displayed in a different colour.

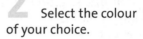

You should already know these colour settings from the desktop in chapter 4.

2 Select the colour of your choice.

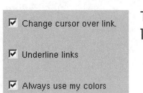

Three further modifications can be made in the lower screen area.

If you tick the *Cursor over link* option, the mouse pointer will be displayed as a hand instead of an arrow as soon as the mouse is dragged over a link. The default *Underline links* option ensures that links are always displayed as underlined. It is recommended that these settings be left alone. *Always use my colors* ensures that the modified colours are applied in the file manager.

Note that clicking on an option already activated (indicated with a check) will deactivate it again.

3 Click on one or more of the three options, depending on which one you wish to activate.

4 Then click on *Apply*.

The two remaining settings can now be activated.

1 Click on *Other*.

Click on *Allow per-URL settings* and ensure that the *File navigation view* is applied.

Using *URL-specific settings* means that KDE window settings (e.g. window sizes, view menu options and other menu, status and icon bar settings) will be saved as a bookmark.

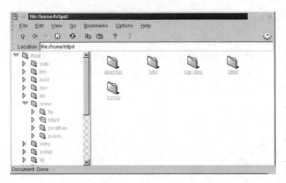

The *File navigation view* option requires the tree view in the file manager to be activated. On the left-hand side of the window the 'contents directory' is displayed. On the right-hand side, the content of the active directory with all sub-folders and files is displayed. In this case the *jonathan* directory is open on the left-hand side, and the files it contains on the right.

2 Click on the *File navigation* window.

3 Then click on *Apply*.

4 Switch to the *File Manager* window and click on a directory containing sub-folders.

The *jonathan* directory is used again in this case. You will see that only the files are shown as the contents of the directory in the right-hand side of the window. The *jonathan* sub-directory on the left-hand side is automatically 'opened'.

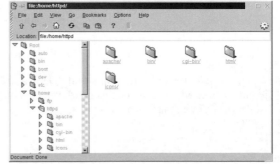

If you are satisfied with your settings, close the KDE control centre.

5 Click on the *Close* button in the upper right-hand corner of the title bar.

Displaying files and directories

In principle, we have already displayed files and directories whilst modifying the file manager view. We will now address this in more detail.

If you followed the steps as outlined above, your file manager should now look similar to the picture opposite. However, you do not have to work with the 'short view'. Large icons or other views can be used if preferred.

It is recommended that the same display be used for the tree structure in the left-hand window. Working with the file manager then becomes clearer.

1 Click on any directory in the left-hand side of the window.

A similar display as shown here appears: files and sub-folders on the selected directory are listed on the right-hand side.

2 Click on one of the blue arrows before the directories in the left-hand side of the window.

The view of the right-hand side of the window does not change. But on the left-hand side the sub-folders of the selected directory appear 'opened'. If you have selected a directory without sub-folders, execute the action until you can see the desired result.

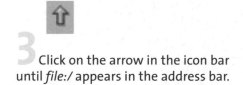

3 Click on the arrow in the icon bar until *file:/* appears in the address bar.

You are now in the root directory. Its content can be seen on the right-hand side.

You may need to move the scrollbar downwards with the mouse.

4 Click on the blue arrow before the root directory, and then on the blue arrow before the *usr* directory.

5 Click on the *doc* directory.

The contents of the *lusr/doc* directory are now displayed in the right-hand side of the window.

6 Move the scroll box on the right-hand side downwards with the mouse until you can see the README file.

7 Click on the name of the file.

As this is a readable text file, this file is 'executed', meaning it is opened in an editor window so you can read it.

You will have already performed such an action in chapter 3 when working with programs. You learned how to start a program or open a window by clicking with the mouse.

Move around in the file tree with the mouse, switch directories and observe the changing displays in the address line and the two halves of the window. You will soon familiarise yourself with the file manager if you take the steps as outlined above.

Creating new files and directories

You have now learned how to modify the appearance of the file manager, how to recognise different views and switch between directories in the file tree. You will now learn how to create new directories and files.

Go back to the file manager in your work directory by 'opening' the */home* directory first, and then your work directory in the left-hand side of the window, for example */home/jonathan*.

1 Click on the plus sign before the respective directory in the left-hand side of the window.

2 Click on the name of your work directory.

The content of the directory is now displayed in the right-hand side of the window.

New ▶		Folder
New Window	Ctrl+N	File System Device
Run...		FTP URL
Open Terminal	Ctrl+T	Mime Type
Open Location...	Ctrl+O	Application
Find	Ctrl+F	Internet Address (URL)
Print...	Ctrl+P	World Wide Web URL
Close	Ctrl+W	

3 Click on *File* in the menu line, then *New*, then *Folder*.

kfm

New Folder:

Company2000

| OK | Clear | Cancel |

4 Enter a folder name (e.g. *Company2000*) in the entry field of the window displayed.

5 Click on *OK*.

You can see the *Company2000* sub-directory in the */home/jonathan* work directory. The view of your file manager should now look similar (it can of course contain more files or directories!).

6 Create a second sub-directory in the same way (called *reports*, for example) in your work directory.

Now create new files.

1 Click on *File* in the menu line, then on *New*, then on *Application*.

2 Enter a filename with the extension *.txt in the entry field of the window displayed (such as *textfile.txt*).

3 Then click on *OK*.

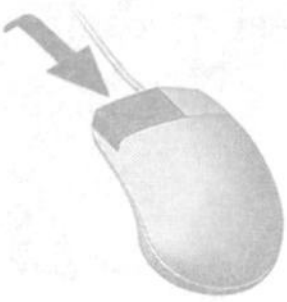

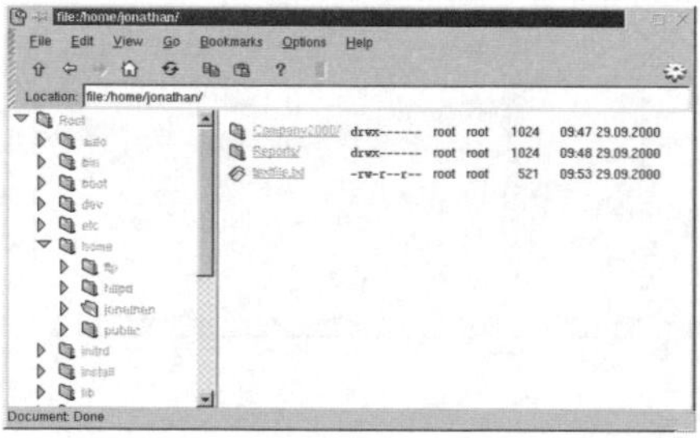

In this image you can now see two sub-folders, *Company2000* and *Reports*, and the text file called *textfile.txt* in the */home/jonathan* work directory. The view of your file manager should correspond to this.

4 Create two more text files called *textfile1.txt* and *textfile2.txt* in the same way.

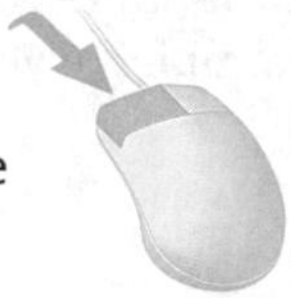

The file manager now looks similar to the example displayed here: two new sub-folders and three new files.

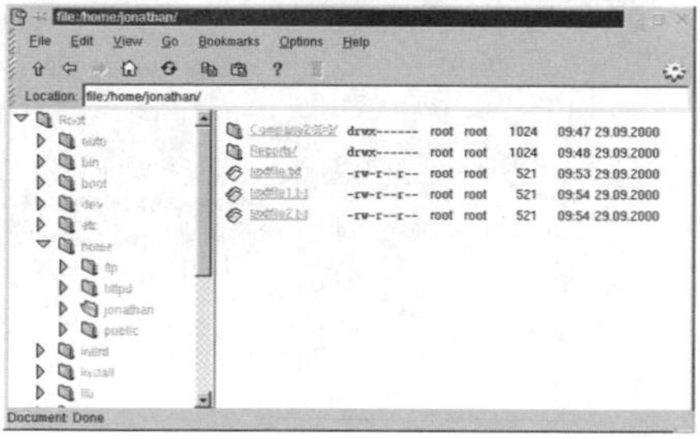

These recently created text files are of course empty. A correct file usually also has content, meaning a text file usually contains some text.

Alternatively, you can also create a text file in the following way – with content this time.

1 Click on the main menu button, and then on the *Editors* and *Kedit Editor* options.

An editor window opens, as in chapter 3. Type in a few words in the text area.

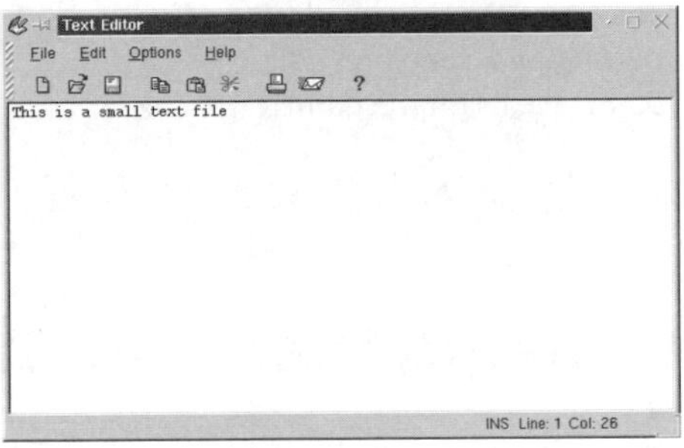

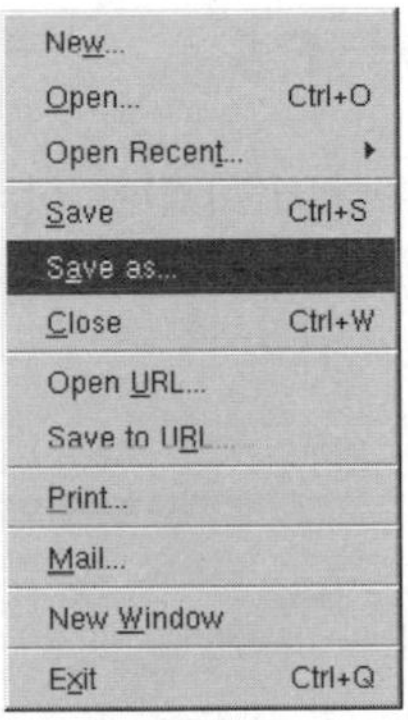

New...	
Open...	Ctrl+O
Open Recent...	▶
Save	Ctrl+S
Save as...	
Close	Ctrl+W
Open URL...	
Save to URL...	
Print...	
Mail...	
New Window	
Exit	Ctrl+Q

2 Click on *File* in the menu line, then on *Save as* in the sub-menu.

The directories of your work directory are displayed here. Type a filename in the *location* entry field **after** the path name (*/home/ jonathan* in this case), such as *editorfile.txt*. Then click on *OK*.

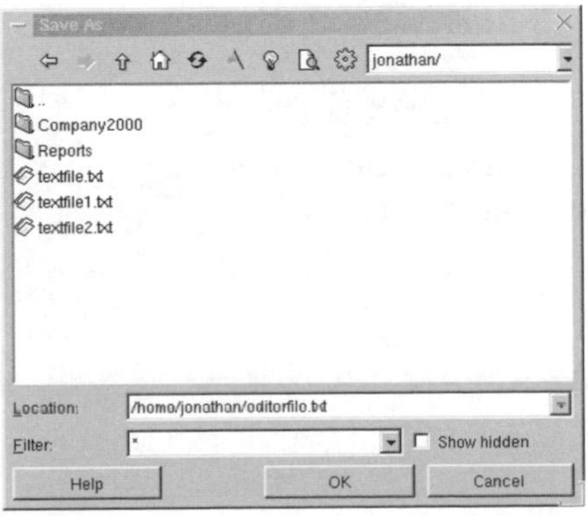

The file manager now displays two new sub-folders and four new files.

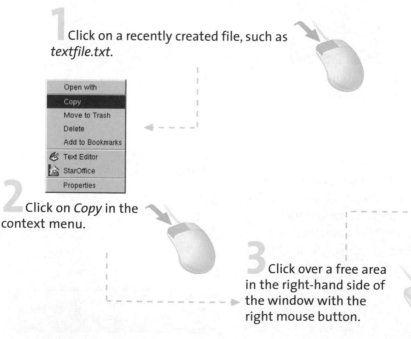

You have now created a file containing text. Alternatively, you can create an empty file as before, and open and edit it using the left mouse button.

Copying files and directories

You may frequently wish to duplicate, or copy, existing files, either to create several copies for security reasons, or to modify files without losing the original file.

1 Click on a recently created file, such as *textfile.txt*.

Open with
Copy
Move to Trash
Delete
Add to Bookmarks
Text Editor
StarOffice
Properties

2 Click on *Copy* in the context menu.

3 Click over a free area in the right-hand side of the window with the right mouse button.

New ▶
Up
Back
Forward
New View
Copy
Paste
Add to Bookmarks
Save settings for this URL
Properties

4 Click on the *Paste* option in the context menu.

An error message will appear, reporting that you may not paste a file of the same name at this point. You should either *Cancel* or *Rename* the file.

— KFM Warning ✕

You try to overwrite

file:/home/jonathan/textfile.txt

with itself. Do you want to rename it to

file:/home/jonathan/textfile.txt

| Cancel | Rename | Skip | Overwrite | Overwrite All |

— KFM Warning ✕

You try to overwrite

file:/home/jonathan/textfile.txt

with itself. Do you want to rename it to

file:/home/jonathan/newtext.txt

| Cancel | Rename | Skip | Overwrite | Overwrite All |

5 Rename the file by clicking behind the existing filename with the left mouse button, then deleting the old filename with the ⟨⇐⟩ key and entering a new name, such as *newtext.txt*.

Try not to delete the necessary filename path by accident (*/home/jonathan* in this case) – otherwise the file will be saved in the root directory. However, if you are registered as the root superuser, you will receive an error message again that the file may not be saved under this name!

The file manager window showing files:

Company2000/	drwx------	root	root	1024	09:47 29.09.2000
Reports/	drwx------	root	root	1024	09:48 29.09.2000
editorfile.txt	-rw-r--r--	root	root	26	10:00 29.09.2000
newfile.txt	-rw-r--r--	root	root	521	10:08 29.09.2000
textfile.txt	-rw-r--r--	root	root	521	09:53 29.09.2000
textfile1.txt	-rw-r--r--	root	root	521	09:54 29.09.2000
textfile2.txt	-rw-r--r--	root	root	521	09:54 29.09.2000

The file manager now displays the copied files, and those renamed once copied.

You may wish to create a copy in a different directory. In the following example we will copy the *testfile.txt* file into the *Reports* sub-directory.

1 Click on the small icon before the file.

2 Drag the file in the left-hand side of the window into the *Reports* directory.

The mouse pointer assumes the form of the file icon. Release the mouse pointer when positioned directly over the directory.

Copy
Move
Link

A small context menu opens again. You can copy or move the file, or create a shortcut (link).

3 Click on the *Copy* option.

4 Open the *Reports* sub-directory in the file manager.

The copied file is displayed here. The original is located in your work directory.

Likewise, an entire directory can be copied. In the following example we will copy the *Reports* directory (containing the *textfile.txt* file) in the *Company2000* directory.

1 Click on the small icon before the directory.

2 Move the directory in the left-hand side of the window into the *Reports2000* directory.

The mouse pointer assumes the form of the directory icon. Release the mouse pointer when positioned directly over the directory.

A small context menu opens. You can move or copy the directory, or create a shortcut (link).

3 Click on the *Copy* option.

Immediately after copying you will see in the file manager that the *Reports* directory is located twice under the *Company2000* directory. Click once with the left mouse button in the left-hand side of the window on the *Company2000* directory.

Copying a directory and file may now seem fairly common. But how can several files or directories be copied at the same time? There is a way of doing so, as copying individually is too time-consuming.

TIP

It would be easiest to proceed as outlined below by switching to the large icons view in the file manager (Click on *View* in the menu bar, then *Icon View*).

You must first specify which files are to be copied.

1 Hold down the Ctrl button and click on the first file to be copied in the file manager.

2 Hold the Ctrl key depressed and click on all other files to be copied.

These will immediately be highlighted.

3 Press the right mouse button directly over one of the marked files.

Open with

Copy

Move to Trash

Delete

Add to Bookmarks

4 Select *Copy* in the context menu.

Files are pasted in exactly the same way as individual files or directories, as already outlined in this section.

Moving files and directories

The icon view will be used here. However, the view with which you work is still your choice. The images will be different from your screen display if you select a different view.

Files do not always need to be duplicated. Sometimes moving them to another directory is enough. In this example, the file *textfile1.txt* will be used.

1 Click on the small icon before the *textfile1.txt* file with the left mouse button.

2 Drag the file in the left-hand side of the window to the *Reports* directory.

207

The mouse pointer assumes the form of the file icon.

3 Release the mouse pointer when positioned directly over the directory.

Copy
Move
Link

4 Click on the *Move* option in the context menu.

5 Click on the *Reports* sub-directory in the file manager.

The file moved is displayed there. It is now located directly in the work directory.

An entire directory is moved in the same way.

If you wish to move a directory or file into another directory in which it is already located, an error message appears. This informs you that you are trying to overwrite a file or directory with the same name. As previously explained, you can cancel the process, or rename the file or directory to be moved.

As with the copying process, several files and/or directories can of course be moved at the same time. Mark all files to be moved with the mouse, as described in the 'Copying files and directories' section.

Renaming files and directories

Files and directories do not need to have a name assigned every time. They can be renamed at any time. The *editorfile.txt* file will now be renamed.

1 Click on the file to be renamed, *editorfile.txt*.

| Open with |
| Copy |
| Move to Trash |
| Delete |
| Add to Bookmarks |
| Text Editor |
| StarOffice |
| Properties |

2 Click on the *Properties* option in the context menu.

The properties of the selected file are now displayed. This includes the name, full name including directory path, file size, date last accessed and date last modified.

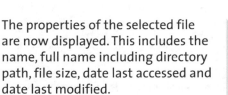

kfm

General | Permissions

File Name

editorfile.txt

Full Name

/home/jonathan/editorfile.txt

Size: 26
Last Access: 10:32 29.09.2000
Last Modified: 10:00 29.09.2000

OK   Cancel

WHAT'S THIS?

The *Last Access* date is when the file was last displayed or its properties viewed. File content is not modified here. The *Last Modified* date signifies the time when the contents of the file were last altered.

3 Click in the text field containing the file name, after the filename.

kfm

General | Permissions

File Name

company-letter.txt

Full Name

/home/jonathan/editorfile.txt

Size: 26

Last Access: 10:32 29.09.2000

Last Modified: 10:00 29.09.2000

OK | Cancel

4 Delete the current filename using the ⌫ key, and type in the new name *company-letter.txt*.

5 Click on the *Permissions* tab.

kfm

General | Permissions

Access permissions

	Read	Write	Exec	Special
User	☑	☑	☐	☐ Set UID
Group	☑	☐	☐	☐ Set GID
Others	☑	☐	☐	☐ Sticky

Ownership

Owner | root

Group | root

OK | Cancel

Access Permissions determines who may read, modify and open (in the case of a program) the file. The *owner* in the lower part of the window is the current user. A user is always assigned to a *group*. The owner and the group have rights to the file. These rights are specified in the upper window area using *Access Permissions*. All other valid system users are labelled *Others*.

These file rights will be explained in more detail later in the book. Rights have to be planned and specified exactly in a network system, so no unauthorised user can read, modify or even delete your files.

Look at the result of renaming in the file manager in your work directory. There is no longer a file called *editortext.txt*, only a file called *company-letter.txt*.

What are links and how are they created?

It is often practical to have some files or directories available in several places. In different directories, for example, as different users work with them, or in a directory directly on the desktop. You should always work with the original file or directory, or several divergent copies will be created.

This problem is solved in Linux by creating a link somewhere (also known as a shortcut). This link is simply a signpost to the original file or directory. A link file contains only the location of the original file (or directory), i.e. its full directory path together with filename.

Imagine a link as a signpost at a crossroads. If you see the sign 'Sheffield' and follow it, you will come to Sheffield at some point. So a road sign can point to an arbitrary point and always refer to the original place.

Just as with a road sign, the original file is not affected if the link is deleted. If you remove a road sign to Sheffield, the city remains in the same place – yet the sign will no longer be in the same place. However, if the original file is deleted, the link points nowhere. The system will report an error message if you try to open the original file via this link.

A link is always indicated in a certain way in Linux. The file icon has a small black arrow in the bottom left-hand corner on the desktop.

In the following example the file *textfile2.txt* is used.

1 Click on the small icon before the file *textfile2.txt*.

2 Drag the file in the left-hand side of the window to the *Reports* directory.

The mouse pointer assumes the form of a file icon.

3 Release the mouse pointer when positioned directly over the directory.

Copy
Move
Link

4 Click on the link option in the context menu.

In this way a shortcut to the original file is created.

Open the *Reports* sub-directory in the file manager. The link is then displayed. Your program icon willl contain the small black arrow in the lower left-hand corner which refers to shortcuts. As this is not a normal file like the other text files, the name of the link is displayed in italics.

5 Click on the shortcut file *textfile2.txt*.

The editor window opens with the content of the file *textfile2.txt*.

If you modify the text, you will modify the original content of the original file *textfile2.txt*. The shortcut file remains unchanged; it contains only the file path (not visible to the user) and name of the original file as before.

A shortcut to an entire directory is created in exactly the same way. A directory is just a special type of file.

Not only can files and directories be moved or copied elsewhere, they can also be placed on the desktop.

The file manager window should be reduced so a portion of free desktop space remains.

1 Move either the left or right window margin inwards using the mouse.

2 Click on the *company-letter.txt* file and drag it onto the desktop using the mouse.

Release the mouse button. The small context menu appears again.

3 Click on the *Link* option.

Note that the link to the original file will be lost if you select the *Copy* option. A further file will then be created, which can be modified independently of the original file.

Avoid using the *Move* option at some point. Placing original files on the desktop is dangerous, as these can easily be deleted by mistake!

The shortcut file appears immediately on the desktop, and is labelled as a shortcut by the black arrow on the icon.

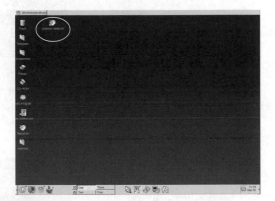

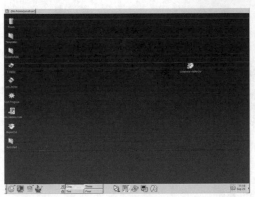

Sometimes icons dragged onto the desktop using the mouse are not arranged as neatly as displayed above. The recently created icon could be located anywhere on the desktop.

The icons must be rearranged on the desktop manually. However, the icons do not need to be placed individually. The following menu helps:

1 Click in a free area of the desktop with the right mouse button.

New	▶
Bookmarks	▶
Help on desktop	
Execute command	
Display properties	
Refresh desktop	
Unclutter windows	
Cascade windows	
Arrange icons	
Lock screen	
Logout	

2 Select the *Arrange icons* option in the context menu.

The system checks to see if you have made the right selection by asking if you really wish to rearrange the icons. You can cancel by clicking on *No*.

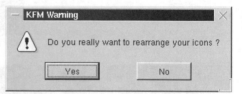

KFM Warning

⚠ Do you really want to rearrange your icons ?

Yes   No

The icons will now be arranged neatly on your desktop.

Deleting files and directories

There is no point in keeping all files for ever. As soon as your filing cabinets start to fill up, you clear them out. Old and/or unimportant documents are usually thrown out. The same applies to files and directories on your PC.

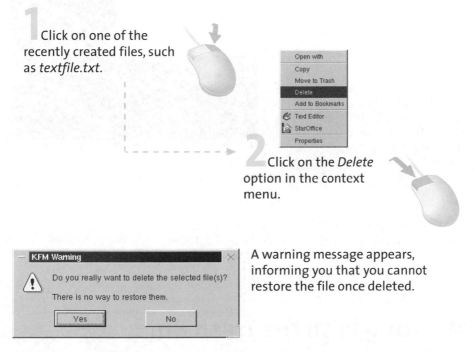

1 Click on one of the recently created files, such as *textfile.txt*.

2 Click on the *Delete* option in the context menu.

A warning message appears, informing you that you cannot restore the file once deleted.

As you have created this file yourself, you can make sure that this can be deleted.

3 Click on *Yes*.

System warning messages should not usually be ignored. If you have the slightest doubt as to whether you really wish to delete the file, click on *No* to cancel the delete process.

The *textfile.txt* file is no longer visible in the file manager. It has been irretrievably deleted.

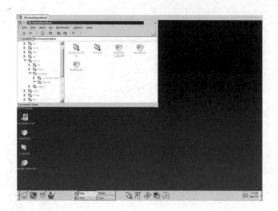

Working with the Trash Bin

When clearing out a filing cabinet, you may not be sure if you really can throw away something immediately. You may well place something in a pile for a certain amount of time before you make a decision. There is a similar process in Linux: something can be deleted without being irretrievably lost (as in the previous section). It is placed in the *Trash Bin* instead. You can then decide whether it should be restored from the *Trash Bin* or deleted permanently.

1 Click on one of the recently created files, such as *company-letter.txt*.

Open with
Copy
Move to Trash
Delete
Add to Bookmarks
🐸 Text Editor
📋 StarOffice
Properties

2 Click on *Move to Trash* in the context menu.

No warning message appears this time. The file is removed from the directory.

3 Click on the *Trash Bin* icon on the desktop.

A file manager opens containing the *Trash Bin* path in the address bar. The *company-letter.txt* file you removed can be seen in the window.

In order to restore the file, reduce both file manager windows so they both fit on the desktop. They should no longer overlap.

4 Move the left or right margin of the window inwards until both windows fit on the screen.

219

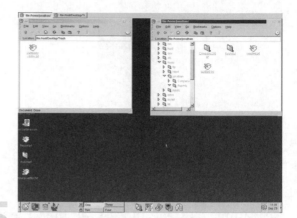

5 Click on the file to be restored in the *Trash Bin*.

6 Drag the file into the right-hand side of the window of the file manager first opened.

Before restoring (actually moving), you should prepare the view of the second file manager. The directory into which the file is to be restored should be open.

7 Release the mouse button when the file is located in the desired place in the directory tree once again.

Once the file has been restored, it is no longer visible in the *Trash Bin*.

If there are other files in the *Trash* folder which you know can be irretrievably deleted, then empty the *Trash Bin*.

1 Click on *File* in the *Trash Bin* file manager.

Empty Trash Bin	
New Window	Ctrl+N
Run...	
Open Terminal	Ctrl+T
Open Location...	Ctrl+O
Find	Ctrl+F
Print...	Ctrl+P
Close	Ctrl+W

You will **not** be asked here if you are sure. Check to see exactly which files are in the recycle bin before they are irretrievably deleted!

2 A sub-menu appears. Click on *Empty Trash Bin*.

You do not have to empty the entire Trash Bin. As with deleting files in your work directory in the file manager, just one or several files and/or directories can be deleted. Open the Trash Bin and select all files to be deleted as described in the 'Deleting files and directories' section.

Finding files and directories

So far you have learned how to organise your computer so that files and directories can be found at any time. However, you will still need to look for something now and again, as in real life. As this occurs fairly frequently, Linux has a search program.

1 Click on the main menu button. Select *Utilities*, then *Find Files*.

A window opens in which more search details can be entered.

Let us assume you wish to find a file, and all you know about it is that it ends with *letter*.

2 Enter the search string **letter*
in the *Name* entry field.

If a search string is already entered, delete it using the ⌫ key.

> You may wonder what the special character * means. This acts as a **wild card** or **dummy**. If you only enter *letter*, the system searches for a file called exactly that. The dummy * stands for an arbitrary number of further characters following the search string. The system could theoretically find the following files (and many others):
>
> *Letter, LETTER, letter, letter1, successfullysentletter, letter.txt, new-leTTEr.txt, 3399letter.doc, 2398letter.sdw, company-letter.txt* and so on.
>
> You will notice that the first five letters of all listed possibilities are identical **(no distinction is made between upper and lower case letters)**. These can be followed by nothing at all, or any number of arbitrary characters, numbers or special characters.
>
> Do not forget to use the wild card if you know only part of the filename, or your search will be in vain.

3 Type a search path in the *Look in* entry field.

If you have no idea as to where the file could be, look in the root directory '/'. Type in / in the entry field. If an entry is already present, delete it using the ⌫ key.

You could usually enter */home* here, as the user's work directory is located here. If you enter a sub-directory, the search will be shortened.

If you use the search function more frequently, you can re-use old search patterns. Click on the black arrow on the right-hand side of the entry fields with the left mouse button. A drop-down menu opens in which old entries are located. These can be selected with the mouse.

Click on the *Browse* button. You can then see the search path in the file manager.

4 Click on the *Include subfolders* option in the lower window area.

Otherwise only the specified directory will be searched.

There are yet more ways to limit the search, or search in a different way, even if part of the filename is missing. Can you perhaps remember the date the file was created?

1 Click on the *Date Modified* tab.

You can limit the search to when the file was created or last modified. A precise period of time, or an estimated number of days or months, can be entered.

2 Click on *Find all files created or modified.*

3 Enter the estimated period of time or the estimated number of days or months.

Further search criteria can be entered in the third tab, *Advanced*.

1 Click on the *Advanced* tab.

You can specify at this point whether only files or directories, or both, should be searched. You can also search for a file containing specific text. The final option is searching for a file of a certain size.

If you wish to limit the search for files or directories to certain types of document, use the *Of type* selection menu.

2 Click on the black arrow to the right of the *Of type* selection field.

3 Select the desired setting from the selection menu.

4 Type some text contained in the file in the *Containing Text* field.

This text should of course not occur frequently in almost every text file. You should use a word rarely mentioned, or you will receive an unmanageable number of results.

If an entry already exists, delete it using the ⌫ key.

If you are looking for a file of a certain size, use the *Size is* selection field.

5 Click on the black arrow to the right of the *Size* field.

A drop-down menu opens, from which you can select the options *(none)*, *at least* or *at most*. If you choose *at least* or *at most*, a file size in kilobytes can be entered.

If you type in a simple text in the editor, then one character (a letter, number or special character) takes one byte of memory space. A file of 50 characters in total will theoretically have a size of 50 bytes. It will actually take slightly more memory space to manage the file (assigning the filename, remembering its location, etc.). It will probably take up 60-70 bytes.

A **kilobyte** is the next large unit of measuring memory space. A kilobyte is 1024 bytes. The pattern continues in the same way: a megabyte is 1024 kilobytes, i.e. around a million bytes, and a gigabyte is 1024 megabytes.

Searching for files of a certain size makes sense only if the file size is vastly different from other files. This means it could make sense to search for a large file by specifying *at least 1000 KB* as an option. This corresponds to a file of around 1 MB in size.

Once all options have been entered, leave the system to search for the file.

TIP

Alternatively, you can start the search from the menu. Click on *File* in the menu line, then on *Start search*.

1 Click on this button in the icon bar.

Depending on the search criteria, the search can last a few seconds or even minutes.

Find Files
File Edit Options Help
Name&Location Date Modified Advanced
Named: *letter
Look in: /home   Browse...
☑ Include subfolders
0 file(s) found

The traffic light icon in the icon bar shines red while the system processes the command. The search result is finally displayed.

TIP

The number of hits is displayed in the status line in the lower window margin. If the system finds *no* corresponding file or directory in the search pattern, the message 'o file(s) found' appears. In this case the search pattern should be reworked. It sometimes happens that too many search criteria are given at the same time.

Working with floppy disks and CD-ROMs

You have already used a floppy disk and CD-ROM at installation. That may have been the first time you worked with data carriers. This section addresses working with floppy disks and CD-ROMs.

WHAT'S THIS?

There used to be different formats of disk. Do you remember the soft black A5-sized disks? Those were **5" disks** rarely used today. The smaller, more sturdy disks, usually grey or black (or sometimes coloured), have replaced these, as they are not quite so sensitive and take up less space in the computer. These are called **3" disks**, or simply floppy disks, as the larger disks used to be called.

A disk has a metal slide on the lower margin, which protects the synthetic disk with a magnetic layer in the plastic cover from dirt and damage.

CAUTION

If you work with disks, you should never remove this metal slide and/or touch the plastic disk. This can damage data stored on the disk. Furthermore, you should always keep the disk from being exposed to dust, heat, magnetic fields or liquid – this can also result in loss of data.

WHAT'S THIS?

There is a small rectangular opening in the upper right-hand corner of every disk which can be closed with a plastic slide. This is known as **write protection**. Opening this gap (slide the plastic tab upwards with your thumbnail) protects the disk from being overwritten. To save data on a disk, write protection should **not** be activated.

When inserting a disk, you should touch it where the sticker is attached. Push it into the drive until it clicks. To eject the disk, press the eject button next to the floppy drive.

You will certainly recognise a CD-ROM because you will be used to music CD-ROMs. A data CD-ROM looks identical. The data is deposited on the underside of the CD-ROM. You should prevent this from becoming scratched or dirty. Never touch the underside of the CD-ROM containing the data. Store the CD-ROM in the same way as a floppy disk after use.

Open the CD-ROM drive by pressing the small rectangular button. The CD-ROM drawer is ejected. Insert the CD-ROM and press the button again so the drawer closes. Remove the disk from the drawer by opening it in the same way.

Until now you have only displayed the contents of your hard drive. You can also view the contents of floppy disks and CD-ROMs. Files and/or directories can be copied from and to disks, files deleted or moved from disks, or placed in the trash bin. The same options are available on a floppy disk. With CD-ROMs, files can usually only be displayed and copied.

TIP

The above operations can be performed only if the floppy disk is not write protected.

Use the icons installed on the desktop by the KDE Configuration Wizard to work with CD-ROMs and floppy disks.

1 Click on the floppy drive icon on the desktop.

If you have not inserted a disk, the following error message appears:

The system is trying to find and read a disk in the floppy drive.

— ⊞ kfm · □ ×

Trying to open
file:/auto/floppy

Cancel

— KFM Error ×

⚠ Could not read
file:/auto/floppy
File does not exist or access denied

Cancel

After several attempts the system gives up and reports a corresponding error message.

If there is no CD-ROM inserted in the drive and you click on the CD-ROM icon on the desktop, the same thing happens. The only difference is in the name of the device. In this case the system tries to access *file:/auto/ floppy*, and with a CD-ROM, *file:/auto/cdrom*.

Error messages can appear if the disk is not formatted for Linux.

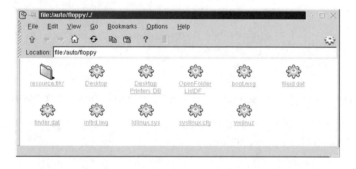

If a readable (i.e. Linux-formatted) floppy disk is inserted in the drive, its content is displayed in the file manager. In this case the Caldera OpenLinux boot disk is inserted and read.

You can now copy, delete, rename, move and create shortcuts for these files, just as with files on the hard drive. However, the disk should not be write protected. It is recommended that the file manager for the work directory be opened at the same time, in case you wish to copy from or to the work directory.

CAUTION

If error messages appear when you try to access the CD-ROM, it may be because, as a normal user, you may not place the CD-ROM drive in the file tree. This problem is easily resolved – consult the chapter on troubleshooting technical problems.

Only use a boot disk for displaying files! Leave the write protection as it is. If you accidentally damage your boot disk, you may have problems when reinstalling the system.

TIP

How to format a disk for use with Linux, so you can read from and write to it, will be explained later in the book.

What's in this chapter:

The KDE graphic interface offers an array of different tools. Simple texts can be created and saved in files to be reused later. Small graphics programs are available with which drawings, images and sketches can be created. Important meetings can be planned with the scheduler, and addresses stored in the address book. There are also many other useful programs, such as the calculator and a clock, as well as entertainment, various games and toys.

Creating text with the editor

By now you will want to create **simple texts**, such as notes, lists and so on, using the computer rather than by hand. Printouts of such texts usually look tidier than handwritten papers and also have the advantage of being able to be reused and/or modified. In addition, several copies of a text file created with a computer can be printed out. A simple text can be created in Linux using an **editor**.

An **editor** is a simple tool used to create a text. Most editors do not allow text to be **formatted**. Formatting makes text appear 'nicer', such as displaying bold or italic text, different fonts and font sizes. Proper **word processing programs** such as StarWriter by Stardivision can do all of the above and even embed images in text. A summary of **StarWriter** will be given later in the book.

1 Click on the main menu button in the program bar.

2 Then select *kedit Text Editor* from the *Editors* menu.

Linux now starts the program for the editor (*kedit*). An editor window opens. This window contains items such as the title bar, menu line and scrollbars. You will recognise these items from the previous chapter.

There are many editors in Linux. There are KDE graphic interface editors, such as the one outlined below. There is also an 'advanced editor', designed especially for programmers. **Klyx** and **Grok** are two other editors. There are also editors which can be started directly from the Linux command interface, including **vi**, **emacs**, **joe** and **elvis**.

However, the white inner area of the window is a special feature of the editor in which text can be created. If you start the editor, a white sheet appears containing no text. A cursor can be seen in the upper left-hand corner.

The **cursor** is a vertical flashing black line. It indicates where the next character will be inserted on the screen. As soon as a character is entered, it is displayed, and the cursor moves one position to the right. Cursors are used wherever text can be inserted, for example in entry fields, as you have already learned.

Point with the mouse to the entry area and the mouse pointer changes: a line resembling the letter 'I' appears instead of the arrow. This mouse pointer is known as the text cursor. The text cursor can point to or click on a word, or select something.

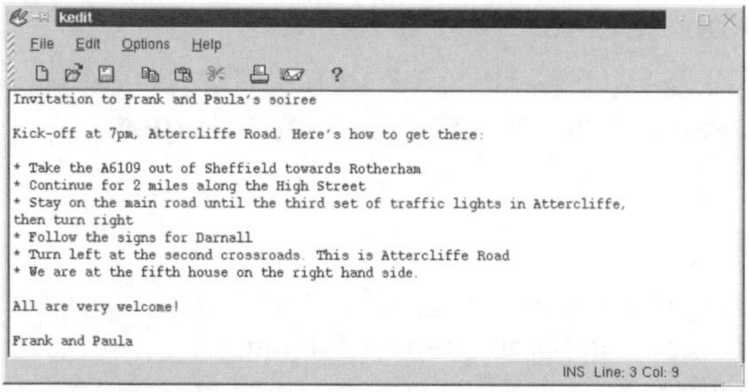

A small sample text is entered here. Simply type the following exercises. Don't worry if you make a mistake: you will learn how to correct this in one of the following sections.

Are you having problems with the **keyboard**? You may find the following tips useful:

▪▸ When you enter letters, they usually appear in lower case. If you wish to type upper case letters, hold the ⬆ key down and press the desired key.

▪▸ To separate words from each other, press the ⬚ button after the word. This is the bottom key of the keyboard, and is wider than all the others.

▪▸ When your line has reached a certain length, the cursor jumps to the next line, together with an unfinished word if necessary. If you wish to begin a new line yourself, press the ⏎ key.

▪▸ If the distance between two lines becomes larger, press the ⏎ key twice or more. In the above image the first line is separated from the second by pressing this key twice.

TIP

An exact keyboard summary can be found at the start of the book.

Editing text in the editor

Errors often occur when entering text. If this happens, you may wish to revise the text. You could also use a saved text which can be modified. You will learn how to do so in this section.

The text already created for the invitation should be modified. Several details were omitted from the text, meaning lines have to be modified and supplemented.

The exact date of the event should be entered first.

1 Click with the mouse in the second line before the word 'at'.

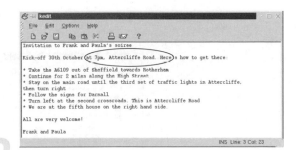

2 Type in the date '30th October' here.

The editor automatically moves the existing text to the right of the cursor as soon as new text is entered. The result looks as above.

Increase the distance between the second and third lines of text.

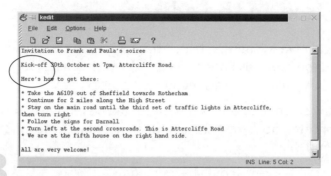

3 Click behind 'Attercliffe
Road' and press the ⏎ key.

You wish to insert a line break after the words 'traffic lights', so both
sections can be clearly represented.

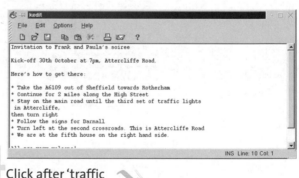

4 Click after 'traffic
lights' and press the
⏎ key.

The result is not quite yet satisfactory. Firstly, there is a space at the start
of the line before 'in', and the following line break is disruptive.

5 Click on the start of the line beginning with 'in'.

6 Delete the space using the Del key.

7 Click on the start of the line containing the text 'then turn right'.

8 Delete the line break using the ⇦ key.

> **TIP**
>
> Delete the character to the right of the cursor using the Del key. Delete a character to the left of the cursor using the ⇦ key.

The result of the editing now looks as shown.

```
kedit                                              □ ×
File   Edit   Options   Help
🗋  📂  💾   📋  📑  ✂   🖨 📧   ?
Invitation to Frank and Paula's soiree

Kick-off 30th October at 7pm, Attercliffe Road.

Here's how to get there:

* Take the A6109 out of Sheffield towards Rotherham
* Continue for 2 miles along the High Street
* Stay on the main road until the third set of traffic lights
in Attercliffe, then turn right
* Follow the signs for Darnall
* Turn left at the second crossroads. This is Attercliffe Road
* We are at the fifth house on the right hand side.

All are very welcome!

                                        INS  Line: 10 Col: 17
```

The cursor can be positioned at any place in the text. Either click with the mouse before the corresponding character, or position the cursor using the keyboard.

Here is an overview of how to move within the text using the keyboard:

Key(s)	Effect
⬆	Moves the cursor up one line.
⬇	Moves the cursor down one line.
⬅	Moves the cursor one space to the left.
➡	Moves the cursor one space to the right.
Home	Moves the cursor to the beginning of the line.
End	Moves the cursor to the end of the line.
Pg⬆	Moves the cursor one page up.
Pg⬇	Moves the cursor one page down.

It may happen that you wish to modify the sentence construction in a text, or even delete entire sentences. It would be very time-consuming if you had to work with the Del and ⬅ keys. It is much easier to select and delete the corresponding text sections at the same time.

> **Marking** means indicating text areas, image sections, files, directories or icons with the mouse. Marked items are assigned a blue background by default in Linux. You will have learned the function from the last chapter as you copied several files at once.

No doubt you will already have marked texts with a highlighter, or simply with a coloured pencil on a sheet of paper. This process is the same as marking text in a text editor or when working with files. The mouse replaces a highlighter when working with a PC. If you mark (highlight) elements in KDE, the system knows that it needs to execute an action concerning these items.

1 Click at the beginning of the passage to be marked.

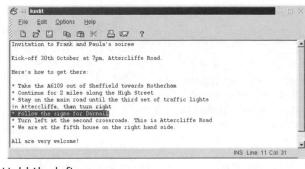

```
kedit                                                    □ ×
File   Edit   Options   Help
  🗋 🗁 🖫   🗈 🗈 ✂   🖶 🗊   ?
Invitation to Frank and Paula's soiree

Kick-off 30th October at 7pm, Attercliffe Road.

Here's how to get there:

* Take the A6109 out of Sheffield towards Rotherham
* Continue for 2 miles along the High Street
* Stay on the main road until the third set of traffic lights
in Attercliffe, then turn right
* Follow the signs for Darnall
* Turn left at the second crossroads. This is Attercliffe Road
* We are at the fifth house on the right hand side.

All are very welcome!
                                    INS  Line: 11  Col: 31
```

2 Hold the left mouse button depressed and drag the mouse to the end of the text to be marked.

3 Release the mouse button.

TIP

Alternatively, you can click on the scissors icon ✂ in the icon bar. Or you could press S + x or click on *Edit* in the menu bar, then on *Cut*.

The selected passage will be highlighted in colour. Now press the ⌨Del key, and the entire passage will be deleted.

To 'deselect' the passage, click anywhere outside the marked text.

TIP

Texts can also be marked using the keyboard. Move the cursor using the cursor keys to the start of the passage to be marked. Then hold the ⌨⇧ key down and move the cursor in the desired direction.

241

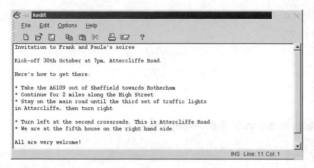

The marked sentence is no longer visible. As long as you do not delete anything else, the deleted passage is stored in an intermediary **buffer** and can be inserted later.

 If you click on the *Paste* icon in the menu line immediately after deleting, the deleted text is re-inserted.

In this way text can be re-inserted at a different position. You need only position the cursor in the right place before insertion. In the following example you will move a line of text further down in the passage by cutting and pasting.

1 Click at the position where you wish to insert text.

In our example click after the line ending in 'is Attercliffe Road'.

2 Click on the ⏎ key to create space for the text to be inserted.

3 Click on the *Paste* icon.

The deleted section of text is inserted at the cursor.

Now remove the empty lines where the text was previously.

4 Position the cursor on the empty line and press the Del key.

The text sequence has been changed by cutting and pasting.

Alternatively, you could click on *Edit* in the menu bar, then on *Paste*. Or use Ctrl + V.

```
kedit                                                    _ □ X
File   Edit   Options   Help
  ▭ ▱ ▭   ▥ ▧ ✂   ▤ ▱   ?
Invitation to Frank and Paula's soiree

Kick-off 30th October at 7pm, Attercliffe Road.

Here's how to get there:

* Take the A6109 out of Sheffield towards Rotherham
* Continue for 2 miles along the High Street
* Stay on the main road until the third set of traffic lights
in Attercliffe, then turn right
* Turn left at the second crossroads. This is Attercliffe Road
* Follow the signs for Darnell
* We are at the fifth house on the right hand side.

All are very welcome!

Frank and Paula

                                          INS  Line: 12 Col: 31
```

You can also duplicate a line of text, or copy it without cutting it. Use the following procedure:

1 Click on the beginning of the passage to be marked.

```
kedit                                                    □ ×
File   Edit   Options   Help
 □  ⬚  ▢   ▯ ▨ ✂  ▤ ▱   ?
Invitation to Frank and Paula's soiree

Kick-off 30th October at 7pm, Attercliffe Road.

Here's how to get there:

* Take the A6109 out of Sheffield towards Rotherham
* Continue for 2 miles along the High Street
* Stay on the main road until the third set of traffic lights
in Attercliffe, then turn right
* Turn left at the second crossroads.  This is Attercliffe Road
* Follow the signs for Darnell
* We are at the fifth house on the right hand side.

All are very welcome!

Frank and Paula

                                          INS  Line: 12 Col: 1
```

2 Hold the left mouse button depressed and drag the cursor to the end of the passage to be marked.

3 Click on the *Copy* icon.

TIP

Alternatively, you can click on *Edit* in the menu bar, then on *Copy*. Or use Ctrl + C.

The selected passage is stored on the clipboard.

4 Place the cursor where you wish the text to be inserted.

In our example, click after the line ending in 'then turn right'.

5 Click on the ⏎ key to create space for the text to be inserted. - - - - - - - - - - ►

6 Click on the *Paste* icon.

The copied section of text is inserted at the cursor.

In this example the section of text is copied back to its original place. However, the copied line is now duplicated.

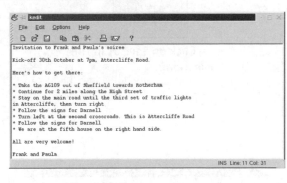

Entire sections can also be copied to the clipboard, not just single lines. The copied section of text can then be inserted anywhere in the document as often as you like.

You can also insert items stored in the clipboard into another window. Open a second editor window. Then mark some text in the first window and use the *Copy* function. Now switch to the second window and click on *Paste*.

Saving and loading text

As opposed to a typewritten item, a computer document can be saved and used later on, or modified if required.

245

1 Click on *Save as* in the
File menu.

Your work directory is
suggested as a saving
location for your file in a
window similar to the file
manager. You can only
change the saving
location by clicking on the
corresponding directory.
You will see the directory
path under which the file
will be saved displayed in the *location* field.

You can switch to a sub-folder by clicking on it once with the left mouse button.
The parent directory is indicated by a folder icon, labelled with two dots. Click on
this to return to the parent directory.

In an office situation, you would remove a folder from a filing cabinet and open
it. This is the same as opening a directory. When you had finished working with
it, you would close it again and place it back in the filing cabinet. This is the same
as closing a directory.

2 Click in the *location* field after the directory path and type in a filename.

It is not necessary to enter the *.txt file extension. The system will recognise that you have created a text file, and will display a corresponding icon in the file manager.

In this example the filename is *invitation.txt*.

3 Then click on *OK*.

The editor has now created a file with the given name.

New...	
Open...	Ctrl+O
Open Recent...	▶
Save	Ctrl+S
Save as...	
Close	Ctrl+W
Open URL...	
Save to URL...	
Print...	
Mail...	
New Window	
Exit	Ctrl+Q

4 Close the editor using *File* then *Close*.

This file can be recalled at any time.

There are other ways of opening a text editor file:

247

1 Select *Editors* from the main menu, then click on *KEdit Editor.*

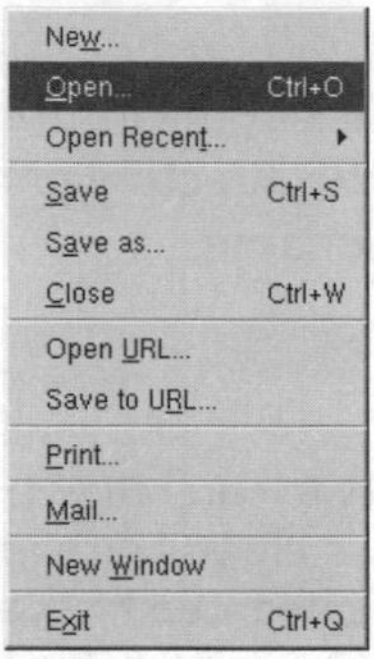

New...	
Open...	Ctrl+O
Open Recent...	▶
Save	Ctrl+S
Save as...	
Close	Ctrl+W
Open URL...	
Save to URL...	
Print...	
Mail...	
New Window	
Exit	Ctrl+Q

2 Click on *Open* in the *File* menu.

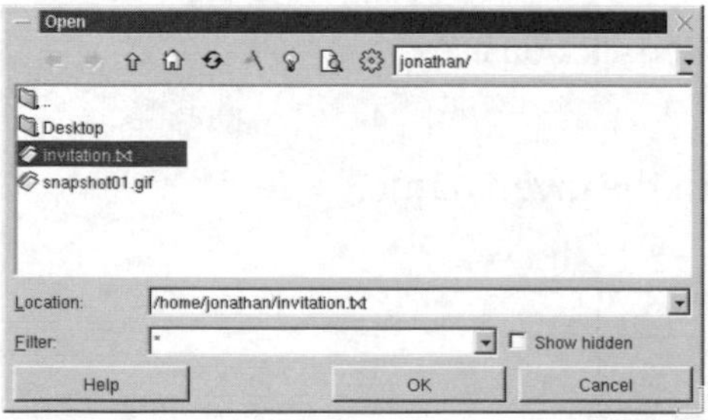

Another window appears displaying the contents of your work directory. The *invitation.txt* file can be opened in two different ways:

Open	×

Desktop
invitation.txt
snapshot01.gif

Location: /home/jonathan/invitation.txt
Filter: *   ☐ Show hidden

| Help | OK | Cancel |

3 Click on the file to be opened.

4 Once marked (as in the above image), click on *OK*.

5 Alternatively, click twice on the file to be opened.

This has the same result – the file can be edited in the editor.

The second option for opening a modified file is also found in the *File* menu.

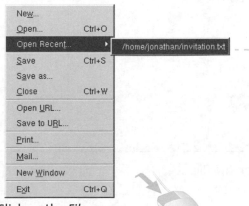

Click on the *File* menu.

Click on the *Open Recent...* option, then choose the desired file from the list.

This option is available only if the file has been opened once and saved again after it was originally saved. Only then will the file appear in the list of recently opened files. If you have opened five or more files in the meantime, this file will fall out of the 'hit list'.

The third option for opening a text editor file is through the file manager.

Open the file manager in the program bar.

Location: file:/home/jonathan/invitation.txt

```
Root
  auto
  bin
  boot
  dev
  etc
  home
    ftp
    httpd
    My Home
      Desktop
  initrd
  install
  lib
```

Desktop/   invitation.txt   invitation.txt~   snapshot01.gif

Document: Done

2 Click once on the file to be opened.

Searching text

Occasionally, you may need to make changes in a text several pages long. For example, you may wish to replace a certain word in the text with another. It would be very time-consuming to browse the text sentence by sentence. The editor therefore has a tool for this process.

Open the editor using the main menu (*Editors – KEdit Editor*), and then the most recently edited document.

Select *Find* in the *Edit* menu.

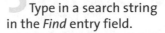

Type in a search string in the *Find* entry field.

Text is searched forwards (i.e. downwards) by default, and no distinction is made between upper and lower case letters.

4 Click on the *Case Sensitive* and *Find Backwards* options if need be.

5 Now click on *Find*.

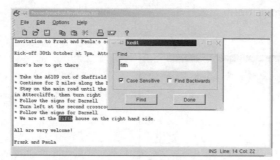

Search strings found in the text are highlighted. You can then close the search window and edit the text.

If you wish to find the term again, leave the search window open and click on *Find* until your search is finished. Alternatively, click on *Find again* in the *Edit* menu.

6 Click on *Done* to close the window.

If the search string cannot be found anywhere in the text, the editor informs you.

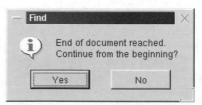

7 Close the window by pressing *No*.

If you want the search string to be replaced by something else, use the *Replace* option.

1 Select the *Replace* option in the *Edit* menu.

The search window contains several more options. Enter a string to replace the original search string. You can also replace each search string found individually, or replace all of them, depending on which button you press.

kedit		
Find:		
fifth		
Replace with:		
Fouth		
☐ Case Sensitive	☐ Find Backwards	
Find	Replace	Replace All	Done

CAUTION

Note that with the **Replace** function the **Replace All** option can lead to errors. If for example you wish to replace the word 'is' with 'are', then every time the letters 'i' and 's' appear side by side, such as in the words 'organise' or 'noise', they will be replaced by the letters 'are'.

TIP

How to print texts will be addressed later in the book, as you have not yet learned how to set up a printer.

Creating images with Paint

There are also small graphics programs in KDE with which simple drawings or images can be created.

The KDE graphics programs are different in the way they function. The **Paint** program, which admittedly has a restricted performance range, will be used to explain all graphics programs. However, working with Paint will give you a feel for graphics programs and their capabilities.

As well as Paint, there is a very powerful but more complex graphics program called **Gimp** (many extensive books have already been published on Gimp, should these interest you). There is also **Xfig**, a program for CAD constructions, **Image Viewer** for displaying graphics, **XV** for creating screenshots, **Icon Editor** for creating your own icons, and many others. A summary of **StarDraw** will be given later in the book. This graphics program is part of the StarOffice pack.

Click on the main menu button in the program bar.

Development	▶
Documentation	▶
Editors	▶
Games	▶
Graphics	▶
Internet	▶
Multimedia	▶
Office	▶
Toys	▶
Utilities	▶
Settings	▶
System	▶
COAS	▶
Applications	▶
KDE Help	
Home Directory	
KDE Control Center	
Disk Navigator	▶
Panel	▶
Lock Screen	
Logout	

DVI Viewer
Fax Viewer
Fractals Generator
Gimp
Icon Editor
Image Viewer
KIllustrator (vector drawing program)
Paint
Pixmap
PS Viewer
Snapshot
TGif
Xfig
Xmgr
XV

Paint is part of KDE version 1.1, which is used as a basis for this book. It is recommended for practising and as a beginner's program.

Then click on the *Paint* option in the *Graphics* menu.

Linux now opens the *Paint* program window. This window contains items such as the title bar, menu line and icon bar. You will recognise these items from the previous chapter.

The window is fairly small by default when opened.

3 Click on the *Enlarge* icon in the upper right-hand corner of the title bar.

The special feature of the graphics program is the white inner area of the window, in which graphics can be created.

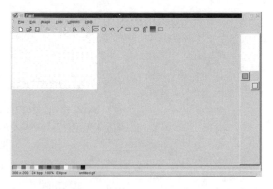

The representation of the white hard-clip area can be enlarged using the ⚲ button in the icon bar.

When the window is opened, the ellipse icon appears 'pressed' by default in the menu bar. We will draw this shape in the first exercise.

255

1 Click in the left-hand side of the window and hold the mouse key depressed.

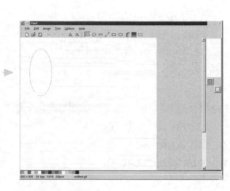

2 Now drag the mouse up, down, left and right.

This is how to define different ellipses. When you are satisfied with the shape and position, release the mouse button.

You have now drawn an ellipse. This has a red border, as red is the default colour. You will recognise this from the red button on the right margin.

Paint is only configured to display the selected shapes in lines by default. This can be altered as follows:

1 Click on *Tools*, then *Tool Properties*.

You can now select the line style and width on the first tab of the window.

2 Open the selection menu by clicking on the black arrow to the right of the selection field.

3 Click on the *Fill Properties* tab.

4 Click on the selection menu of the *Fill Pattern* option and click on the *Solid* setting.

5 Click on *OK*.

6 Click on the rectangular icon in the icon menu, then in the upper area of the white graphics area.

257

7 Now drag in any direction whilst holding the mouse button depressed.

Release the mouse button when you are satisfied with the rectangle.

The result now looks as follows. The rectangle is also drawn in red, but its interior is filled in.

We will now alter the colour of the image.

1 Click on the red button on the right-hand margin.

2 Click on any colour in the window.

You will recognise the *select color* window from previous chapters. The colour chosen now will be displayed in the preview area.

3 Then click on *OK*.

4 Click in the upper area of the white graphic area.

5 Now drag in any direction whilst holding the mouse button depressed.

Release the mouse button when you are satisfied with the rectangle.

You may no longer wish to work with rigid shapes, but may wish to draw 'freehand' instead. The results may be clumsy, because working with the mouse is somewhat cumbersome.

1 Click on the icon with the hand-painted line on the right-hand side of the circular icon.

2 Click anywhere in the hard-clip area.

3 Hold the mouse key depressed and move the mouse in the desired direction.

When you wish to end the line, release the mouse button.

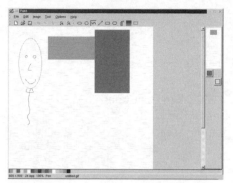

In the image a balloon with a 'face' is drawn by hand from the ellipse. You will probably have noticed that it is very difficult to draw lines correctly by hand.

Sometimes a graphic may have to be inscribed. This will now be explained.

1 Click on the blue icon to the right of the icon with the spray can.

2 Click at the point in the graphics area where you wish to insert text.

3 Type in your text.

If you wish to type text in another place, click at the corresponding point with the mouse.

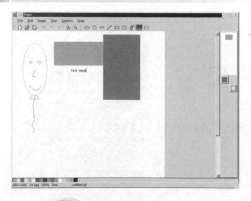

You can see an inserted text in this image.

We will now refine the image a little, giving a brief explanation.

1 Click on the icon with the line running between two points.

2 Click at the position in the graphic where you wish to insert lines.

3 Hold the mouse key depressed and move the mouse in any direction.

Release the mouse button when you wish to end the line.

> If you wish to supplement the graphic further, test the other icons. Switch between colours to test the entire array. The shapes speak for themselves, and the spray can icon gives an aerosol effect.

In this image, the street names are supplemented as well as the sketch map, and the direction is indicated with a hand-drawn arrow.

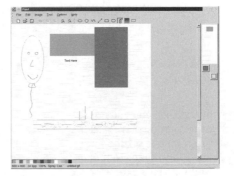

Are you satisfied with your result? Then save the drawing.

Open Image...
New Image...
Save Image
Save Image As...
Image Format...
Open from URL...
Save to URL...
New Window
Close Window
E_xit

1 Click on the *File* menu, then on *Save image as.*

Save

Location: file:/home/jonathan/Plan.gif
Filter: *.gif   ☑ Show hidden

Help   OK   Cancel

Your work directory is suggested as a saving location for your file in a window similar to the file manager. You will see the directory path under which the file will be saved displayed in the *Location* field.

2 Click after the path name in the *Location* field.

3 Enter a filename after the path name.

In this case you will not see other files displayed, as the program has set the filter *.gif. This means that only files with this extension are listed.

Planning events

If you use the StarOffice program package from Stardivision, you can use the built-in scheduler to plan events. It is briefly mentioned in the chapter on StarOffice, and functions similarly to the event planner addressed here.

KDE has a tool with which you can plan events.

An **organiser** or **scheduler** is a program which shows your scheduled appointments. You can also plan, browse, move and delete appointments.

1 Click on the main menu button in the program bar.

2 Then select the *KOrganizer* option in the *Office* menu.

Linux now starts the *KOrganizer* program and opens a window with a calendar view.

The daily view corresponds to that of a calendar, whereby entries can be made against every hour in the day. A monthly view is displayed on the left-hand side.

3 Double-click **twice** on the desired period of time to enter an appointment.

A window opens in which more details of your appointment can be entered. You can enter the reason for the appointment, the time, and even set a reminder note.

4 Type the reason for the appointment in the *Summary* entry field.

5 Click on the small buttons next to the date fields, and enter a date in the window which appears.

You can change the months (left for previous and right for forthcoming months) and years (up for previous and right for forthcoming years) using the buttons with the black arrows.

6 Select the times from the menus opened by clicking the black arrow to the right of the time field.

If you select *No time associated* then you have created an appointment for the same day, yet with no specific time.

If you click on *Recurring event*, the third tab, *Recurrence* is activated. A series of appointments is then created. This will be explained in more detail later in this section.

Do you wish to be reminded of the appointment before the event?

The reminder by tone works only if your soundcard is correctly installed, and if you have speakers connected to your PC.

7 Click on *Reminder* and select a corresponding time period.

8 Click on *Categories* and select one or more categories which you would like to assign to the appointment.

Click on the desired category, then click *Add*. The category is then taken from the *Available Categories* list to the *Selected Categories* list. A new category can be created by entering it in the *New Category* field and clicking *Add*.

9 End category selection by clicking on *OK*.

265

10 Now click on the *Details* tab.

Enter the name of the attendee, and their e-mail address, role and status (both from a selection menu). If you wish, you can create more categories and assign a priority for the appointment (using a selection menu).

11 Click on *Add*.

The attendee is now entered in the *Attendee Information* list.

Alternatively, you can enter an attendee using the address book, provided it already contains an entry. Click on the *Address Book* button and select a contact. Then click on *Add* again to include the attendee in the list above.

You will learn how to use the address book in more detail in the next section.

Do you wish to delete an attendee from the list?

12 Click on the corresponding entry, then on *Remove*.

You may now wish to enter regularly recurring appointments, or a series of appointments.

1 The *Recurring event* has to be activated on the first tab by clicking.

The third tab, *Recurrence,* is now activated.

2 Click on the *Recurrence* tab.

Specify how often the event is to take place by clicking the desired option (daily, weekly, monthly, annually etc.), when it should start and end, and whether there should be any extra meetings.

3 To save a meeting, click on the *Save and Close* button in the upper screen area.

A scheduled appointment looks as follows in the daily view.

You can also reschedule appointments as in real life.

1 To reschedule an appointment on the same day, click on the white area of the event.

The mouse pointer assumes the form of a cross whilst being moved.

2 Hold the mouse key depressed and drag the appointment to the desired position.

Move the appointment to three hours later in the calendar. Release the mouse button when the desired time has been reached.

Alternatively, the appointment can be rescheduled for a different day.

If the appointment
is currently active,
the area appears
blue.

1 Click on the grey button
on the far left-hand side.

2 Hold the mouse button
depressed and drag the
appointment to the small calendar
preview on the left-hand side.

3 Release the mouse
button when the desired
day is marked in blue.

The mouse pointer again assumes a different form, that of an appointment
icon. Try to drag the appointment somewhere outside the small calendar, and
the mouse pointer assumes the form of a 'No Entry' sign.

Alternatively, appointment times can be rescheduled using the appointment
window. Open the corresponding appointment by double-clicking, then alter
the times.

Appointments and events can of course be deleted at any time.

1 Right-click on the appointment to be deleted.

Edit
✕ Delete
🔔 Toggle Alarm

2 A context menu appears. Select the *Delete* option.

You can select a view other than 'daily' using the *View* option.

📋 List
1 Day
5 Work Week
7 Week
31 Month
📋 To-do list
Update

1 For example, click on *View* and select the *Month* option.

A summary of appointments for the entire month is displayed.

Series of appointments are indicated with this icon: ↻

Before you finish working with the appointment calendar, you should always save your entries.

🗐 New Window	Ctrl+N
🗁 Open	Ctrl+O
Open Recent	▶
Close	Ctrl+W
🗐 Save	Ctrl+S
Save As	
Import From Ical	
Merge Calendar	
Archive Old Entries	
Print Setup	
🖨 Print	Ctrl+P
Print Preview	
Quit	Ctrl+Q

1 Click on the *File* menu, then on *Save as*.

Assign the appointment calendar a name in the same way as you did the editor and graphics files. The appointment calendar can then be restored if problems occur. When you come to modify it later, you need only click on *File* and *Save*. The file will then be updated.

2 Click on *File – Exit* to end the scheduler.

If you have activated the scheduler once during a KDE session, it will remain in the background in the program bar throughout the entire session – even after you have used *File – Exit*. It looks like this:

It can be opened again using the left mouse button. It will be closed down properly when you shut down the system.

Creating an address book

You can also manage addresses on your computer. This KDE function is called the address book, and can be compared with a real address book.

1 Click on the main menu button in the program bar.

2 Then click on *Address book* in the *Office* menu.

Linux now opens the *kab* program and opens either (the first time) an empty window, or a window with the address last used.

TIP

If you have already created addresses, you can browse these using the black arrow on the lower margin. Use the left cursor key to search backwards through the alphabet, and the right cursor key to search forwards. The double arrow goes all the way to the beginning or the end. The small binoculars help you search.

TIP

Addresses can also be revised (*Edit entry*) or deleted (*Remove entry*) using the same menu.

kab		
File	Edit	About

Alick Robertson

Dr Alick Robertson

◀◀ ◀   ▶ ▶▶   🔍

1/1

Copy	Ctrl+W
Add entry	Ctrl+N
Edit entry	Ctrl+E
Remove entry	Ctrl+R
Mail	Ctrl+M
Talk	Ctrl+T
Browse	Ctrl+B

3 To create an address, click on *Add entry* in the *Edit* menu.

Edit the current entry

| Name | Address | Organization | Contact | Others |

Title: Mr

First name: Paul

Additional Name:

Name: Watkinson

Formatted Name:

OK   Cancel

4 A window opens in which the title and name of your new entry can be entered.

5 Click on the *Address* tab.

Edit the current entry

| Name | Address | Organization | Contact | Others |

Address: Attercliffe Road

Town/City: Sheffield

State: South Yorkshire

Zip/Postal Code: S9 3QS

Country: England

OK   Cancel

6 Enter the address of your new contact.

7 Now click on the *Organization* tab.

Edit the current entry

| Name | Address | Organization | Contact | Others |

Organization: Cybertechnics Limited

Department: Publishing

Sub-Department: Typesetting

Job/Role: Boss

OK   Cancel

8 Enter the business details of your new contact here.

9 Click on the *Contact* tab.

Edit the current entry ✕

| Name | Address | Organization | Contact | Others |

Edit email addresses

Edit talk addresses

Telephone: 0114 2431000

Fax: 0114 2433000

Modem:

Homepage (URL): www.cybertechnics.co.uk

OK   Cancel

10 Enter the telephone numbers and website address (if applicable) of your new contact.

11 If your new contact has an e-mail address, click on *Edit email addresses*.

Edit email addresses ✕

paul@cybertechnics.co.uk   ✕

paul@cybertechnics.co.uk

🗑

OK   Apply   Cancel

12 First click on the icon with the black cross in the upper right-hand corner.

Enter one or several e-mail addresses for your new contact. Enter these in the upper entry field.

For every new e-mail address you create here, you must first click on the cross. The previously entered address will then be applied to the list. To delete an address, mark it using the left mouse button, then click on the trash bin icon in the lower right-hand corner. The address will immediately be deleted.

13 End the e-mail address creation process by clicking on *OK*.

14 Click on the *Others* tab.

```
┌─────────────────────────────────────────────────┐
│ ☐ Edit the current entry                      ✕ │
├─────────────────────────────────────────────────┤
│ ┌─────┬────────┬──────────────┬─────────┬───────┐│
│ │Name │Address │ Organization │ Contact │Others ││
│ └─────┴────────┴──────────────┴─────────┴───────┘│
│            ┌──────────────────────────────────┐  │
│            │Book project leader               │  │
│            │                                  │  │
│  Additional Comment:                          │  │
│            │                                  │  │
│            │                                  │  │
│            │                                  │  │
│            └──────────────────────────────────┘  │
│  Birthday:  ┌──────────────────────────────────┐ │
│             └──────────────────────────────────┘ │
│                      ┌──────────┐  ┌──────────┐   │
│                      │    OK    │  │  Cancel  │   │
│                      └──────────┘  └──────────┘   │
└─────────────────────────────────────────────────┘
```

15 Notes and the date of birth of your contact can be entered here.

The notes can then be inserted into the corresponding field.

16 Enter the date of birth by clicking in the appropriate field.

A small calendar appears, similar to that of the scheduler function.

```
┌─────────────────────────────────────┐
│ — Select birthday               ✕  │
├─────────────────────────────────────┤
│ ┌─┐┌─┐              ┌─┐┌─┐          │
│ │↑││←│  October 2000 │→││↓│         │
│ └─┘└─┘              └─┘└─┘          │
│ Sun Mon Tue Wed Thu Fri Sat        │
│  25  26  27  28  29  30  31        │
│   1   2   3   4   5   6   7        │
│   8   9  10  11  12  13  14        │
│  15  16  17  18  19  20  21        │
│  22 [23] 24  25  26  27  28        │
│  29  30  31   1   2   3   4        │
│       Today: 10/5/2000             │
│ ┌─────────────────────────────────┐│
│ │        Mon Oct 23 2000          ││
│ └─────────────────────────────────┘│
│ ┌──────────┐      ┌──────────┐     │
│ │    OK    │      │  Cancel  │     │
│ └──────────┘      └──────────┘     │
└─────────────────────────────────────┘
```

17 Enter the date of birth of your contact, then click on *OK*.

You will notice that the date is immediately applied to the *Birthday* field.

18 Click on *OK* in the *Edit entry* window if you have finished altering your entries.

The entries are applied to the address book, and the most important, such as the name and address, are listed in the title page.

As well as the option of finding an entry using the binoculars icon, you could also open the selection menu above the address card by clicking the black arrow on the right-hand side. The entries are arranged alphabetically. Click on the desired entry with the mouse.

You should always save your new entries in the address book by using *File – Save*.

Using other useful tools

There are countless other KDE tools, most of which can be put to some use.

Some will be outlined in this section. You may well have tested some already, such as the calculator.

The program which formats disks proves particularly useful. However, there are also commands on the Linux command level, but these are far more complicated to use.

1 Click on the main menu button and select the *KFloppy* option from the *System* menu.

Linux now starts the *KDE Floppy* Formatter program and opens a window in which formatting settings can be modified.

Formatting a disk to DOS format is suggested by default.

A disk must be formatted so it has a file system with which an operating system can work. For example, **DOS** uses the **FAT** file system, though it is usually just referred to as DOS. Linux uses the *ext2fs* file system.

Do you remember the problems which can arise when working with the disk icon on the desktop? If you try to read a DOS-formatted disk using this icon, the errors described in the previous chapter can arise, as the program behind the disk icon expects a Linux-formatted disk with the *ext2fs* system.

2 Open the small *File System* menu by clicking the black arrow on the right-hand side, and select *ext2fs*.

This is how to format a Linux disk.

We do not need to concern ourselves with the other options. The *HD* (High Density) memory capacity is recommended, as is the *Full Format* option.

You can observe the progress of the formatting process in the lower area of the window.

The disk is examined after formatting for safety reasons.

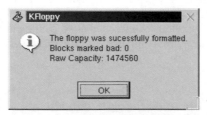

When the formatting process has completed successfully, a corresponding message appears. Click on *OK*.

You now have a disk formatted with a file system from which Linux can read and to which it can write.

The **Notepad** program is also a useful little program. You can make notes on little yellow pieces of paper, rather like Post-it® notes.

1 Click on the main menu button, and select the *KNotes* option from the *Utilities* menu.

Linux starts the *knote* program and opens a small yellow window, into which your notes can be entered directly. Write and delete notes as you would in the editor.

> knote 1
> Meetting at 12:30pm

2 If you right-click on the *Close* button in the upper right-hand corner, the note is placed in the background.

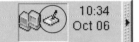

10:34
Oct 06

3 It can be reopened at any time by clicking the icon in the program bar.

knote 1
Insert Date
Operations ▶
Options ▶
Sticky
To desktop ▶

A small context menu opens which gives you the option of creating a new note (*New KNote*) or editing the existing note (*KNote 1*). If you have created several notes, these will be numbered appropriately.

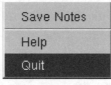

Save Notes

Help

Quit

4 Another context menu appears after you click the right mouse button.

The program can be closed using this option.

A neat little function will now be outlined to conclude this section. Do you wish to have a clock visible on your desktop? Simply use the *Xclock* program!

1 Click on the main menu in the program bar and select the *Non KDE application* option in the *Utilities* menu, then click on *X Clock*.

An analogue clock is displayed which can either be enlarged or reduced (by dragging or moving the window margin), and placed in the desired position.

KDE games and toys

You have toiled enough now – it's time for some entertainment. Linux has countless toys and games to amuse you!

1 Select *World Watch* from the *Toys* menu.

A world map is displayed, indicating different time zones. You can also see exactly where daylight hours are across the globe.

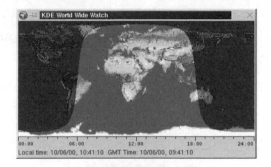

2 You can see the exact time in individual countries by pointing the mouse at the desired position on the map.

The time then appears in a small yellow QuickInfo box.

The *X Eyes* program is very funny, though not actually very useful.

1 Click on *X Eyes* in the *Tools* menu.

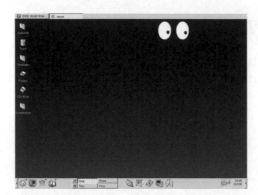

A large set of eyes now appears on the desktop, which follows the movement of the mouse.

Do you wish to remove the eyes from the desktop? Not a problem. Look at the taskbar on the upper margin – you will see an entry for the *X Eyes* program.

Maximize
Iconify
Move
Resize
Sticky
To desktop ▸
Close

2 Right-click on this entry. A context menu appears.

3 Now click on *Close* and the eyes disappear again.

The second toy is called *XEarth*.

1 Select the *XEarth* option from the *Toys* menu.

The globe appears as a background image, and you can see exactly where daylight hours are. If you leave this background image activated long enough, the globe turns correspondingly.

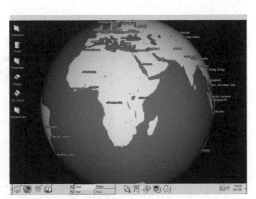

TIP
This background image disappears again when you log on and off from KDE.

Now let's look at the games. They can all be found in the *Games* option in the main menu. Have a look at *Mahjongg* first.

TIP
Each of the following games can either be closed using the *File – Close* menu, or *Game – Quit*. Alternatively, you could click on the *Close* icon in the upper right-hand corner of the menu bar.

Select the *Mahjongg* option from the *Games* menu.

This is a game with playing pieces laid out, each bearing an icon. It is similar to *Memory*, the difference being that not only are the tablets larger and wider, they are placed on top of each other and face upwards. You may only ever remove 'free' tablets. Tablets are 'free' when not covered by other tablets, and when they can be removed from the left or the right, meaning when there are no neighbouring tablets either side.

TIP
Help is also available. You can ask for a tip from the *Game – Help Me* menu, or start a new game using *Game – New Game*, where you can choose how the stones are arranged.

The aim of the game is to remove all the tablets.

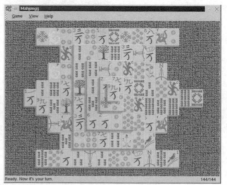

2 Simply select two matching tablets on the edge by clicking them.

If the move is allowed, both tablets are removed. The tablets should always be on different levels.

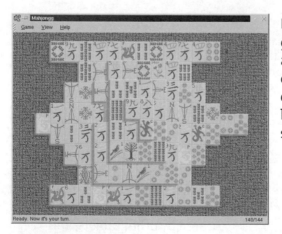

If this works, there is gradually more space to clear away the tablets. If the game cannot be finished, a corresponding message will be displayed. Click on *OK* to start a new game.

Is this game too tame for you? Do you need more excitement? Then opt for *Minesweeper*.

1 Click on the
Minesweeper option in the
Games menu.

In this game you have to uncover hidden mines in
a field. Uncover the squares at your own risk. If a
mine lies beneath, the game is of course over. If
not, a figure appears telling you how many mines
there are in neighbouring squares.

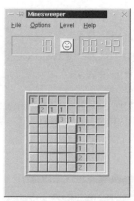

1 means that one mine lies beneath one of the
squares immediately surrounding the one you
have just uncovered. 2 means there are two mines,
and so on. If no number appears, there are no
mines in the surrounding area.

You can place a mine icon on a covered field with
the right mouse button if you suspect a mine may
be underneath. If you are unsure, you can also place
a question mark.

Once you have found all the mines, the smiley face in the upper area of the window beams at you, and you have the honour of being included in the hall of fame if the time achieved was a personal best. If you can complete the 'easy' level in less than ten seconds, you can consider yourself an expert.

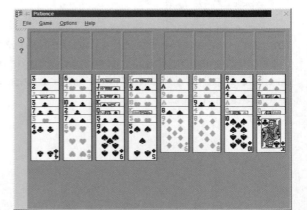

Too much excitement? Then maybe you should try the next game – *Patience*. And it does take a lot of patience!

1 Select the *Patience* option from the *Game*s menu.

Patience is a card game in which cards are dealt and must be rearranged in a strict order. If you can place all your cards, the game is won.

There are different forms of Patience from which you can select in the *Game – Choose new game* menu. The following example is called *Free Cell*.

Cards can temporarily be placed in the four spaces on the left-hand side if they are in the way.

The four spaces on the right-hand side are where the cards will eventually be placed, beginning with the respective aces. The two of the same suit comes next, then the three, and so on, until the jack, queen and king complete the pile. Once all cards have been placed, the game is won.

If all four spaces on the left-hand side are occupied, and no cards can be placed on the right, and no cards in the lower field can be moved, then the game is over. You will have to restart this game, or begin a new one entirely.

Cards may be placed on top of each other in the lower area. The cards must alternate between red and black, and a card may only be placed if its value is one less than that of the top card. The cards must be in ascending order, as mentioned above.

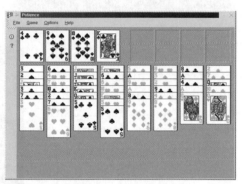

Try it for yourself. The system lets you know if you try to make a false move.

The card of the highest value must lie on the bottom, i.e. the king underneath the queen, the nine underneath the eight, and so on.

Are you not yet satisfied? Do you want a more leisurely game with more brains involved? Then click on *Sokoban*, the 'box sliding' game!

1 Select *Sokoban* from the *Games* menu.

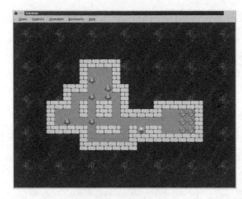

You will see a little man who has to move the boxes into the green storage areas. The only difficulty is that only one box may be moved at a time.

The box may be moved in any direction. However, if placed in the corner, it can no longer be moved and the game is over. If all boxes have been placed in the storage area, the game proceeds to the next level.

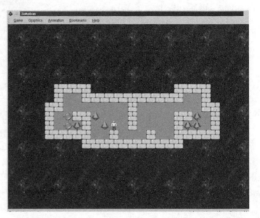

There are different levels of difficulty. You can choose using *Game – Level Collection*. However, you may not proceed to a higher level if you lost the previous game!

Still not right for you? What did you think of Tetris on installation? This game is the last one outlined in this section.

1 Click on the *Sirtet* option in the *Games* menu.

Tetris is started by clicking on *File – Restart Game*. Blocks fall in a chamber, which can be rotated as they fall. If you have completely filled a level of blocks, the pile moves down and you score one point.

Blocks are moved and turned using the cursor keys. Just test the moves, or consult chapter 1 on how to use the cursor keys.

What's in this chapter:

You will learn how to manage and configure the OpenLinux operating system. You will learn how to switch from being a normal user to becoming root user to perform certain tasks, without having to log on again. After this chapter you will be able to install a printer and print out documents. You will also be able to create new users and edit existing ones if required. You will then learn how to summon further system information, become familiar with a terminal window, and master a few important Linux settings.

You already know about:

You are going to learn about:

291

Switching to super user without logging on again

Some system settings may only be made by the super user. This is justifiable in that a normal, inexperienced user could modify system settings by accident to such an extent that the system becomes damaged. The super user setup thereby acts as a kind of system protection.

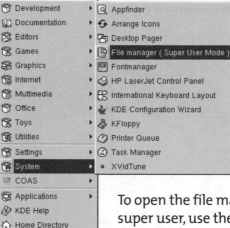

To open the file manager as the super user, use the following procedure:

1 Click on *System* in the main menu, then on *File Manager (Super User Mode)*.

A terminal window opens in which the password of the root super user should be entered.

2 Type in the password.

If this is correct, you are entered into the Linux system.

TIP

If you make a mistake when entering the password, you will be prompted to re-type.

```
kfmsu2                                                        □ ×
File  Sessions  Options  Help

Allowing ALL (!) local users to use this display
non-network local connections being added to access control list

Logging in as super user
Password:

Welcome to your OpenLinux system!
```

```
file:/root/                                                  □ ×
File  Edit  View  Go  Bookmarks  Options  Help
⇧  ←  →  ⌂  ↻  ⧉  ⧉  ?  ▌
Location: file:/root
▷ 📁 Root
▷ 📁 My Home
▷ 📁 Desktop          Desktop/

Document: Done
```

The file manager is opened in super user mode when the welcome note appears. This means you have unrestricted access to the file manager: you may modify, delete, distribute and create files anywhere in the file tree.

TIP

It makes sense to switch to the super user mode in this way if you wish to edit a system file to perform an action. It takes much longer to log off as a normal user first and then log on again as the root super user, just to perform this function.

There is another way of modifying system settings as the super user whilst still logged in as a normal user.

1 Open the *Settings* option in the main menu, and then the sub-program *COAS*.

Network ▸
Peripherals ▸
System ▸
Commercial Products
Kernel
kpackage
X-Server

2 Click on the
System option,
then on *Accounts*.

The super user normally has the right to start the program for system
settings. You need to log on as an authorised user for this program.

COAS su wrapper ✕

Please enter root password:

*****

Ok   Cancel

3 Type the password for the
root user in the entry field.

4 Then click
on *OK*.

Installing a printer

One of the most important system administration tasks is setting up a
printer. A printer is something of a necessity with PCs these days – what
good is a letter which you cannot print out and send?

Installing a printer with Linux is either very easy, as you will see, or almost impossible. It partly depends on which type of printer you have.

You are advised to consult the 'hardware' section in the Appendix. A list of all printers for which **printer drivers** are available is displayed here. All postscript printers are easy to install. A third option is setting up a printer using a software program, such as StarOffice. This option is explained in more detail in chapter 9.

WHAT'S THIS?

Printer drivers are special programs which enable communication between the operating system and the printer. Your printout can only be produced in a specified form using these programs. Printer manufacturers distribute driver programs for their printers for certain operating systems. Unfortunately, Linux has been somewhat overlooked, which is why you should obtain a list of Linux-compatible printers before purchasing.

CAUTION

It is almost impossible to install special GDI- or Windows printers. These are directly controlled by Windows software, which is not available with Linux. For example, it is not possible to install Lexmark ink-jet printers to a Linux operating system.

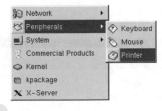

2 Select the *Printer* option from the *Peripherals* menu.

1 Open the COAS menu using the program bar.

295

This welcome note always appears when the COAS program is summoned.

Welcome to COAS ✕

Welcome to the Caldera Open Administration System!
In order to help you find your way around COAS, online help is available for most dialogs by pressing the F1 key. Also, most input fields provide additional help via the F2 key.

OK

3 End this by clicking on *OK*.

Printer configuration ✕

Printer   Daemon

Configure the printers connected to your computer or network.

Name	Description

OK   Cancel

A window appears in which printer installation and configuration can be specified. Printers can be edited, installed or uninstalled (removed) here.

Edit...
Add...
Remove...

4 Click on *Add*.

Now select your printer model.

Select printer model ✕

Select your printer, or a model close to it.

Generic remote printer
Generic postscript printer
Generic raw printer device
Apple Dot Matrix Printer
Apple Image Writer hires
Apple Image Writer lowres
Apple Image Writer LQ

Cancel

5 Use the scrollbar on the right-hand side to find your printer.

6 Select it once you have found it.

Printer name ✕

Please enter the logical name for the new printer, e.g. lp1, ps1 etc.

Name   E3C400

| OK | Cancel |

7 Select a name for the printer and type it in the name field.

8 Then click on *OK*.

A few printer properties must now be specified.

Printer attributes ✕

Modify the attributes of the printer

Name	E3C400
Paper size	DIN A4 ▾
Device	/dev/lp0 ▾
Speed	57600 ▾
2 pages/sheet	☐

| OK | Cancel |

9 Open the selection list for each setting to be modified by clicking on the black arrow.

You should set the *Letter* paper size as *DIN A4*.

The *Letter* paper size is the default American paper size. The *Device* field contains the device names of Linux printers. The first printer device name should always read */dev/lpo*. If you install several printers, then refer back to the other device names in the list. The *Speed* field applies only to printers installed via a serial interface, rather than the usual parallel interface, and can be ignored.

10 Click on OK.

Save

? Save modified information?

| Save | Discard | Cancel |

11 Then save the settings by clicking on *Save*.

Create printer queue

? Should I create the printer queue for "ESC400"?

| OK | No |

12 Let the system set up a queue for the printer. Click on OK.

If several people send several print jobs to the one printer at the same time, these must wait in a queue, just as you would when buying goods in a supermarket – not everybody can be served at once. Print jobs sent first are usually first in the queue and are therefore printed first.

An error message may appear at this point as shown.

The *lp* module is a **system process** (also known as a **daemon**) responsible for starting the print process. Printing cannot occur without this process.

This problem is easily eliminated. However, the recently installed printer is displayed in the next window:

Click on *Daemon*, then on *Done*.

The print service is halted. It contains the lp module required for printing.

Click on *Daemon*, then on *Start*.

The print service is then
restarted.

Stopping Service ×

INFO Stopping service Print server (LPD)...

Done

The printer is now set up –
you will test to see if it works
in the next section.

Printing out documents

To print out a document, open it with the text editor.

1 Click on *Editors* in the main
menu, then on the *KEdit Editor*
option.

A blank editor window appears.

2 Click on *File*,
then *Open*.

Open ×

jonathan/

snapshot01.gif
Desktop
nsmail
invitation.txt
invitation.txt~

Location: /home/jonathan/invitation.txt

Filter: *   ☐ Show hidden

Help   OK   Cancel

The files in your home
directory are displayed. Open
the practice file created in the
last chapter, called
Invitation.txt.

3 Select this with the left mouse button, then click on *OK*.

/home/jonathan/invitation.txt

File   Edit   Options   Help

New...
Open...   Ctrl+O   Paula's soiree
Open Recent...   ▶
Save   Ctrl+S   7pm, Attercliffe Road.
Save as...
Close   Ctrl+W   Sheffield towards Rotherham
Open URL...   Long the High Street
Save to URL...   until the third set of traffic lights
                            a right
                            arnell
Print   crossroads. This is Attercliffe Road
Mail...   arnell
New Window   se on the right hand side.
Exit   Ctrl+Q

Frank and Paula

INS   Line: 1 Col. 1

4 Now select *File* from the menu line, then *Print*.

Print Dialog

⦿ Print directly using lpr

○ Print using Command: enscript –2rG

⦿ Print Document

○ Print Selection

OK   Cancel

The default printer settings displayed in this window are usually correct.

5 Click on *OK* to begin the print process.

Most programs have a *Print* option, usually listed in the first menu line option.

Your file is now printed out. Proceed in exactly the same way to print documents from other programs.

Supervising printing

If you have sent several print jobs to the printer, you may well not remember which ones you have sent. Or you may wish to cancel a print job for a large file. The *Print Queue* administration program should be used in these cases.

The print queue can be opened in two ways. The first option is to use the main menu in the program bar.

🗄 Development ▶	🔍 Appfinder
📕 Documentation ▶	✦ Arrange Icons
🗄 Editors ▶	🗇 Desktop Pager
🎮 Games ▶	🗇 File manager (Super User Mode)
🗄 Graphics ▶	🖼 Fontmanager
🗄 Internet ▶	🖨 HP LaserJet Control Panel
🗄 Multimedia ▶	🖭 International Keyboard Layout
🗄 Office ▶	🖌 KDE Configuration Wizard
🎮 Toys ▶	🗄 KFloppy
🗄 Utilities ▶	🖨 Printer Queue
🗄 Settings ▶	🕓 Task Manager
🗃 System ▶	• XVidTune
🗄 COAS ▶	
🗄 Applications ▶	
🗄 KDE Help	
🏠 Home Directory	
🖳 KDE Control Center	
🗄 Disk Navigator ▶	
🗄 Panel ▶	
🔒 Lock Screen	
✕ Logout	

1 Click on *System*, then on *Printer Queue*.

Alternatively, click on the printer icon on the desktop created using the KDE Configuration Wizard.

You will see the print queue window with which print jobs can be viewed and deleted if necessary. If no print jobs have been sent, the window appears empty.

You will see a second smaller display window in the lower area, showing the print system status. At this point you can also check for errors if your printer does not react to a print command. Such a message could look as follows:

Printer: ESC600@caldera
Queue: no printable jobs in queue
Status: server finished at 16:22:20

To eliminate this particular problem, open the COAS menu in the program bar, click on *Peripherals*, then *Printer*. First click on *Daemon*, then on *Stop*; then on *Daemon*, then *Start*. The error message in the print queue window should now have disappeared.

You will see three processed print jobs in this window.

'**Spooling disabled**' means that the print queue is not accepting any print jobs.

2 If you wish to delete a print job, click on it, then press *Remove*.

Klpq ✕

ⓘ Remove Job No. 0

| Yes | No |

The system asks you if you are sure.

3 Click on *Yes*.

The print job is removed from the queue.

The print queue view is updated regularly, meaning recent entries are displayed. You can specify this period of time yourself.

Auto update
Spooler

1 Click on *Configure* in the menu, then on *Auto update*.

You can now specify the update rate by dragging the scroll box left or right using the mouse.

Configure Auto Update

Update frequency in seconds:

OK   Cancel

Then click on *OK*.

An advanced user can also specify the spooling system, meaning the way in which a print job joins the queue and is sent to the printer.

Auto update

Spooler

Click on *Configure* in the menu, then on *Spooler*.

Select your spooling system

Select your spooling system

It is recommended that the default *BSD* setting be left as it is.

Paths of spooling commands:

⊙ BSD

○ PPR   lpq: lpq

○ LPRNG   lpc: /usr/sbin/lpc

               lprm: lprm

OK   Cancel

Click on *OK* to close the window again.

Creating and editing users

You have already had the option of creating one or more users alongside the super user on installation. If you passed up the opportunity to do so then, you can still create new users now.

Why would several users be required at all? If you live alone or nobody else uses your computer, then you should really require only two users: the super user for modifying system settings, and a normal user.

Assuming your entire family wish to use Linux, it is a different situation entirely. If both your children and your partner use your username, they can modify or delete your files. You certainly would not want your reports to be deleted by mistake by a family member. You should therefore take the precaution of setting up a user account for each family member. Then nobody can delete anybody else's files.

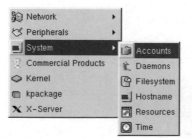

1 Click on *System* in the COAS menu, then on *Accounts*.

Login	UID	Group	Name	Home Directory
root	0	root	root	/root
bin	1	bin	bin	/bin
daemon	2	daemon	daemon	/sbin
adm	3	adm	adm	/var/adm
lp	4	lp	lp	/var/spool/lpd
sync	5	root	sync	/sbin
shutdown	6	operator	shutdown	/sbin
halt	7	root	halt	/sbin
mail	8	mail	mail	/var/spool/mail
news	9	news	news	/var/spool/news

A list of all current users is displayed. It contains the login names, the user ID numbers assigned by the system, full user name and the name of the home directory.

When you edit current users, or wish to modify their data, the same window appears as when creating a new user. How to create a new user will now be explained in detail.

WHAT'S THIS?

The system automatically assigns a user ID number to a new user. It works with these numbers rather than the usernames. **UID** stands for user identification number. An advanced user can assign a UID to a new user, though this is not possible with this system program.

TIP

If you have no interest in the user used by the system, you can also change the view. Click on *View* in the menu, then on *Regular users*. The list is shorter, and displays only normal users.

Edit user
Create user
Delete user

2 Click on *Create user* in the *Actions* menu.

307

The *Create user account* window opens.

Create user account

Please specify the name of the user to be created.

Login Name   Alick

OK   Cancel

3 Enter the login name of the new user here, then click on *OK*.

Edit User

:USER_EDIT_NEW:

Account name	Alick
Full name	Alick Robertson
UID	501
Group ID (GID)	501
Other groups	<click to edit>
Login shell	GNU Bourne Again Shell
Password	<not displayed>
Home directory	/home/Alick
Disabled	Enabled
Shadow information	<Click to edit>

OK   Cancel

4 Enter the full username in this window.

Apply the UID and login shell as displayed.

The home directory is automatically created and can usually be left as it is.

The **Group Identification Number** is configured by default so that each new user is allocated a separate personal group with his name. This is useful for individual users, but not for a network.

Users are **summarised** in groups in Linux so administration tasks can be performed more easily. This is not really of any use with single-user computers, yet saves the system administrator a lot of time with large networks.

Imagine a network with 200 users. All users require access to a file with job advertisements regularly updated by the personnel department. If the group concept did not exist, the system administrator would have to grant access to this file to each of the 200 users individually. But, with the group concept, the system administrator need only grant access to the group, thereby saving time.

You can modify the default setting as follows:

5 Click on the black arrow to the right of the Group ID (GID) selection field and select the users group.

This group is only considered 'usual' until otherwise specified by the system administrator (only on your own computer). In a company, the system administrator may configure groups by department. The new employee *Smith* in accounts would be assigned to the *Acc* group.

A password can now be assigned to the new user. This should be done at all costs. A user without a password is a serious security problem, especially in a network.

6 Click on *Not displayed* next to *Password*.

Change Password ✕

Please change Alick's password. The password is not displayed while you type it, so in order to make sure you haven't mistyped it, please enter it twice.

Enter password   `*****`
Re-enter password

| OK | Cancel |

7 Enter the password for the user twice in this window.

The word is displayed in 'stars'.

8 Then click on *OK*.

If you are the system administrator, you should also give a password to a new user. This should immediately be modified when you first log on. A password should always be kept secret, even from the system administrator. The administrator cannot help you if you forget your password – they can only assign a new one. You will learn how to modify a password later in this chapter.

The *Disabled* field means that the user account is deactivated. It is enabled by default, so you should leave it be when working with the username.

The *Disabled* function is only of any meaning to the system administrator in large networks. Sometimes an employee may be away or ill for a long time. To prevent an unauthorised party from logging in as the absent employee and damaging the system, the account can be temporarily disabled. When the employee returns, the account can be enabled again. This process again saves the system administrator time, as the alternative would be to delete the account and then create a new one.

The last option in this window is *Shadow Information*. The name refers to the file in which password information is contained. Other password settings are also available.

9 Click on *Click to Edit* next to *Shadow Information*.

The *Password Expiration* window enables a password expiration date to be set.

The fields have the following meaning:

Field name	Meaning
Last changed	The date the password was last modified (marked grey here, as the new user has not yet modified it).
Min. days for change	The minimum number of days before a password can be changed (this is for security reasons: users should change their passwords regularly. They often change it back afterwards. The system administrator can prevent this by entering 7, for example: the new password may then only be altered after 7 days).
Max. days for change	The number of days after which the password must be changed.

Field name	Meaning
Warn before expire	The number of days after which the user receives a message to say the password will soon expire. You then have time to think of a new password.
Disable after	The number of days after which the user account should be disabled. This can be used if a trainee is placed with a company for only three months, for example. –1 is entered here, meaning no value is set.
Expiration date	The password expiration date. Never is entered here, meaning the password never expires. In this case users should change it themselves.

> You will see that these password settings are of great use to companies with many employees using Linux. You can of course experiment with the settings. However, you should avoid modifying super user settings. The system may become damaged and you may have to reinstall everything!

10 Click on *OK* to close the window.

Close the *Create New User* window. The recently created user will now be displayed in the *User Accounts* window.

You will remember that a new user is assigned a specific username in a group by default. It would be silly to create a new group for every user, so change the group to *users*. You can then configure the system so that the users group is always automatically assigned to each newly created user.

Proferonces...
Disable shadow passwords
Enable NIS lookups

1 Open the *Options* menu, then click on *Preferences*.

Default preferences can be specified for new users in this window. The following options are available.

Edit Preferences

Please set the user administration preferences. Help for the individual items is available via the F2 key.

Minimum UID	500
Group Assignment Policy	User Private Group
Default group	
Default Shell	GNU Bourne Again Shell
Default Password lifetime	30
Home Directories	/home

OK   Cancel

Field	Meaning
Minimum UID	New user identification numbers are assigned from this number onwards. This number is always set to 100 or higher, as lower numbers are reserved for system user accounts.
Group Assignment Policy	Here you can specify to which group a new user should be assigned by default. The corresponding group number is indicated in the next field, *Default group*. The operating system works with group identification numbers rather than names at this stage.
Default Shell	The default shell for a new user can be specified here.

Field	Meaning
Default Password lifetime	Contains the setting for password validity in days.
Home Directories	The path in which the home directories of the new user should be placed.

Most default settings are correct. Just change the value in *Group Assignment Policy*.

2 Open the corresponding selection menu and select *User Private Group*.

New users are then assigned to the users group.

Users should be deleted from time to time. It would be best to create a sample user, following the steps outlined above. This user can be deleted as described below:

1 Click on the name of the user to be deleted in the list.

The name is surrounded by a frame.

Edit user
Create user
Delete user

2 Click on the *Delete user* option in the *Actions* menu.

The system does not delete the user immediately, but asks if you are sure.

3 Click on *Yes*.

You are then asked if you wish to delete the user's home directory.

4 Click on *Yes*.

You should think carefully before answering this question: important files may be located in the home directory. If you are unsure, click on *No* or copy the files into another directory before deleting the user account!

Modifying a user account works in the same way as creating a new user. However, you will not be asked for the username. Instead, select a user from the list before editing. Then click on the Edit User option in the Actions menu.

5 Close the *User Accounts* window by clicking on the *Close* button in the upper right-hand corner.

315

Mounting file systems with COAS

You can place other hard drives in your file tree using the COAS program. You have already learned how to place a CD-ROM drive in the file tree using the *KDE Configuration Wizard* CD-ROM icon.

If you know DOS or Microsoft Windows well, you will soon realise that Linux does not use the ABC drive letter specifications for floppy, CD-ROM and hard drives. Linux uses a mount command which places these devices straight in the file tree, so that the files and directories on these devices (e.g. on the CD-ROM) become a part of the file tree. You need not enter the mount commands yourself. You can use the KDE Configuration Wizard icons for CD-ROMs and floppy disks, and the COAS program for hard drives.

Click on *System* in the COAS menu, then on *Filesystem*.

All mountable file systems (such as CD-ROM and floppy drives) are displayed on the left-hand side of the window, and those already mounted on the right-hand side.

CD-ROMs and floppy drives are not mounted into the file tree automatically as there is not always a data carrier (a CD-ROM and/or floppy disk) in the drive. The hard drives used are mounted by default. Assuming you have mounted a new hard drive in your computer which has been recognised by the system, this will be listed on the left-hand side. This hard drive can then be mounted in the file tree in the same way as described below in the case of the CD-ROM drive.

If you have SCSI hard drives, the drive specification will be slightly different, such as /dev/sdd.

2 Click on /dev/hdc in the left-hand side of the window, then on Mount.

The term /dev/hdc stands for the CD-ROM drive. This can vary from one computer to another.

Mount File System

Please edit the file system information

Device	/dev/hdc
Directory	/mnt/cdrom
FS Type	iso9660
Options	ro,user,noauto

OK   Cancel

Here you can specify where the files on the CD should be mounted in the file tree, and what type of file system the drive to be mounted uses.

When you mount a hard drive you can choose under which directory you wish to see it in the file tree. The directory must be an empty one created by the user.

The CD-ROM drive could be mounted in the /mnt/cdrom directory. Likewise the file system iso9660.

3 Click on the Options button.

The options are activated by clicking the corresponding check field. They contain a blue check when activated.

```
┌─ File System Options ──────────────────────── ✕ ┐
│ Please edit the mount options for file system /dev/hdc. │
│                                                         │
│ Don't mount at boot time                          ☑     │
│ Mount read-only                                   ☑     │
│ Any user can mount                                ☑     │
│ No set-uid binaries                               ☐     │
│ No /dev files                                     ☐     │
│ No Rockridge extensions                           ☐     │
│                  ┌──────────────────────┐               │
│                  │         OK           │               │
│                  └──────────────────────┘               │
└─────────────────────────────────────────────────────────┘
```

The following essential options are available when mounting a device:

Option	Meaning
Don't mount at boot time	The device should not be mounted in the file tree at startup. This option is recommended for the CD-ROM and floppy drive, though a hard drive should not be checked at this point.
Mount read-only	The mounted device should be accessed as read-only. This option is set for CD-ROMs by default (as these can usually only be read and not written to). A hard drive should not be checked at this point.
Any user can mount	When this option is enabled, any normal user can mount a device. Only the super user is normally permitted to mount devices in the file tree.

The options displayed above are correct for a CD-ROM drive.

4 Click on *OK*.

The system informs you that the CD-ROM drive is mounted. The report disappears from the screen as soon as the process is finished.

The following errors can occur during this process:

The system reports that the CD-ROM drive cannot be mounted.

The process is cancelled with an error message.

This error message is displayed if you have not placed a CD-ROM in the drive. The system tries to find a disk with files, but cannot find any. Repeat the process once you have inserted a CD-ROM. This error message can also appear using badly scratched or burned CD-ROMs, or CD-ROMs without an ISO format.

This time mounting the CD-ROM drive worked: it is listed on the right-hand side under the mounted devices.

319

Removing a CD-ROM drive or other device is a similar process:

1 Click on the device to be removed in the right-hand side of the window, then click on *Unmount*.

You can mark whether the device should no longer be listed in the *fstab* file (*Remove from fstab*) and/or whether the device should be mounted at the next startup.

```
Unmount File System                                    ×
Unmounting file system /dev/pts, which is listed in the /etc/fstab file.

Remove from fstab              ☐
Remount on next boot           ☑


         OK                              Cancel
```

TIP The */etc/fstab* system file contains a list of all devices to be mounted. Only alter this list at this point if you are sure that you will not wish to mount this device again. This will probably not be the case with the CD-ROM drive.

CAUTION With hard drives, you should never check Remove and always check Remount.

2 Click on *Remount on next boot*, then on *OK*.

CAUTION You cannot open the CD-ROM drive and remove the CD as long as the drive is mounted. It must first be opened by the system.

The CD-ROM drive (*/dev/hdd*) is now no longer displayed in the table of mounted devices in the right-hand side of the window. It is listed on the left-hand side with the unmounted devices.

3 End the program with *OK*.

Displaying or modifying the hostname

You can display or modify the hostname assigned to your computer using the COAS program. The hostname of the computer is particularly important in a network.

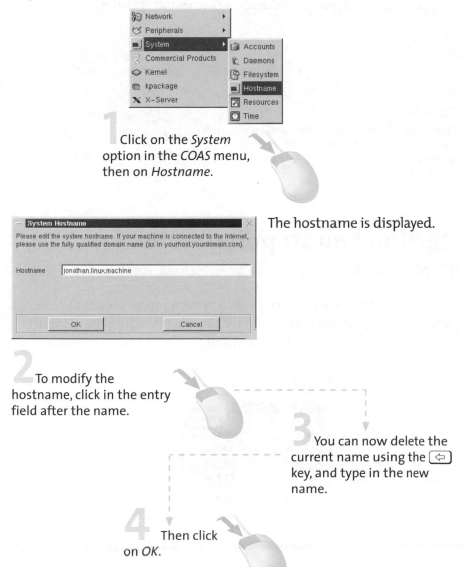

Click on the *System* option in the *COAS* menu, then on *Hostname*.

The hostname is displayed.

To modify the hostname, click in the entry field after the name.

You can now delete the current name using the ⌫ key, and type in the new name.

Then click on *OK*.

321

Warning

⚠ You changed your hostname while in an X Windows session. This may completely confuse all applications and/or the X server. If this happens, you will not be able to start any new applications, or even terminate your X session properly (except by pressing Ctrl-Alt-Backspace).
You can therefore choose to either postpone setting the run-time hostname, continue with setting it, or reboot now.

| Postpone | Update now | Reboot |

The system reports that this alteration may cause problems in the graphic interface. You can *Postpone* the alteration, *Update now* despite the warning, or *Reboot*.

The second option is not recommended. If you need to modify the computer name, click on *Reboot*. Otherwise cancel by pressing *Postpone*.

5 Click on *Postpone*.

Starting and stopping system processes

As the super user you can specify which system processes (also known as daemons) should be started automatically when starting the computer. This is also done using the COAS program.

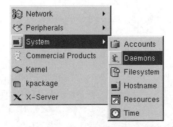

🖧 Network ▶
🖂 Peripherals ▶
▪ System ▶   📁 Accounts
 Commercial Products   🐾 Daemons
◇ Kernel   🗒 Filesystem
🖿 kpackage   ▪ Hostname
✕ X-Server   🖼 Resources
  ⏲ Time

1 Click on *System* in the *COAS* menu, then on *Daemons*.

System processes are listed here. Use the scrollbar on the right margin to see all of them.

System services

Use this list to select which system services will be activated after system boot.

- ☑ Print server (LPD)
- ☐ Very large filesystem support (delayed & backgrounded)
- ☑ Basic IP services (normally enabled!)
- ☑ Networked file-systems support
- ☑ Network devices
- ☑ Redirect console/tty0 to tty1 for booter (normally enabled!)
- ☑ Auto Mount Daemon (NFS & local)
- ☑ WEB server
- ☑ Batch Server (atd)
- ☐ Internet domain name server (named)
- ☐ DHCP and BOOTP boot server
- ☐ GPM Console Mouse Driver
- ☐ InterNetNews news transport system (innd)
- ☐ Internetwork Packet eXchange (ipx)

[OK] [Cancel]

2 The option is enabled or disabled by clicking in the small box before the process name.

TIP

If the box is already marked with a blue check, this means that the system process is loaded at startup. You should only enable or disable system processes with which you are familiar. Disabling important processes can lead to unexpected errors when operating Linux. There is no system response when a process is enabled or disabled.

3 Click on *OK* to end the application.

Displaying system information

WHAT'S THIS?

The term **interrupt** is used to mean internal system processes connected to hardware devices. You will hardly come into contact with interrupts, as these are usually managed by the system automatically.

It may happen that you require detailed system information for whatever reason (maybe when installing hardware), such as the make of your processor or interrupt settings.

323

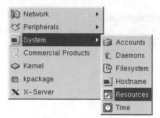

Click on the *System* option in the *COAS* menu, then on *Resources* (resources or installed hardware).

Most information hidden behind this menu entry refers to the hardware, and is of a highly technical nature. The program only displays this hardware information. It cannot be modified at this point.

A window opens containing processor information. In the example you will see an Intel processor running at 450 MHz.

Further system information can be retrieved using the *Info* menu entry.

System Resource Information

Info

This table shows you several information about your system cpu(s). You can access more information on other components over the info menu.

system resource	resource value
processor	0
vendor_id	GenuineIntel
cpu family	6
model	7
model name	00/07
stepping	2
cpu MHz	451.031593
cache size	512 KB
fdiv_bug	no
hlt_bug	no
sep_bug	no

OK

Block devices
Character devices
Interrupts
System load average
IOports
DMA

Click on *Info*, then on the desired menu entry.

This could be *Block Devices*, for example.

major	device
1	ramdisk
2	fd
3	ide0
9	md
22	ide1

System Block Devices

This is the list of the registered block devices in your system.

OK   Cancel

All system block devices only display the device number (major) by which the system recognises them. The device number corresponds to the driver.

WHAT'S THIS?

A distinction is made between *block devices* and *character devices* in Linux. Block means that the devices can process data in entire data blocks (such as the hard drive), while character devices can read one character after the other (such as the monitor).

TIP

The menu entries *Interrupts*, *IOPorts* and *DMA* (direct memory access) are special types of hardware addresses required by the system to be able to respond to the hardware. The entry *System Load Average* displays the average system load of three different measurement times. As the evaluation of this hardware information requires very detailed technical knowledge, detailed information will not be outlined in this book.

3 Click on *OK* to close the display of block devices.

4 Close the *System Resource* window by clicking *OK*.

325

Setting system time

Your computer usually displays the current time. This is programmed during the manufacturing process and functions even when the computer is shut down, by means of an internal battery. This 'system' time may begin to deviate from actual time – usually with older computers when batteries are running out. Or you may have specified the wrong time zone on installation. For this reason, the time and time zone can be corrected manually.

🔯 Network ▶	
✄ Peripherals ▶	
■ System ▶	🗔 Accounts
⚙ Commercial Products	🕯 Daemons
◇ Kernel	🗋 Filesystem
🖿 kpackage	■ Hostname
✗ X–Server	🖾 Resources
	🕓 Time

System Time

Please set the system clock, and your system time zone.

Current time	Mon, 9 Oct 2000 13:18:05
Set current time	Mon, 9 Oct 2000 13:18:52
Your time zone	Europe/London

OK   Cancel

1 Click on *System* in the *COAS* menu, then on *Time*.

2 Click in the *Set current time* field containing the date and time.

Modify the values accordingly. Use the left and right cursor keys to position yourself at the value to be altered. Then delete the value, such as 18:52, and type in the new value, such as 17:59.

As soon as you click on *OK*, the new settings are applied. You can also enter a number instead of a month, such as '9' or '10' instead of Sep or Oct. The system then converts the number into a month. If you make an invalid entry, such as deleting the month and not entering a new value, or entering 25:33 in the time field, the program simply retains the old settings.

3 Click on *Your time zone*.

Continent

Please select which continent you live on.

Arctic Ocean
Asia
Atlantic Ocean
Australia
Europe
Indian Ocean
Pacific Ocean

Cancel

Select the geographical area applicable to you. You can alter the display using the scrollbar.

4 Click on the desired geographical area, then on *OK*.

The country can be selected in the next window.

Country

Please select which country you live in.

Albania
Andorra
Austria
Belarus
Belgium
Bosnia & Herzegovina
Britain (UK)

Back

5 Click on the corresponding country, then on *OK*.

The selected time zone (e.g. Europe/London) will now be displayed on the *Your time zone* field.

6 Click on *OK* to end the application.

327

KDE control centre information

If you require more system information, open the KDE control centre. The COAS menu provides information and further details, such as the available system partitions.

1 Click on the *KDE Control Centre* icon in the program bar.

2 Click on the plus symbol before the *Information* entry.

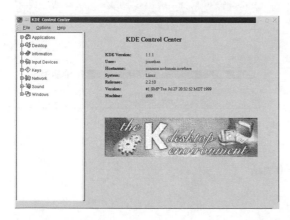

The sub-menu appears. You will see that several KDE control centre system information entries agree with those of the COAS menu.

Two of the extra menu entries are particularly interesting.

3 Click on *Memory*.

A window displaying the values of your working memory appears (also called RAM memory). The display comprises the output of your total and available memory, as well as virtual memory details.

4 Click on *Partitions*.

In this example the system has a hard drive (hda) with six partitions, HDA1, HDA2, HDA3, HDA4, HDA5 and HDA6, and a CD-ROM device, hdc.

TIP

You can deal with both the COAS menu and the KDE Control Centre information menu in detail. You should consult the appropriate manual for further hardware information.

5 Click on *OK* to end the application.

329

What's in this chapter:

Until now you have only worked with the programs and tools placed on the hard drive automatically during the installation of Linux (Chapter 1). However, some of these programs may not be required. First, you will learn how to display the pre-installed software using the *kpackage* program. You will then uninstall and re-install a program. Finally, you will install the StarOffice software package.

You already know about:

You are going to learn about:

331

Displaying installed programs

All programs installed on your system can be displayed using the *kpackage* application.

To do so, you have to be logged in as the *root* user. Otherwise the COAS administration tools window appears, asking for the root password. It is recommended that software only be installed by the *root* user. Normal users do not usually have the necessary rights required to install or create new system directories and files.

1 Open the main menu.
Click on COAS, then on *Kpackage*.

The programs installed are listed in categories. The category sub-entries can be opened by clicking on the plus symbols before the names, as in the file manager.

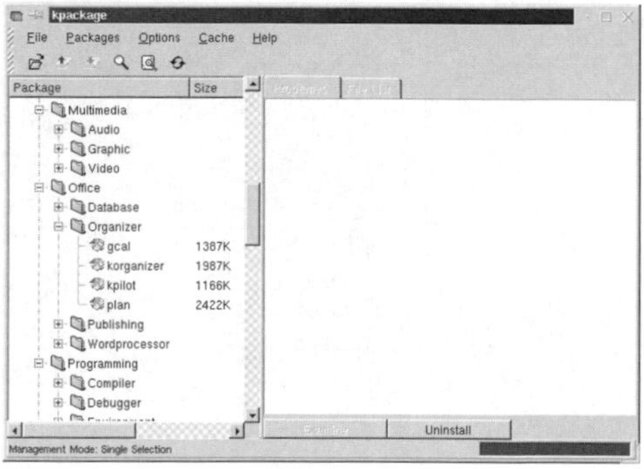

2 Click on the *Office* category, then on *Organizer* and *KPilot*.

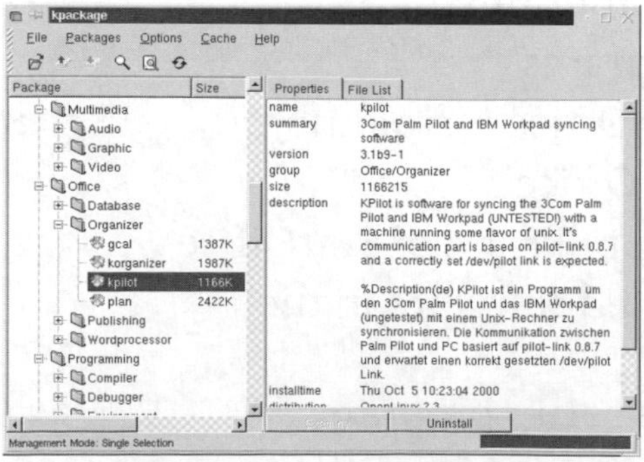

The programs are listed in categories on the left-hand side, and a description of the selected program, *kpilot*, can be seen on the right.

3 Click on the *File List* tab.

All files listed here are component parts of the *kpilot* package.

Uninstalling programs

Programs can easily be removed using *kpackage*. This process is known as uninstalling. The *kpilot* is uninstalled as follows.

The *kpilot* software package should still be displayed in the *kpackage* window. If not, reopen it.

1 Click on the *Uninstall* button (in the lower right-hand corner of the window).

Several settings can be made for uninstalling. The *Use Scripts* and *Check Dependencies* options are recommended. The *Test* option does not actually uninstall, but only simulates uninstallation.

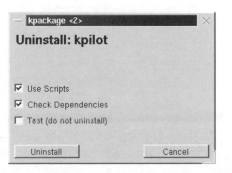

2   Click on *Uninstall* if the *Use Scripts* and *Check Dependencies* options are enabled.

The *kpilot* program will no longer be displayed following successful uninstallation.

You can search for the *kpackage* program using the search function.

3   Click on *File* in the menu and then on *Find Package*.

4   Enter the name of the program (*kpilot*), then click on *Find*.

As the program is no longer available following uninstallation, the following message appears:

5 Click on *OK* and close the *kpackage* application.

The *Kpilot* option can still be found in the main menu under *Utilities*. No error message will appear when you try to start the program. Right-click in the program bar and select *Restart* in the context menu. The menu contents are then updated.

Installing programs

Programs can also be installed using *kpackage*.

1 Place the *Linux Installation CD1* in the CD-ROM drive.

2 Click on the CD-ROM icon on the desktop.

The files and directories on the CD-ROM are displayed. Click on the *cdrom* directory in the left-hand side of the window, then on *Packages*, then on *RPMS*. All installable packages are listed in the right-hand side of the window.

Alternatively, you could use the *Find* option in the *Edit* menu and search for the *kpilot* program. Enter 'kpilot*' as a search string.

3 Drag the scroll box to modify the view of the right-hand side of the window.

4 Click on *kpilot-3.1b9-1.i386.rpm* file.

The *kpackage* program opens to install the new software. A program description is displayed. The options offered on the left-hand side can be enabled by clicking on them. Several options are only used for updating purposes.

kpackage
File   Packages   Options   Cache   Help

Install Package

	Properties	File List
	name	kpilot
☑ Upgrade	summary	3Com Palm Pilot and IBM Workpad syncing software
	version	3.1b9-1
	group	Office/Organizer
☑ Replace Files	size	1166215
	description	KPilot is software for syncing the 3Com Palm Pilot and IBM
☑ Replace Packages		Workpad (UNTESTED!) with a machine running some flavor of unix. It's communication part is based on pilot-link 0.8.7 and a correctly set /dev/pilot link is expected.
☑ Check Dependencies		
		%Description(de) KPilot ist ein Programm um den 3Com Palm Pilot und das IBM Workpad (ungetestet) mit einem Unix-Rechner zu synchronisieren. Die Kommunikation zwischen Palm Pilot und PC basiert auf pilot-link 0.8.7 und
☐ Test (do not install)		erwartet einen korrekt gesetzten /dev/pilot Link.
	distribution	OpenLinux 2.3
	vendor	Caldera, Inc.
	packager	Matthias Hoelzer-Kluepfel <mhk@caldera.de>
	build-time	Wed Jul 28 02:10:53 1999

Install	Cancel

Updating File List

Updates are new versions of programs. Old program files are therefore frequently overwritten, i.e. replaced.

5 Click on the *Check Dependencies* option, then on the *File List* tab.

The program files are now displayed.

Now click on *Install*.

The *kpilot* program is now reinstalled.

Alternatively, commercial software can also be installed using the *Commercial software* option in the COAS menu, though this is more time-consuming.

Open your CD-ROM drive and remove the installation CD.

The reinstalled *Kpilot* option cannot yet be found in the main menu under *Tools*. Right-click in the program bar and select *Restart* in the context menu. The menu content will then be updated.

Preparing StarOffice installation

There are two ways of installing StarOffice: either from the Linux installation CD, or from a separate CD-ROM program. The StarOffice program is usually found in the /cdrom/Packages/RPMS directory on the Linux installation CD-ROM. The program package name begins with StarOffice.

The program itself can be installed in two ways. The first option is single-user installation. This means that the program will only be available to the person who installed it. Installing the program for two users in this way amounts to two full installations, which takes up a lot of memory space.

The second option is a network installation. This means that StarOffice only needs to be installed on one computer once, then configured for each individual user. This saves a lot of memory space on the hard drive, and is strongly recommended for use on a network, or on computers used by several users.

The second option is described below. First, you need to prepare the StarOffice installation.

1 Place the *StarOffice* CD-ROM in the CD-ROM drive. The file manager opens and shows the contents of the CD-ROM.

The files and directories on the CD-ROM are displayed. When software is installed as new, it is recommended that the text file with installation instructions be read. These files are usually called *readme*.

2 Click on the *Linux* directory, then on *office51* and on the README file.

The file is opened in the text editor and shows you how to follow the installation through. Always read through such files attentively and follow the advice.

According to the file, you need to start the program *setup* with the option */net*, if you want to carry out a network installation.

3 Open an appointment window by clicking on this symbol in the control strip.

TIP

Observe the blank in front of */net*.

4 Enter *cd /auto/cdrom/linux/office51* and then */setup /net*.

The preparations are completed and the installation can start.

339

Installing StarOffice

The StarOffice 5.1 installation program is started.

1 Click on *Next*.

This window contains information about the program which should be read through carefully.

2 Then click on *Next*.

The licence agreement for the software program is shown, which you should read through.

3 If you agree, click on *Accept*.

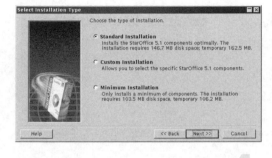

A standard installation is best.

4 Then click on *Next*.

You have already selected an installation size with the installation of Linux. The minimal configuration contains only the minimal program parts and the custom installation requires good system knowledge. The standard installation which contains all necessary program parts therefore is recommended.

5 Type the directory under which the program packet of StarOffice shall be saved on the hard disk.

It is part of the optional software and should be installed therefore under */opt/office51*.

6 Then click on *Next*.

You will get an error message saying that the directory doesn't exist and asking if you want to create it.

StarOffice 5.1 Installation

? Folder '/opt/office51' does not exist. Create it now?

Yes   No

7 Click on *Yes*.

You have now carried out all of the tasks needed for the installation.

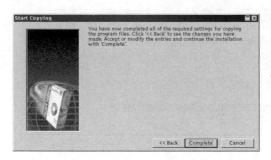

Start Copying

You have now completed all of the required settings for copying the program files. Click '<< Back' to see the changes you have made. Accept or modify the entries and continue the installation with 'Complete'.

<< Back   Complete   Cancel

You can correct the previous sections by returning to the corresponding screens with the help of the back button.

8 If you don't want to carry out any changes, then click on *Next*.

The installation still checks the system before starting.

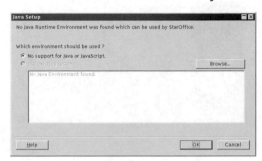

The installation program looks for Java running on your machine. This is a special program which is not necessary for using StarOffice.

9 Click on *No support for Java or JavaScript* and then on *OK*.

The installation starts now and you can watch its progress.

The first step consists of copying the programs. Information about StarOffice is simultaneously displayed on the screen.

343

When this window is displayed, the installation is complete.

Installation Complete

The installation has been successfully completed. We hope you enjoy working with StarOffice 5.1!

Click 'Complete' to end the installation program.

Sun microsystems   STARDIVISION

[Complete] [Cancel]

1 Click on *OK*.

2 Then open your CD-ROM drive and remove the StarOffice CD again.

Single-user installation of StarOffice

StarOffice is now located on your computer, but is not yet configured for individual users. Use the following procedure for each user wishing to use StarOffice:

1 Log on to the system using the desired username.

2 Open the file manager using this icon in the control bar.

3 Click on the *opt directory*, then on *office51* and *bin,* and finally on the *setup* file.

The StarOffice 5.1 single-user installation program is now started. It begins with a welcome screen, just as with the multi-user installation.

4 Click on *Next*.

Important information is displayed again.

5 Click on *Next*.

Software License Agreement

Read the following License Agreement carefully. Use the scroll bar to view the entire text.

Sun Microsystems, Inc.

Binary Code License Agreement

READ THE TERMS OF THIS AGREEMENT AND ANY PROVIDED SUPPLEMENTAL LICENSE TERMS (COLLECTIVELY "AGREEMENT") CAREFULLY BEFORE OPENING THE SOFTWARE MEDIA PACKAGE. BY OPENING THE SOFTWARE MEDIA PACKAGE, YOU AGREE TO THE TERMS OF THIS AGREEMENT. IF YOU ARE ACCESSING THE SOFTWARE ELECTRONICALLY INDICATE YOUR ACCEPTANCE OF THESE TERMS BY SELECTING THE "ACCEPT" BUTTON AT THE END OF THIS AGREEMENT. IF YOU DO NOT AGREE TO ALL OF THESE TERMS, PROMPTLY RETURN THE UNUSED SOFTWARE TO YOUR PLACE OF PURCHASE FOR A REFUND OR, IF THE SOFTWARE IS ACCESSED ELECTRONICALLY, SELECT THE "CANCEL" BUTTON AT THE END OF THIS AGREEMENT.

If you accept all terms of the license agreement, click the 'Accept' button. Otherwise, click 'Cancel' to cancel the installation.

`<< Back`   `Accept`   `Cancel`

The licence agreement must be accepted again.

6 Click on *Accept*.

Enter User Data

Company			
First and Last Name/Initials	Jonathan	Mitton	M
Street			
City/State/Zip code			
Country	United Kingdom		
Title/Position			
Tel. (Home)			
Tel. (Work)			
Fax			
E-mail			

Help   `<< Back`   `Next >>`   `Cancel`

7 Several details of the current user need to be entered in the next window so you can be registered as the program owner.

StarOffice Setup

Name, Last name, Street, Post Code and city where not entered

`OK`

Enter at least your name, surname, address and postcode before clicking on *Next*. Otherwise this error message will appear. Your user details will then be displayed for editing.

In this window you are prompted to choose either *Standard* or *Custom* installation. You are recommended to opt for Standard.

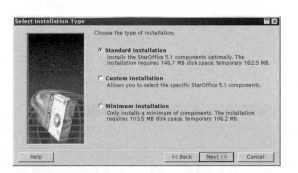

8 Then click on *Next*.

You will doubtless already be familiar with the installation process, especially from the first installation of the Linux operating system. Minimal installation contains only the essential program components, and custom installation requires a good system knowledge. Standard installation is therefore recommended, as all necessary program components are present.

9 Type in the name of the directory in which the StarOffice program should be saved on the hard drive.

In the case of user installation, it should be installed in the home directory of the current user.

347

10 Then click on *Next*.

StarOffice 5.1 Installation ▭ ▣ ✕

② Folder '/opt/office51' does not exist. Create it now?

Yes   No

An error message appears, informing you that this directory does not exist, and asks whether you would like to create it.

11 Click on *Yes*.

You have now created all the necessary steps for installation.

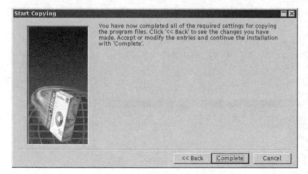

Start Copying ▭ ▣ ✕

You have now completed all of the required settings for copying the program files. Click '<< Back' to see the changes you have made. Accept or modify the entries and continue the installation with 'Complete'.

<< Back   Complete   Cancel

At this stage you can amend the details entered so far by using the *Back* button to return to the required position.

12 If you do not wish to make any more amendments, click on *Complete*.

A system check is now performed before installation.

The installation program now searches for a Java run-time environment. This is a special program environment, but it is not required for use with StarOffice.

Java Setup

No Java Runtime Environment was found which can be used by StarOffice.

Which environment should be used ?

◉ No support for Java or JavaScript.
○ Use existing system   Browse...

No Java Environment found.

Help   OK   Cancel

13 Click on *No support for Java or JavaScript*, then on *OK*.

The installation now begins. You can follow the progress of the installation process and see

StarOffice Setup

ⓘ During the installation StarOffice was added to the KDE-Panel. Make sure to restart your KDE in order to complete the integration.

OK

exactly which operations are taking place at what time.

At the end of the installation process you will receive a message informing you that the StarOffice program has been inserted into the main menu. Right-click in the program bar and select *Restart* from the context menu. The content of the menu is then updated.

1 Click on *OK*.

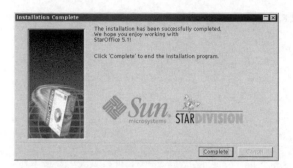

2 Click on *Complete*.

With this window the installation is finished.

Finding installed software in the main menu

TIP
You will learn the basics of working with the *StarOffice* program in the next chapter.

TIP
If the *Personal* entry does not appear in the main menu, right-click in the control bar, and then left-click on the *Restart* option.

> Development ▶
> Documentation ▶
> Editors ▶
> Games ▶
> Graphics ▶
> Internet ▶
> Multimedia ▶
> Office ▶
> Toys ▶
> Utilities ▶
>
> Settings ▶
> System ▶
> COAS ▶
>
> Applications ▶
> KDE Help
> Home Directory
> KDE Control Center
> Personal ▶   🖳 Setup
> Disk Navigator ▶   SPAdmin
> Panel ▶   StarOffice
> Lock Screen
> Logout

1 Click on *Personal* in the main menu, then on *StarOffice* to start the StarOffice program.

If the installation is successfully completed, the program should now be started. If not, repeat the installation process.

StarOffice will try to configure internet settings on first use. If you have not yet set up an internet connection (see chapter 10) then cancel the process by clicking on *No Internet connection*.

2 Close *StarOffice* again by clicking on *Close* in the upper right-hand corner of the title bar.

If you wish to work with *StarOffice* frequently in the future, insert the program as an icon in the program bar.

3 Click in the main menu on *Panel*, then on *Add application – Personal – StarOffice*.

The *StarOffice* program now appears in the program bar:

The StarOffice setup program

When installing StarOffice, the *StarOffice* setup program is installed at the same time. This program can be used if you wish to install or uninstall other *StarOffice* components at a later date. It can also be used for repairing or uninstalling *StarOffice*.

1 Click on *Personal* in the main menu, then on *Setup*.

If you opted for standard installation of StarOffice, then it is not necessary to install any further programs using the *Setup* options. Take a quick look in the next window to view the *Setup* options, in case you need to use one of them.

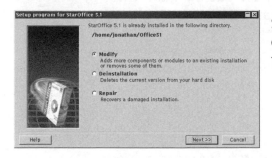

Should this be the case, click on the option you wish to perform.

2 Then click on *Next* and execute the corresponding program instructions.

Close the window again, as there is no need to use the setup program at present.

3 Click on the *Close* button in the upper right-hand corner of the title bar.

Installing printers for StarOffice

The printers already installed must be made 'known' to *StarOffice*. This means that several more printer details have to be entered.

1 Click on P*ersonal* in the main menu, then on *SPAdmin*.

Alternatively, click on *Printer Setup* in the StarOffice window.

In both cases a window opens, in which the printer can be configured for StarOffice.

File: /home/jonathan/Office51/xp3/Xpdefaults

If your printer has so far functioned properly with Linux, proceed as follows.

1 Click on *Connect*.

File: /home/jonathan/Office51/xp3/Xpdefaults

2 Enter the following in the *Existing queues* field: Printername=lp -d printername.

Replace the word *printername* with the name assigned to your printer in both cases. In this example the printer name is *lp-d Apple*.

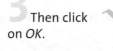 Then click on *OK*.

The *Printer Installation* window now contains the following entry in the *Printers* area:

Generic Printer in Queue printername(lp –d printername)

Printer Installation

Default printer
Generic Printer
n queue Apple=lp –d Apple

Installed printers
Generic Printeron queue Apple (lp –d Apple)

Default Printer

Existing printer drivers
Adobe LaserJet II Cartridge
Agfa–Compugraphic 9400P
Agfa Matrix ChromaScript
Agfa TabScript C500 PostScript Printer
Apple LaserWriter
Apple LaserWriter IIf
Apple LaserWriter IIq
Apple LaserWriter II NT
Apple LaserWriter II NTX

Add new printer

Install new driver...   Deinstall driver...

Close
Connect...
Configure...
Remove...
Rename...
Test Page

Edit Font Attributes...
Add Fonts...
Store Settings Locally

File: /home/jonathan/Office51/xp3/Xpdefaults

The name of your printer will be displayed in this entry instead of *printername*.

4 Click on *Test Page*.

You should print out a test
page to see if the printer works.
The system advises you that
the settings must be saved.

Printer Installation

Default printer
Generic Printer
n queue Apple=lp –d Apple

Installed printers

Generic Printer on queue Apple (lp –d Apple)

Close

Connect...

Configure...

Remove...

Rename...

Query

To print a test page, the defined settings must first be saved. Do you
want to continue?

Exis
Ado
Agf
Agf
Agfa TabScript C500 PostScript Printer
Apple LaserWriter
Apple LaserWriter IIf
Apple LaserWriter IIg
Apple LaserWriter II NT
Apple LaserWriter II NTX

Yes   No

Edit Font
Attributes...

Add
Fonts...

Add new printer

Install new driver...   Deinstall driver...   Store Settings
Locally

File: /home/jonathan/Office51/xp3/Xpdefaults

5 Click on *Yes*.

If the test page prints successfully, you can end the *StarOffice* printer
installation.

6 Click on *Close*.

TIP

If the test page does not print out, or printing using *StarOffice* causes problems, then consult the section in Troubleshooting on alternative printer installation and print problems using *StarOffice*.

Working with StarOffice

What's in this chapter:

Using the StarWriter word processing program, you can write, edit, save and format documents. You will learn the basics of the StarCalc spreadsheet program, filling in cells, creating a table and entering formulae. You will then be given a brief insight into the StarDraw graphic program. You will create a simple graphic. Finally you will set appointments and series of appointments with the StarOffice task scheduler.

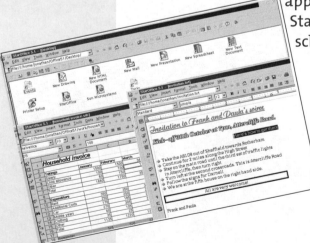

You already know about:

You are going to learn about:

An overview of StarOffice

Before you work with StarOffice, you should get to know the program interface.

 Start the program via the main menu.

Alternatively, you can start StarOffice by clicking the corresponding button in the program bar.

This assumes you have already installed the program in the program bar as outlined in the previous chapter.

The StarOffice interface consists of two parts: all programs can be seen in the upper area, and a tip is displayed in the lower area when StarOffice is opened.

TIP

If you do not wish tips to be displayed in future, click on *Do not display tips* in the lower left-hand corner.

The StarOffice program window consists of a title bar, a menu bar and different icon bars, as do most windows.

2 Close the tip window.

Click on the small *X* button (Close) on the left of the text, *Did you know?*.

The StarOffice program window corresponds to a shelf containing various books. A number of StarOffice programs are hidden behind these books.

StarOffice offers the following options: word processing (StarWriter), spreadsheet analysis (StarCalc), graphics creation (StarDraw), presentation editing (StarImpress), planning tasks and appointments, configuring a printer, editing HTML documents, writing messages and calling internet pages. Some functions must be configured before they can be used.

All homepages and web pages are written using HTML documents. **HTML** is a special language used for this purpose.

You usually need to double-click to start a program in StarOffice, as opposed to the single click required in KDE.

All functions can be started from the desktop using the mouse.

Alternatively, the different StarOffice programs can be started using the *Start* button in the lower left-hand corner of the window.

This is handy if you have already opened a program and wish to start another at the same time.

3 Click on *Start*.

The start menu now displayed contains all StarOffice program functions. The main functions are listed in the upper part of the menu. Other functions can be found in the respective sub-menus.

The StarOffice program interface can also be called a desktop interface. Just as with the KDE interface, other icons can be added, or existing icons deleted or moved.

4 Click on a free area of the desktop.

The StarOffice desktop context menu appears. The actions mentioned above can now be performed.

Arrange Icons	▶
Find...	
New	▶
Copy	
Show	▶
✓Desktop	
Update	
Properties...	

TIP

These actions correspond to KDE desktop functions. If you are having problems executing these actions, consult the section on 'KDE configuration' in chapter 4.

Opening a text in StarWriter

StarWriter is a word processing program. This means that not only can text be written, modified, deleted and printed as with the editor, but the text can be edited in different ways, such as specifying the type, colour and size of the font. This is known as **formatting**.

TIP

Alternatively, StarWriter can be opened using the *Start* and *Text Document* buttons.

1 Start the StarWriter program using the *New Text* desktop icon.

As with the editor, a window opens with different bars and a large white area in which text can be written. Text can be created or deleted at the cursor point.

The formatting bar underneath the icon bar is new. This can be used to alter the font size, style and colour.

Do you still have the *invitation.txt* text? Then open it. Otherwise you will need to type it in again.

2 Click on *File*, then *Open* in the menu list.

StarWriter usually prompts you to save work in the StarOffice */work* sub-folder. This sub-folder will therefore be opened on the assumption that the file to be opened is located here.

This is not a problem. You need only remember where you saved the text file. It may be in your home directory, marked under */home*. In our example the *invitation.txt* file is located in the */home/jonathan* directory.

You can also modify the standard StarOffice home directory if you wish. Open the *Tools* menu entry, then *Options*. Now open the *General* option by clicking on the minus symbol. Click on *Path*, then on *Home directory*. If you click on *Edit*, you can overwrite the default path name of your home directory, such as */home/jonathan*. The new settings can be saved using *Select* then *OK*.

The */opt/Office51/work* folder is open, or you may wish to use your own home directory.

3 Click three times in sequence on the *One folder up* button.

It is located in the upper right-hand corner of the window and has this icon:

You are now located in the uppermost directory level, the root directory, and can see all subordinate folders.

4 Now click on */ home*, then on the name of your home directory.

The text file *invitation.txt* is
still located in this directory
(as long as you have not
deleted it).

5 Click on *invitation.txt*,
then on *Open*.

The document is opened and
can now be edited.

Modifying the text view

Text can be displayed in different ways. Until now, a large proportion of
the screen has been taken up by the window and its bars. The text does
not occupy much space. This can be modified.

1 Click on *View*, then on
Online Layout.

2 Repeat the step for both the
Integrated Desktop and *Full Screen*
entries.

The entire screen is now available for text.

3 Click on the small screen
icon in the upper left-hand corner.

Revert to *Online Layout*. This will now be explained in detail.

367

Editing text

You will now edit the existing text to make it more appealing. Use the formatting functions.

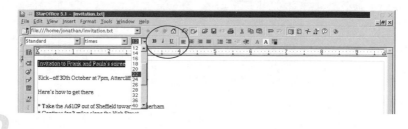

1 Mark the text heading with the mouse.

It is then highlighted in black. First alter the font size using the formatting bar.

2 Click on the selection field currently showing the number 12. Now select font size 22.

Format the text using the *Bold, Italic* and *Underlined* options in the following steps.

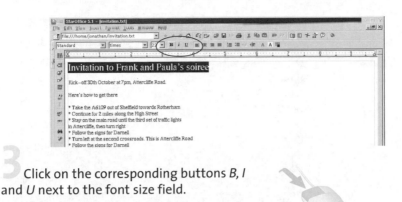

3 Click on the corresponding buttons *B*, *I* and *U* next to the font size field.

Finally, alter the text colour.

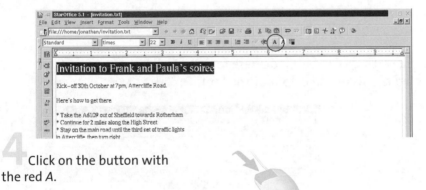

4 Click on the button with the red *A*.

The result now looks more striking and appealing than the simple text.

Formatting using the format bar is very quick and easy. However, it only contains the most important formatting functions. Other functions can be called using the *Format* menu.

369

5 Click on *Format*, then on *Character*.

Different settings can be made here for selected sections of text, including the style and colour of the font.

6 Click on *Color*, then select any colour you prefer.

The marked text now appears in the desired colour in the preview field on the right-hand side of the window.

Now select another text size and effect, such as *Shadow* or *Outline*.

Click on the desired font, such as
arioso, then on *Shadow* and *Underline*.

The preview shows the new settings. Further font settings can
also be made.

Click on the *Font
Effects* tab.

Click on the desired effect,
such as *Title*.

You can observe the changes made using the preview. Finally, you can
choose a background colour.

Character

Font | Font Effects | Hyperlink | **Background**

Background color

No Fill

White

Preview

OK   Cancel   Help   Reset

11 Select any background colour and click on *OK*.

The result now looks quite different from the original simple text. Now alter the remainder of the text.

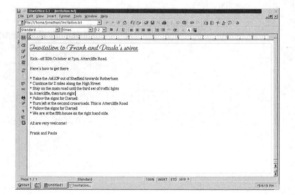

1 Click on the first line of text to be altered, beginning with 'Beginning at...'.

2 Now drag the mouse to the last line to be formatted.

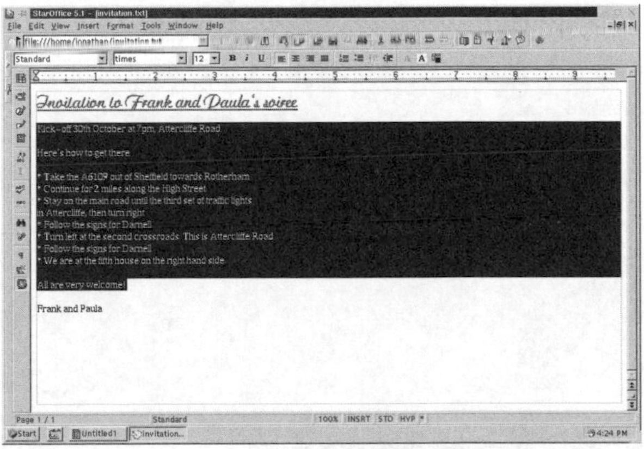

The selected text is
marked in black.

Select a font from
the menu.

Click on the black
arrow next to the selection
field containing the type
name (*times*).

Utopia is selected in
this example.

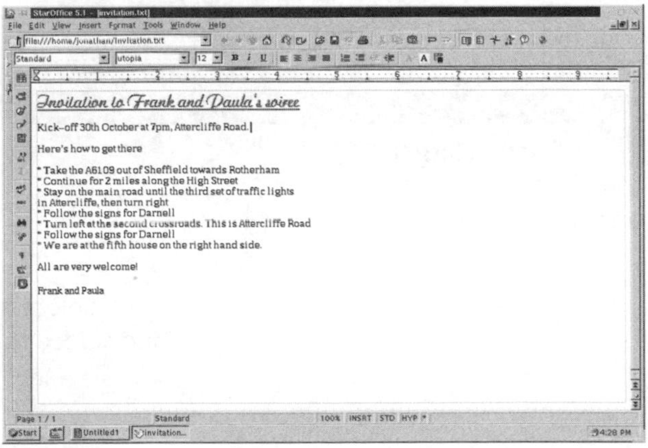

Now make further alterations to the text. Indent the date.

Click before the line 'on
30th October…' and press the
[⇆] key.

373

The line is indented with a tabulator.

2 Now mark this line.

3 Click on *Format*, then on *Character*.

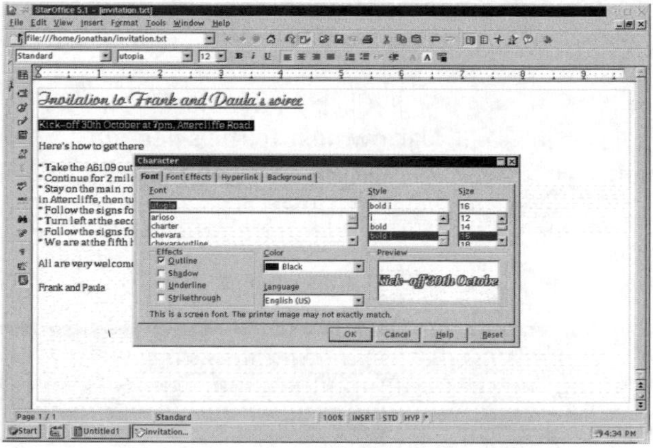

Select a larger font for this section and the *Outline* option.

4

Select another font, and select *Bold* and *Italic*.

5

6 Click on the *Background* tab and select a red background.

7 Click on *OK* to apply the format settings.

The date line now looks quite impressive.

In the next steps you will format the directions.

1 Click on the first line of directions and drag the mouse as far as the last line.

The selected lines are now marked black.

```
Format  Tools  Window  Help
Default

Character...
Paragraph...
Page...

Numbering/Bullets...

Styles              ▸
Stylist        F11
AutoFormat          ▸
```

2 Click on the *Format* menu, then on *Numbering/Bullets*.

```
Numbering/Bullets                                    _ □ ×

Bullets | Numbering style | Outline  Pictures | Position | Customize |
 ─ Selection ─────────────────────────────────────────
   ●              ■              *              ➜
   ●              ■              *              ➜
   ●              ■              *              ➜
   ────────────────────────────────────────────────────
   ●              ◆              ■              *
   ●              ◆              ■              *
   ●              ◆              ■              *

        OK    Remove   Cancel    Help    Reset
```

3 Now select the appearance of your bullet points in the *Pictures* tab.

375

4 Then click on *OK*.

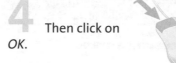

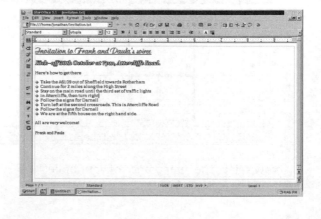

The directions are now indicated by bullet points. However, the old points entered manually will need to be deleted.

1 Click on each line before the old bullet points in the form of a *.

2 Delete each * using the ⟨⇐⟩ key.

The result looks as follows.

Insert a new line underneath the title:

1 Click in the line below the title.

2 Enter a blank line using the ⏎ key.

When typing in a new text, a word is usually offered from a suggestion list which corresponds to the letters already entered. This happens when typing the word 'octagon' for example. The word 'October' appears in the suggestion list, marked in blue once you have typed in the first three letters. If you wish to accept the suggestion, click on the ⏎ key. Otherwise just type the next letter of your word and the suggestion simply disappears.

Selecting and cutting text works in the same way as in the text editor.

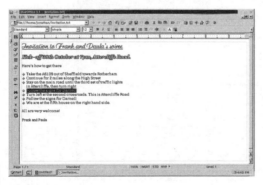

1 Mark the phrase 'Follow the signs for Darnall'.

TIP

Alternatively, you can remove the phrase using the *Cut* option in the *Edit* menu.

2 Remove the phrase using the ⌈Del⌋ key.

The bullet point remains in place. This and the extra line of spacing must also be removed. The cursor is currently placed directly behind the bullet point.

3 Delete the bullet point and the line spacing using the ⌈⇦⌋ key.

The line is now completely removed.

The invitation will now be smartened up by surrounding the phrase 'All are very welcome!' with a border and placing it in the centre of the page. This is known as **centring**.

1 Mark the phrase.

2 Click on *Insert*, then on *Text Box*.

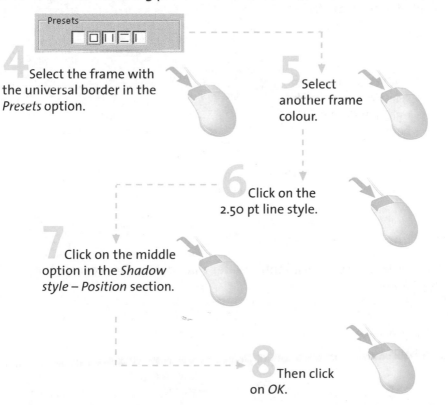

3 Click on the *Borders* tab.

Let us assume you prefer a fairly wide, coloured frame which casts a shadow. Use the following procedure:

4 Select the frame with the universal border in the *Presets* option.

5 Select another frame colour.

6 Click on the 2.50 pt line style.

7 Click on the middle option in the *Shadow style – Position* section.

8 Then click on *OK*.

The frame is a touch too narrow. This can easily be rectified. Use the green rectangles marking the border.

1 Click on the green selection point on the right-hand side of the border.

2 Drag towards the right until the border has reached the desired size.

The border is now considerably wider than before. Now centre the text in the frame.

1 Click on the text outside the frame.

2 Now click on the text in the frame.

3 Click on the *Centred* button in the format bar.

The group of four buttons to which *Centred* belongs is used to place text on the left, on the right, in the centre or justified. Test the individual options to see their effects.

You are now satisfied with the border. Finally, you wish to format the section 'Here's how to get there' as right-aligned.

1 Click in this area of text.

2 Click on the *Right-aligned* button in the format bar.

The text is immediately moved towards the right.

You have now finished editing the document. These amendments should now be saved.

1 Click on *Save As* in the *File* menu.

When you save a file for the first time, you will always be asked for a name under which to save the file. Every document saved requires a name so you and the system can find it again. After you have made any amendments, the document should be saved again. Clicking on *Save* is usually sufficient. As your text was created with the editor and edited with StarWriter, you should save the file as a StarWriter file, or your formatting will not be applied. This is why you should use the *Save As* function.

2 Open the *File type* selection list and select *StarWriter 5.0*.

The program suggests saving the text as *invitation.sdw* instead of *invitation.txt*.

3 Click on the *Save* button to confirm.

You can now close the StarWriter program as you have finished editing the file.

> If you forget to save the amendments to your file before closing a StarOffice program, it is not a matter of life and death. The program always asks you if you wish to save the changes made to the document before ending the program. Confirm by clicking on *Save*.

Click on the *File* menu,
then on *Close*.

First steps with StarCalc

In this section you will get
to know a **spreadsheet
analysis program**. As you
probably know, this type of
program is part of every
standard program
package for office
applications.

Open the *StarCalc* program
by clicking on the *New Table*
icon on the desktop.

The program window is identical to the StarWriter window. Different bars for title, menu, format and status display can also be seen.

The calculation bar is new: this contains the names of the active cells (in the example, *A1*) and their content, which can be either text, figures or formulae.

WHAT'S THIS?

Imagine your old maths book in primary school: that was divided into individual boxes in which numbers could be written. StarCalc is very similar: every **cell** or box has its own content.

The fundamentals of the program are cells, meaning that all entries are made using cells. Each cell has a name made up of its row and column number. In the image you can see that the first cell has a thick border. It is marked as the active cell, and the cell name *A1* is displayed in the calculation bar.

The use of StarCalc is best demonstrated by an example. In the following steps you will create a small budget, where the calculations are performed automatically by the program.

Text can be entered in a cell just as in an editor. However, the cell must be activated before text can be entered. The cursor is usually placed in cell *A1* when a new file is opened (as shown in the example).

2 Type out the example displayed.

You can switch between the individual cells in different ways:
either use the mouse and click the next cell, use the cursor keys, or
⇧ to move right and ↵ to move down.

Don't worry if the value entered is longer than the space in the cell
permits. You will learn how to alter the size of the cells. If the cell to the
right is empty, the text will
extend beyond the cell border. If
the cell to the right contains an
entry, as much text as the cell
width allows will be displayed.

Ensure that you enter the exact same
values in exactly the same cells as
displayed in the example. Otherwise,
you will have difficulties later on when
performing calculations referring to
specific cells.

3 To widen column A, move the mouse
(without pressing any buttons) to between
the column titles A and B.

The mouse pointer assumes the form of an arrow pointing to both left and right at the same time.

4 Now press the left mouse button, hold it down and move the mouse to the right.

Release the mouse button as soon as column A has reached a sufficient width to display the text entered.

5 Click in cell *B3*.

6 Type the three months in cells *B3*, *C3* and *D3*.

Have you made a mistake? Just delete the mistake as you would in the Editor using the ⬅ key. If you notice the error after leaving the cell, proceed as follows.

1 Click in the cell once more.

As soon as you make a new entry, you delete the old cell content. However, you may merely wish to correct an error.

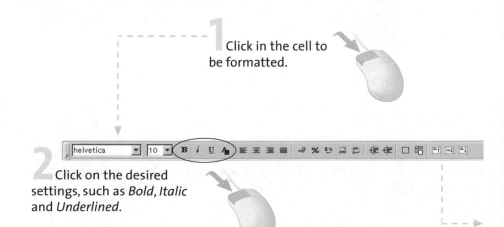

2 Click in the calculation bar in the entry line field after the error.

3 Delete the character in the normal way using the ⌫ key and type in the correct character.

As soon as the cell is disabled either using the cursor keys or by clicking another cell, the alteration is confirmed.

Text or cell contents can also be formatted in a spreadsheet analysis program in exactly the same way as in StarWriter. The title is formatted in the example displayed.

1 Click in the cell to be formatted.

2 Click on the desired settings, such as *Bold*, *Italic* and *Underlined*.

3 Now open the *Font size* menu.

4 Select font size *16*.

You will format several cells at once in the next step, as well as the budget column headings.

1 Click in the first cell to be formatted.

2 Hold the mouse key depressed and drag the mouse to the last cell to be formatted.

389

Release the mouse button. The selected cells are marked in black.

3 Select the *Bold* format.

Now record the budget figures.

| StarOffice 5.1 - [household invoice.sdc] |
| File Edit View Insert Format Tools Data Window Help |

	A	B	C	D	E	F	G	H	I	J	K
3	Takings	January	Feburary	March							
4	Salary	1500	1500	1500							
5	Child allowance	100	100	100							
6	Other	60	150	40							
7	Total										
8											
9	Expenditure										
10	Rent										
11	Additional Costs										
12	Car										
13	Middle years										
14	Clothing										
15	Other										
16	Total										
17											
18	Remainder										

1 Click on cell B4.

2 Type in the number 1500.

Then correct the rest of the numbers for the monthly takings as shown in the example.

Adding formulae

You may now wish to see the sum of the takings. Leave the calculations to StarCalc.

The sum of cells *B4*, *B5* and *B6* should be displayed in cell *B7*.

1 Click in cell *B7*.

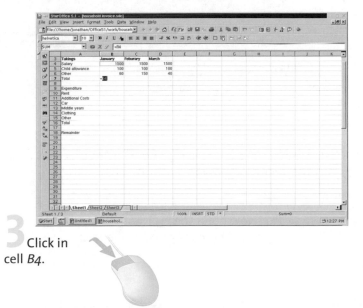

2 Type in the = character.

The word *Total* now appears in the calculation field in the left of the calculation bar, where the cell name (*B7* in this example) had previously been written. This means that StarCalc has recognised that you wish to calculate the sum of several numbers because of the equals sign. You now need to enter what StarCalc should add.

3 Click in cell *B4*.

Cell *B4* now has a red border, and is written after the equals sign in cell *B7*.

4 Enter a plus sign +.

5 Click in cell
B5.

6 Enter another plus
sign +.

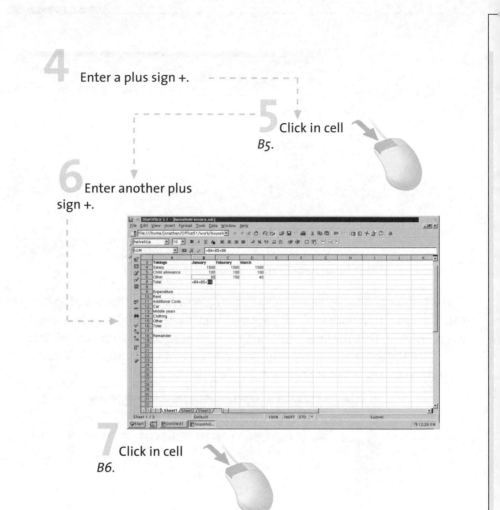

7 Click in cell
B6.

The cell now contains the sum =*B4+B5+B6*. This means that StarCalc
should display the result of this sum in this cell.

8 Now press the ⏎
key to save the formula.

The result of the calculation will be shown in the cell itself: the number 1660. The entry field in the calculation bar only displays the underlying sum.

9 Calculate the total takings for the months of February and March.

The output area must also be filled out. Enter the value from the picture.

The sum of the total output will also be calculated – more efficiently this time.

1 Click in cell *B16*.

2 Now enter the following: =*Sum(*

3 Click on the first value (350) from the
Outgoings list in cell *B10*.

4 Drag the mouse whilst
holding the left button down
from cell *B10* to cell *B15*.

The formula *=Sum(B10:B15* appears in the calculation bar entry field and
in the cell.

5 Now enter the character *)* to close
the formula.

6 Then press the
⏎ key.

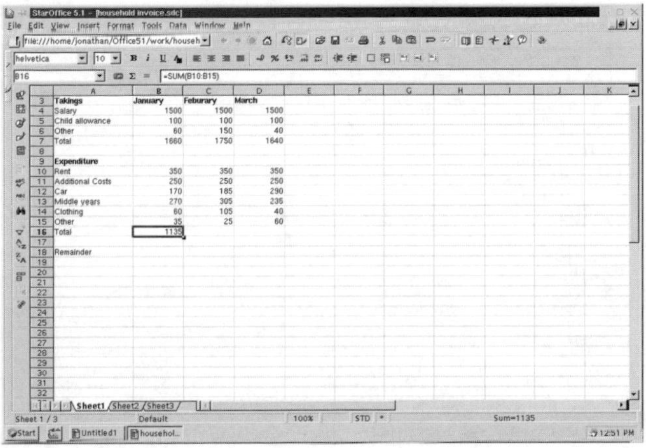

7 Click in cell
B16.

The result of the calculation is displayed in turn in the cell itself. The underlying formula is still displayed in the entry field in the calculation bar. It consists of the *Total* function from the fields *B10* to *B15*.

You need not type the formula again for both *Total February Outgoings* and *Total March Outgoings*. There is an easier option: the StarCalc copy function.

1 Click in
cell *B16*.

2 Move the mouse
to the lower right-
hand corner of the cell
without pressing the
mouse button.

The mouse pointer no longer has the form of a black arrow, but it becomes a cross.

3 Now press the left mouse button and drag the mouse over cells *C16* to *D16*.

The selected cells now have a red frame.

4 Release the mouse button.

Values now appear in cells *C16* and *D16*, which were previously empty. This is the accumulated expenditure per month. In the previous steps you copied the formula of cell B16 to *C16* and *D16*. The formula has not only been copied but also automatically adapted to the new conditions. StarCalc assumes that you do not wish to add the value from column *B* to cell *C16*, but the one from column *C*. The spreadsheet analysis assumes likewise.

Now you wish to establish how much income remains once the outgoings have been accounted for. The rest will be calculated with the *Income – Expenditure* formula.

1 Click in cell *B18*.

2 Enter an equals sign.

3 Click in cell *B7* containing the total income.

4 Now enter a minus sign.

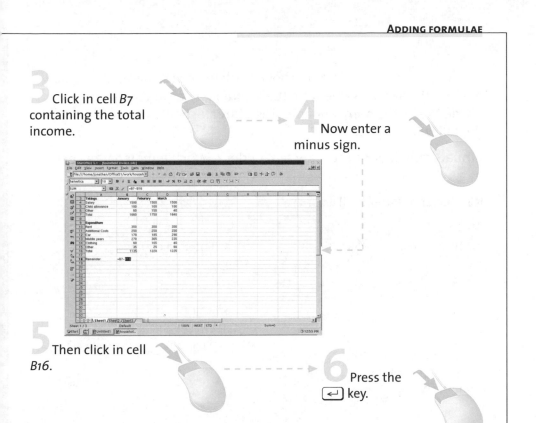

5 Then click in cell *B16*.

6 Press the ⏎ key.

The cell displays the value of the difference between the income and expenditure, but still contains the formula entered.

7 Copy the formula from cell *B18* into cells *C18* and *D18* as described in the previous section.

397

You may be interested to know how much income remains on average per month. Take the value from the *Remainder* line and add it up. Then divide this by the number of months. StarCalc should therefore calculate the following formula:

January remainder + February remainder + March remainder divided by 3.

It is better to enter it all at once.

1 Click in cell *F18*.

2 Enter an equals sign.

3 Click in cell *B18* and enter a plus sign.

4 Click in cell *C18* and enter another plus sign.

5 Click in cell *D18* and enter the division sign (*/*).

6 Click on the ⏎ key.

7 Click in cell
F18.

You will see the formula displayed in the calculation line, and the result in the cell. But can that be so? Should there be an average surplus in excess of almost £1100? That can't be right.

Then you may remember: multiplication and division take precedence over addition and subtraction. This means that in our equation only the value of *March remainder* was divided by 3. The equation is therefore wrong. The sum of the *remainder* values should be placed in brackets.

8 Click in the entry line of cell *F16* in the calculation bar after the equals sign.

9 Enter the character (.

10 Move behind cell *D18* using the *W* key and enter the character).

11 Press the ⏎ key.

12 Click in cell *F18*.

The result is now £490, which seems correct.

Formatting a table

You already know the basics of making a table more attractive. As with StarWriter, the bold, underlined and italic type functions are available, as well as the different types and sizes of fonts.

There are also different options here for defining frames and placing things in different colours.

1 Select cells *A3* to *D7*.

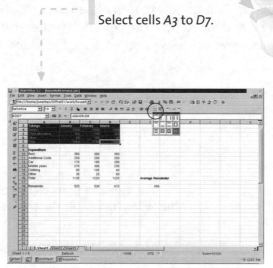

2 Select the *Borders* button in the format bar.

3 Select the option in the lower right-hand corner, which suggests a border for a table.

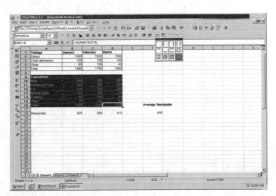

Repeat the same process for cells *A9* to *D16*.

Highlight the cells containing the remaining amount in a background colour.

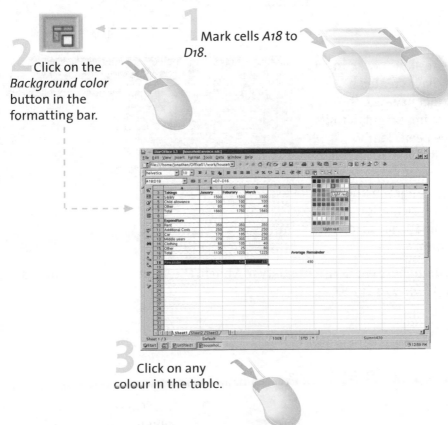

Mark cells *A18* to *D18*.

Click on the *Background color* button in the formatting bar.

Click on any colour in the table.

The *average remainder* should also be highlighted.

1 Mark cells *F16* to *G18*.

2 Click on the *Background color* button in the formatting bar again.

3 Click on any colour in the table.

The result is now correct. You have created a budget in which the most important details have been clearly highlighted. An excellent feature of StarCalc is that any changes in any part of the calculation are automatically taken into account.

Assume there was a rise in salary in March. The value of cell *D4* changes from £1,500 to £1,700.

1 Click in cell *D4*.

2 Type in the number 3400.

3 Press the ⏎ key.

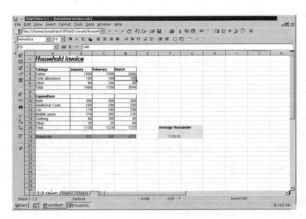

The formula is calculated immediately after leaving the modified cell.

You have now finished editing the budget. As you may wish to edit it at a later date, you should of course save the file.

As you have not yet saved the file, you could also use the *Save* function.

1 Click on *File*, then *Save As*.

StarOffice always saves new files in and opens existing files from the StarOffice *Work* directory by default. This is displayed when the *Save As* window is opened.

2 Click on this button to reach your home directory.

3 If you find yourself in the / directory, click on /home and then on the name of your own home directory.

Save As			
/home/jonathan			

☐ Desktop
☐ nsmail
☐ Office51

| Filename: | household invoice.sdc | ▼ | Save |
| File type: | StarCalc 5.0 | ▼ | Cancel |

☑ Automatic file name extension   ☐ Edit Filter Settings
☐ Save with password

4 Type the name of the document in the *Filename* field, such as *Budget*.

5 Then click on *Save*.

The StarCalc spreadsheet analysis program saves all files in the *StarCalc 5.0* format by default, the extension for which is *sdc*.

Now end the StarCalc program.

6 Click on *File*, then on *Close*.

Drawing with StarDraw

This section outlines a brief introduction to the graphic StarDraw program. The options are similar to the Paint program, but there is a wider range of functions. Much practice is required to master a graphics program.

1 Open the *StarDraw* program by clicking on the *New Drawing* icon on the desktop.

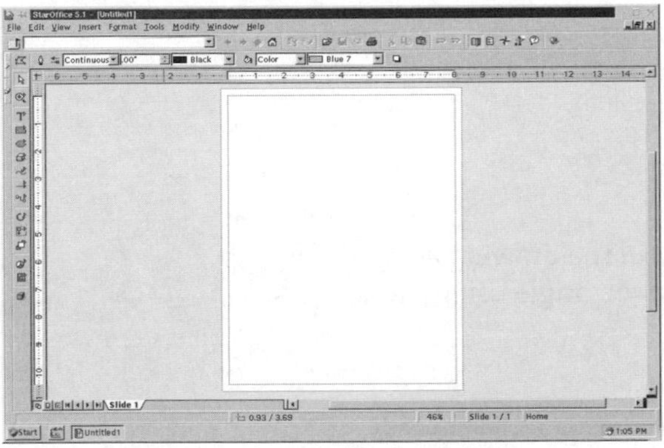

The program window is similar to those of StarWriter and StarCalc. Title, menu, format and status display bars are available.

The graphic toolbar displayed on the left and the colour table on the lower margin are new. You draw in the white area in the middle of the window.

You can begin to create simple graphic shapes, just as with the Paint program.

1 Click on the *Circle* icon in the graphic toolbar.

2 Click in the drawing area and form a circle using the mouse.

You can now see a blue circle. Blue is the default colour. The circle is surrounded by green marker points. You will recognise this from StarWriter: graphic elements are marked in this way.

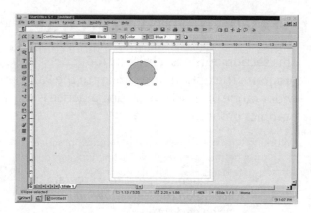

Now draw a rectangle.

1 Click on the *Rectangle* icon in the graphic toolbar.

2 Click in the drawing area and form a rectangle using the mouse.

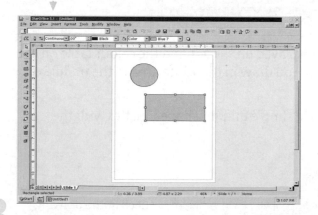

3 Click on any colour in the colour table on the lower margin.

The rectangle is immediately filled with the selected colour.

In the next step you will draw a more complicated shape. First look at the graphic toolbar. Can you see the small green arrow against every item? This arrow can be used to open a menu for each item.

Working with a tiny green arrow requires practice. It will probably take several attempts before the sub-menu is opened. Try to position the mouse pointer directly over the arrow before clicking.

Alternatively, you could hold the mouse button pressed longer to activate the sub-menu.

1 Click on the green arrow on the *3D-Objects* icon.

2 Click on the *Cone* figure in the upper right-hand corner of the menu.

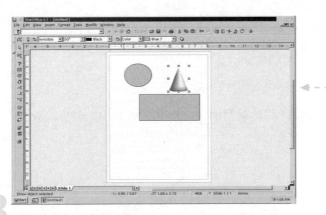

3 Click in the drawing area and form a cone using the mouse.

4 Click on any colour in the colour table on the lower margin.

A StarDraw graphic can of course also contain text. The graphic toolbar contains a button with a large *T* (for text). This icon also has a sub-menu.

1 Click on the green arrow on the *Text* icon.

2 Click on the middle option in the menu, *Fit text to size*.

3 Click in the drawing area and type in any word.

The text entered is marked as active by green marker points. StarDraw regards text as a graphic item like any other shape. You can delete an active text item using the Del key.

Do you wish to format the text? This works in the same way as with StarWriter.

1 Mark the text with the mouse.

The text is now highlighted in black and can be formatted using the icon in the formatting bar.

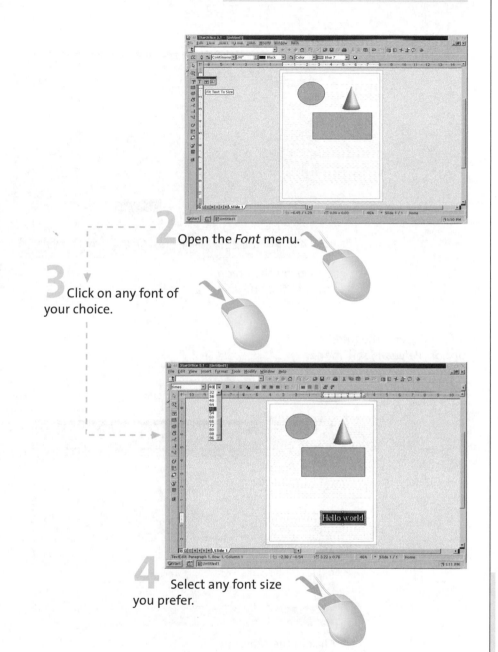

2 Open the *Font* menu.

3 Click on any font of your choice.

4 Select any font size you prefer.

You can also select the bold, italic and underlined options, and whether the alignment should be centred, or on the left or right. Use the colour table on the lower window margin to select the colour.

Then insert a few lines in the image.

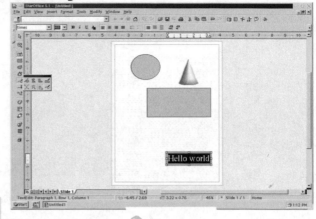

1 Click on the green arrow in the line icon.

2 Click on the middle option, *Polygon (45°)*, in the menu.

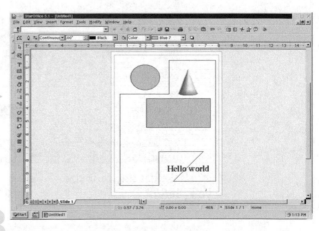

3 Click in the drawing area and draw some lines using the mouse.

When the mouse is clicked, one side of the polygon is fixed and the new one begins. An arbitrary polygon is formed in this way.

If you are not satisfied with the shape, simply delete it using the Del key. Note that the polygon must be marked as active by the green margin points in advance. It is activated by clicking on one of the lines.

4 Editing the polygon is ended by double-clicking.

You have now finished editing the drawing. Do you wish to keep your work? Then you should save it.

1 Click on *File*, then on *Save As* or *Save*.

StarDraw always saves new files in the StarOffice *Work* directory by default. It is now displayed in the *Save As* window.

2 Click on this button repeatedly until you are in the / directory.

3 Now click on */home*, then on the name of your own home directory.

Save As	⬜◻️✕
/home/jonathan	▦ ▦ ↻ ↱ ◿

☐ Desktop
☐ nsmail
☐ Office51

File<u>n</u>ame:	test images	▼	<u>S</u>ave
File <u>t</u>ype:	StarDraw 5.0	▼	Cancel

☑ Automatic file name <u>e</u>xtension
☐ Save <u>w</u>ith password

4 Type the name of the drawing in the *Filename* field, for example, *Test Images*.

5 Then click on *Save*.

StarDraw saves all files as file type *StarDraw 5.0* by default, the extension for which is *sda*.

End the StarDraw program.

6 Click on *File*, then *Close*.

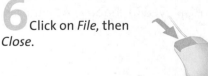

Scheduling appointments with StarOffice

You have already used the KDE tool, *Task Scheduler*, which can be used as an appointment calendar in Linux. If you use the StarOffice software package, you can also use the StarOffice calendar function instead. The advantage is that all programs are on hand.

1 Open the task scheduler by clicking on the *Events* icon on the desktop.

The program window is constructed as the other StarOffice windows. At the same time you will recognise the similarity to the KDE *Task Scheduler* program.

When you first open the program you will see the daily calendar view. In future the program will also be opened with the last view selected. You will learn how to change the view in the next section.

TIP

In this preview the current day is always marked with a red border.

In the daily view there is always a small preview in the upper right-hand corner for the next month. The preview can also be configured for a previous or later month.

413

This is controlled using both black arrows next to the name of the month.

```
    ◀   September 2000   ▶
        S  M  T  W  T  F  S
36     27 28 29 30 31  1  2
37      3  4  5  6  7  8  9
38     10 11 12 13 14 15 16
39     17 18 19 20 21 22 23
40     24 25 26 27 28 29 30
41      1  2  3  4  5  6  7
```

1 Click on the left arrow to display the previous month, September.

You now need to enter your appointment. The current month should be displayed.

2 Click on the right arrow to change to October.

3 Click on the daily planner in the white field behind the time (such as *10.00*).

The field is now marked in blue.

4 Type in the text for your scheduled appointment, such as *Edit Course Material*.

The appointment at 10.00 is currently active. This can be seen from the blue border. However, the appointment will only be assigned to this time once you confirm the entry.

5 Press the ⏎ key to do so.

You can assign additional options to the appointment.

1 Move the mouse to the lower margin of the schedule calendar.

The mouse pointer assumes the form of an arrow pointing in two directions. You will see a small bar in the middle.

2 Now click the mouse button and drag the mouse upwards towards the appointment calendar.

The appointment calendar window reduces in size. You can specify additional appointment options in the lower area.

Additional appointment information is specified in the *Description* field.

3 Type in other key points in the *Description* field.

415

The time of the appointment can be modified using the *Details* option.

1 Click on the *Details* button.

2 Modify the end date using the small arrow button next to the entry field.

3 Type in a category in the *Categories* field, such as *Training*.

Alternatively, you can use the selection menu.

It is also essential that you be reminded of your appointment at the correct time.

1 Click on the *Reminder* button.

This message appears when this is first enabled.

Service Configuration

If you want to make use of reminders, you should start StarSchedule at the same time StarOffice is started. Presently, StarSchedule is only activated when necessary. In the future, do you want to activate StarSchedule automatically when StarOffice is started?

Yes

No

Help

☐ Don't remind

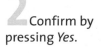
2 Confirm by pressing *Yes*.

The automatic reminder service will always be started with the StarOffice application in future.

Enable the automatic reminder service for the *Edit Course Material*.

TIP

Note that appointments with a reminder mark show a small clock icon on the calendar.

Reminder

Test Appointment

OK

Snooze

Display Appointment

Help

Next Alarm in   5 Minutes

You will be reminded of an appointment by a similar message. The subject of the appointment was called *Test* in this example, and the commentary field was not filled out – hence the blank space.

417

The reminder can easily be removed by clicking on *OK*. If you click on *Sleep*, the reminder reappears after a certain amount of time (5 minutes in this case) in the lower field.

The reminder is then displayed at the specified time.

Some appointments are repeated regularly. These are known as series of appointments.

1 Enter a new appointment, *Conference Project 2000* at 1pm.

2 Click on the ⏎ key.

3 Click on the *Repeat* button in the lower window area.

4 Click on the *Weekly* option.

5 Increase the week counter to 2 using the arrow keys.

Series of appointments have no time limit by default. If you specify an end date in the *Repeat until* field, the series of appointments will be limited. Click on the arrow and select an end date from the small calendar window.

Note that recurring appointments are indicated by a special icon in the calendar. This has the form of two arrows forming a circle.

With an appointment calendar, you can also specify who is scheduled to attend.

1 Click on the *Participants* button.

2 Click on the field containing the name *Mr Robertson*.

419

3 Enter any name and click on the ⏎ adjust button.

The name is added to the list below. Enter another name in the same way.

You now wish to alter the calendar view. Only being able to see appointments for one day is not enough.

Use the button on the second icon bar, marked with numbers.

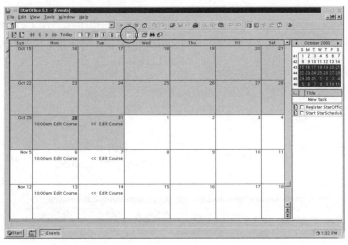

1 Click on the button marked with number 31.

A monthly view with 31 days is then displayed.

End the task scheduler.

1 Click on *File*, then *Close*.

Now close the StarOffice application.

2 Click on *File*, then *End*.

Alternatively, you could use the *Close* button in the upper right-hand corner of the title bar.

You are advised at this point that this chapter does not claim to give an extensive introduction to StarOffice. It intends only to give a short summary of the essential functions and their options.

421

What's in this chapter:

First you will learn the requirements for creating an internet connection with Linux. You will then learn how to establish an internet connection with the KDE graphic interface. Internet jargon will be used, such as *browser* and *surfing the web*. You will also become familiar with Netscape Communicator and make your first steps on the World Wide Web. Finally, you will learn how to use e-mail, with which you can send and receive your mail electronically on the internet.

You already know about:

You are going to learn about:

What are the internet, browsers and the WWW?

Nowadays everybody talks about the *internet*. But what is it exactly? The internet consists of two words, *International* and *Network*, also referring to a global network. Yet strictly speaking, the internet is not a single network, but a worldwide combination of many small networks.

The smallest form of a network is one that connects two computers to each other (see chapter 11). Different computers can usually communicate on a network in a company.
On the internet, not only the computers of a single company can be linked but any computers anywhere in the world.

On the internet, a computer in Sydney can easily and quickly exchange data with computers in Berlin, Kiev and Boston. Instead of a direct data line between the computers in the form of a cable, telephone networks or satellite links are used.

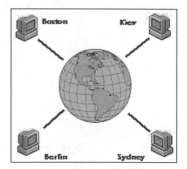

Initially, only several university computers used the internet. The origins of the internet can be found in the ArpaNet, which was founded in 1969 by the US Ministry of Defense. The main reason was to enable a fast and simple interchange of data.

Since an electronic letter, an **e-mail**, is not only faster but also cheaper than conventional postal service, more and more people participate in data connection.

An **e-mail** is created with an e-mail program, such as Microsoft Outlook Express, Pegasus Mail, Netscape Communicator etc. The main parts are: receiver address, subject and text. It is sent to the electronic PO box of an internet user.

Today the internet consists of many thousands of computers, called servers or web servers, and millions of users. As a web server is a relatively expensive computer, not every internet user has such a facility. However, anybody can access the internet by using a *provider*. This usually offers internet access for a fee. You are usually charged for call costs as well as provider costs, as you need to use the public telephone network.

Besides a user account and a password, the corresponding software and hardware are also required for the internet access. On

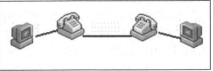

the hardware front you will need either a modem, which establishes the connection between telephone and PC in the case of an analogue telephone connection, or an ISDN card if you use an ISDN connection.

A **modem** is a hardware device which converts computer data, available in digital form, into **analogue** signals. A computer only understands **digital** signals, i.e. numbers. However, analogue signals, in this case tones, which the computer cannot understand, are sent via the conventional telephone network.

As for software for internet access, you need an **internet browser.** Microsoft Internet Explorer and Netscape Communicator, included free of charge with your Linux package, are the two most common browser programs. If you have used standard installation (see chapter 1), the Netscape Communicator should already be installed on your computer.

A particular property of these documents in the WWW is the file format. It has the *.htm* or *.html* file extension. **HTML** stands for the **Hypertext Markup Language,** the special browser programming language. This format can represent not only text but also graphics and multi media elements such as sound, video and active graphics (graphic animation) in a browser.

When you dial the internet through your modem, internet access is given by your provider, then as a rule you are surfing the World Wide Web (WWW). This is the primary internet service most frequently used by private and company customers. There are a countless number of accessible files on WWW computers. All files have an address in the WWW under which they can be found again at any time.

References to other documents are a further special feature of HTML. These special features are also described as hyperlinks. You will already have learned about hyperlinks when working with KDE support. As soon as you place the mouse on a hyperlink, the mouse pointer assumes the form of a hand.

Location: `file:///home/httpd/html/openlinux_help/index.html`

Surfing the internet means that you enter a known internet address in a browser window. The address for a document or a web server on the internet is described as the URL (Uniform Resource Locator).

A URL is always built up in this form:

Internet service://net name.domain name.country characteristics

The internet service is usually the *http* protocol. It is the standard service and therefore does not even have to be entered in the browser address field.

Very frequently the net name is the *www* definition for the World Wide Web. Enterprises and private people who would like to have a permanent area on the internet buy a domain name under which they can be found. The country characteristic, for example, can be *DE* for Germany or *UK* for Great Britain. The USA differs from these names in its role as internet originator: here names like *COM* (commercial), *MIL* (military), *GOV* (government), *EDU* (Education) etc. can be found.

For example, the URL of the Caldera company is:

http://www.caldera.com.

This means it uses the *http* protocol in the *WWW* net, and uses the following domain names: *caldera*, and *commercial* for the USA area.

If you want to visit the websites of specific enterprises or people on the internet, you must know the URL and indicate it in the browser. The browser loads the requested document and displays it on your computer. It makes no difference to the browser whether the address refers to a document from the World Wide Web, an intranet or the computer itself.

TIP

It is often fairly easy to find an address of a known enterprise. All large enterprises usually use *www* as the first part of the address, followed by the company name, such as *caldera*. The third URL part is either *com*, if it is an international enterprise, or the country characteristic for a smaller enterprise. The country characteristic always consists of two letters, such as *uk* for the United Kingdom, *fr* for France and *de* for Germany. It should therefore be fairly easy to guess the URL of a company.

You will probably run into the term **chat** in the internet, which quite simply means that people register at a specific internet address, behind which a chat server or IRC server is located, and then 'chat' with each other. Simple texts are entered and sent between users. Quite simply, the users talk in text.

Newsgroups is another internet term. These include discussion groups on specific topics. The address of a news server is known to participants. You send the newsgroup your enquiries or answers to enquiries about the topic, and contributions can be read at the receiving end.

You have probably heard the term **intranet** frequently. An intranet is an internal company network which is built up and is used just like the internet. Strictly speaking, since intranets are usually accessible only to company employees, they are not part of the internet.

Requirements for an internet connection

A **provider** is a service that rents you internet access. The large providers include online services, such as T-Online or AOL. There are often other regional services providing convenient access.

To access the internet, you must have the necessary hardware and software installed, and internet access via a provider.

Hardware requirements include a modem connected to your computer or an ISDN card. If you only have a traditional analogue telephone connection, you need to connect a modem to your computer. A modem with a transfer speed of 33.6K is usually enough, as the transfer rates of most providers rarely exceed this speed.

If you have an ISDN telephone connection, you will need to install an ISDN card in your computer. Surfing the web with an ISDN card is much quicker than using a modem, as the transfer rate is quicker, and pages can therefore be accessed in a shorter time.

This covers the hardware front. Now for the software. This should not be a problem, as you only require a browser. Netscape Communicator is used as standard on Linux machines, and is installed if you carry out a standard installation.

If you installed Linux in this way, you will see the Netscape Communicator icon in the program bar.

Which provider or online service should you choose? You should follow these criteria: does the online service offer a local call rate? If not, surfing the net can prove costly. Large online services such as AOL, as well as regional providers and high schools, offer different dialling options.

The second selection criterion should be the rates the provider charges. Both a signing-on fee as well as monthly standing charges, and rates for the actual use of the connection, are usually included. These rates are generally charged by the minute. A third selection criterion is the availability and speed of the internet connection.

Ask your friends and acquaintances who already have an internet connection which one they prefer. Even if you often hear different opinions, you can still learn from the negative experiences of others. Alternatively, you can ask consumer protection organisations or get information about provider comparisons in magazines.

In addition, consider how frequently you wish to use your internet connection. Compare the costs of the on-line services with these requirements to find the best provider for you.

Establishing an internet connection

Once you have chosen a provider, you will receive various documents from them. The connection number and password should be contained in these. In the following steps you will use *Force 9* as an example of how to configure an internet connection.

If you have chosen another provider, simply have the documents which contain information on internet access next to the PC and replace the details of the example with your own settings.

When opening for the first time, you will receive a report about improvements to the previous program. Click on the *Don't display this note any more* option and then on *OK*.

It may happen here that an error message is displayed with the contents, saying that *kppp* cannot be started. In this case you should open the file manager and enable the *Display hidden file* option in the *View* menu. Then open the *.kde, share, apps* directory below your work directory. Here you will find a file named *kppp.pid* which should be deleted so that the error message is no longer shown.

Development ▶	
Documentation ▶	
Editors ▶	
Games ▶	
Graphics ▶	
Internet ▶	
Multimedia ▶	Archie client
Office ▶	Biff
Toys ▶	Chat Client (ksirc)
Utilities ▶	Communicator
Settings ▶	kISDN
System ▶	Kppp
COAS ▶	KPPP – Logview
Applications ▶	Mail client
KDE Help	Mail monitor
Home Directory	Network utilities
KDE Control Center	News client
Personal ▶	PWS
Disk Navigator ▶	Seyon
Panel ▶	User information
Lock Screen	X Biff
Logout	

Click on *Internet* on the main menu and then on *kISDN*.

In this window you can determine one or more data sets for your online access.

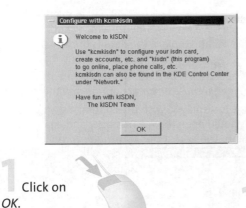

1 Click on
OK.

2 Open the *KDE Control Centre* using this icon in the program bar.

3 Open the *Network* menu entry by clicking on the minus sign with the mouse.

4 Open the *kISDN Configuration* menu entry.

The program usually finds most common ISDN controllers automatically.

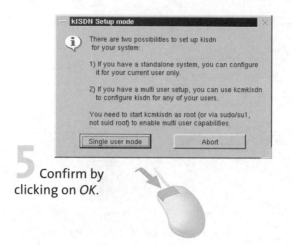

5 Confirm by clicking on *OK*.

You now need to enter the details of your service provider.

1 Click on *New*.

An entry window containing several tabs for registering your provider details is now displayed. In the following example the details of the provider *Force 9* are used.

2 Enter the name of your provider in the *Provider name* field, such as Force 9.

3 Enter your provider telephone number in the ISP number field. In our example, it should read 0845 142 4000 for Force 9.

4 Apply the telephone number to the list below by clicking on *Add*.

Leave the other settings unaltered.

New Account Force 9

Remote | IP | DNS | Auth | Callback | Compress. | More

IP Setup

- ● Dynamic IP Address
- ○ Static IP Address
  - Local IP Address
  - Remote IP Address
  - Subnet Mask

☑ Apply default route

MILLENNIUM   Help   OK   Cancel

5 Click on the *IP* tab.

6 Check that the *Dynamic IP Address* option is enabled.

New Account Force 9

Remote | IP | DNS | Auth | Callback | Compress. | More

DNS Setup

Domain:

IP Address: Add

Address List:
192.1.1.70   Remove

MILLENNIUM   Help   OK   Cancel

7 Now click on the *DNS* tab.

8 Enter the domain name of your provider in the *Search* domains field. In our example, it should read *www.force9.net* for *Force 9*.

9 Click on *Add* to apply the entry to the list below.

10 Enter the DNS IP address of your provider in the *DNS Server details* field. This should read either 169.252.5.11 or 161.252.4.12 for Force 9.

11 Click on *Add* to apply the entry to the list below.

The IP address entered now appears in the DNS IP address bar. If your provider has several IP addresses, then add these individually in turn.

New Account Force 9

Remote | IP | DNS | **Auth** | Callback | Compress | More

Authentication settings

☑ Perform authentication

Username: jmitton

Password: •••••••

☑ Allow users to change this username/password

☐ Send encrypted password

M I L L E N N I U M   Help   OK   Cancel

12 Click on the *Auth* tab.

13 Activate the *Perform authentication* option.

14 Enter the username and password for your preferred provider here (*Force 9* in our example).

15 Activate the *Allow users to change this username / password* and *Send encrypted password* options if necessary.

In this way you allow a user to modify their registration details. It is recommended that passwords always be sent encrypted.

16 End the settings by clicking on *OK*.

Configuration of the KISDN package

1 Click on the *Users* tab.

2 Open the *Users configuration* list using the small black arrow on the right-hand side of the selection field.

3 Click on a user from the selection list who will be allowed to use an internet connection in the future.

437

4 Click on *OK* to end the selection.

Repeat these steps for every system user using an ISDN internet connection.

5 Activate the functions the user may use in the *Allow features* area.

6 Activate the connections the user may work with in the *Enable accounts* area, such as *Force 9*.

1 Click on the *General* tab.

2 Enter the dialling code in the *use area prefix* field should one be required for your ISDN connection.

3 Check the entry in the *D-Channel Protocol* field.

1 Click on the *Driver* tab.

2 Ensure that the *Load driver as a module* option is enabled.

3 Check the entry in the *ISDN Adapter Type* field.

4 Click on *Apply* to save the settings and end the KDE Control Centre.

You are now almost ready for the internet!

439

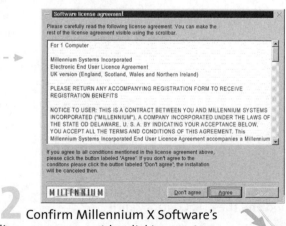

1 Open the kISDN program using the *Internet* menu entry.

2 Confirm Millennium X Software's licence agreement by clicking on *Agree*.

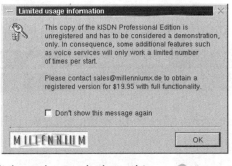

3 Click on the *Don't show this message again* option. Then click on *OK*.

TIP

If you wish to use all special functions of the kISDN program constantly, you will need to obtain the corresponding licence. More information can be found at:

http://www.millennium.co.uk.

The kISDN program connects to the internet when you click on the button.

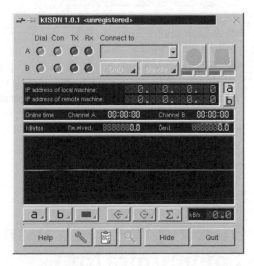

You will recognise a successful and active connection when a green light comes up on one of the channels displayed. Otherwise the *Dial* button will be represented as follows:

441

You will see how long you have been connected to the internet and how much data has been transferred in the middle area of the window:

Online time	Channel A:	88:88:88	Channel B:	88:88:88
kBytes	Received:	8888888.8	Sent:	8888888.8

Further connection information can be obtained using the 📋 button.

A window entitled *kISDN Notebook* opens. Connection times are displayed in more detail here.

TIP

You can place the program in the lower right-hand corner of the program bar using the | Dock | button. It can be reactivated using the right mouse button.

4 If you wish to surf the internet immediately, then go straight to the next section. Otherwise cancel the connection by closing the window.

Surfing the web using Netscape Communicator

You are finally ready to look around the internet. However, the online connection must be established before starting the browser.

CAUTION

Note that for every minute you are connected to the internet, you will have to pay charges to your telephone company. **Never** forget to disconnect once you have finished surfing the web. Otherwise your telephone bill will be huge!

1 Click on *Internet* in the main menu and then on *Kppp*.

2 Then select the online service which you wish to use, and click on *Connect*.

3 Click on the *Netscape Communicator* icon in the program bar.

TIP

When Netscape Communicator is started for the first time, you are asked whether you acccpt the licence conditions. Click on *Accept* and on *OK* in the window.

Netscape: License Agreement

Netscape is licensed software. Its use is subject to the terms and conditions of the license agreement below.

NETSCAPE CLIENT PRODUCTS LICENSE AGREEMENT
Redistribution Or Rental Not Permitted

These terms apply to Netscape Communicator and Netscape Navigator.

BY CLICKING THE ACCEPTANCE BUTTON OR INSTALLING OR USING NETSCAPE
COMMUNICATOR OR NETSCAPE NAVIGATOR SOFTWARE (THE "PRODUCT"), THE
INDIVIDUAL OR ENTITY LICENSING THE PRODUCT ("LICENSEE") IS
CONSENTING TO BE BOUND BY AND IS BECOMING A PARTY TO THIS

If you accept the terms of this license agreement,
press "Accept". Otherwise press "Do Not Accept".

Accept   Do Not Accept

The first thing you receive will be standard Netscape pages. You can of course look at these in more detail, but this can also be done offline. These pages are saved on your computer together with the browser. Now you really want to surf the web.

Enter the address of the page you wish to visit in the browser. In a way, it is rather like giving a taxi driver an address to which you wish to be taken. Simply type the URL in the *Address* field.

Now you have spent such a long time in front of your monitor using Linux, you may well wish to travel at leisure – at least on the internet!

1 Location: http://www.australia.com/

Type the desired URL in the *Location* field, for example *www.australia.com*.

TIP

First of all you have to cancel the entry already in the field. Mark it with the left mouse button and then press the Del button.

2 Confirm the entry by pressing the ⏎ key.

The home page of a website about Australia appears. You can surf to the secondary sites using the hyperlinks there.

3 Click on the *English* hyperlink and then on *Enter*.

The same website now appears in English. The URL of the new site is now in the *Location* field. Now you can look around at will on the internet sites for the Australia information service.

4 Choose *England* as country, for example.

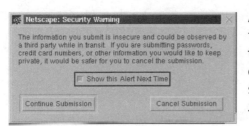

A warning message appears, informing you that you are transmitting non-encrypted data over the internet. As there is no sensitive data, click on *Continue Submission* without worrying.

Take care not to do this when sending bank details or your credit card number over the internet. In this case click on *Cancel Submission* immediately. You should never send non-encrypted important and/or confidential data over the internet.

Another website with information about Australia now appears. This site again contains hyperlinks to other sites – as you can see, you can easily spend hours surfing if you run into interesting information!

Australia was too far away for you? No problem, you can also pay a visit to Munich.

1 Enter the URL *www.munich-tourist.de.*

2 Confirm the entry with the ⏎ key.

You are now visiting the website of the city of Munich. Are you interested in events? Or would you like to book a hotel room? Or just look up some general information about Munich? Simply follow the corresponding hyperlink.

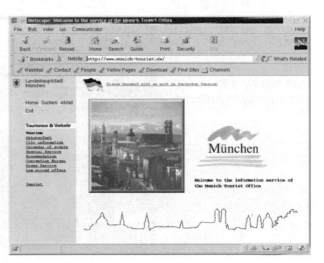

3 Click on the *Tourism & Traffic* hyperlink.

You can now delve into what Munich has to offer on the web.

Do you not care for towns or countries? Maybe you wish to look at the weather forecast instead.

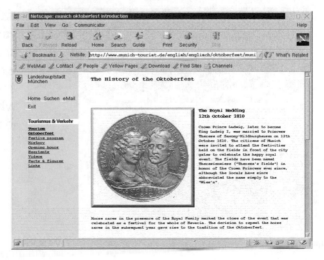

1 Enter the URL
www.bbc.co.uk/weather.

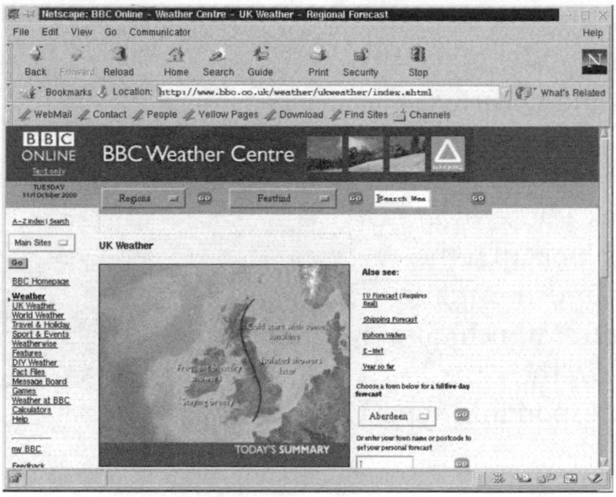

2 Confirm the entry
with the ⏎ key.

3 Click on the *World Weather* hyperlink and
then on your region.

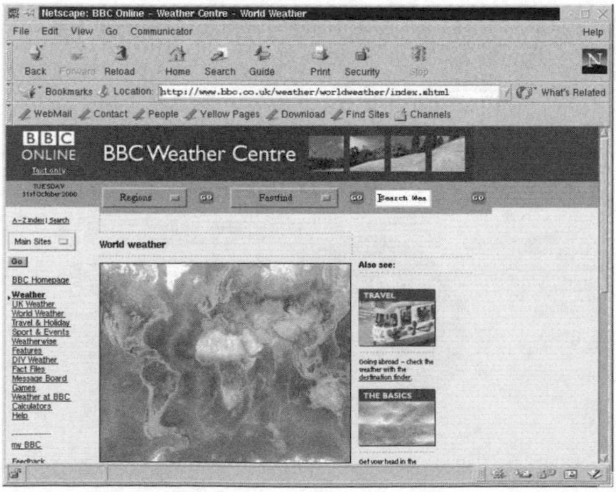

If the weather holds out,
you may wish to visit a
sporting event at the
weekend. However, you
are undecided about
which one to choose. Just
look on the web!

1 Enter the URL *www.bbc.co.uk/sport*.

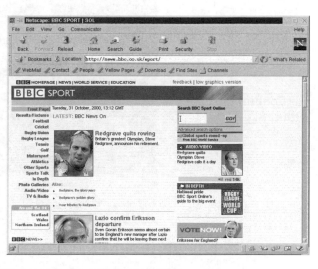

2 Confirm the entry with the ⏎ key again.

3 Click on the *Results/Fixtures* link.

Does this not grab you? Would you like to learn more about Linux, for example tips and tricks? Then go to one of the private sites of a Linux fan.

1 Enter the URL
www.kde.com.

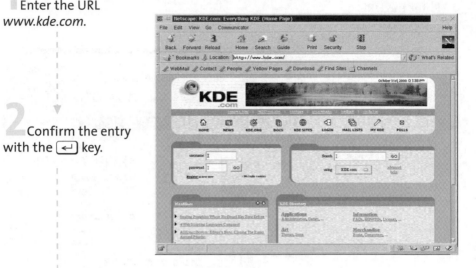

2 Confirm the entry
with the ⏎ key.

3 Click on the *Documents* hyperlink.

This is an example of
a typical homepage.

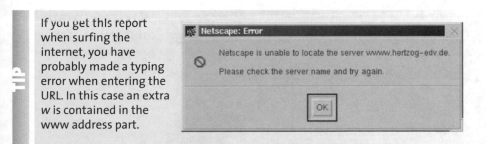

If you get this report when surfing the internet, you have probably made a typing error when entering the URL. In this case an extra *w* is contained in the www address part.

Or would you like to purchase secondary books on Linux from *Pearson Education?* Then pay a visit to the publishing house on the internet.

1 Enter the URL *www.pearson-education.com.*

2 Confirm the entry with the ⏎ key.

3 First click on the *Global Publishers* hyperlink, then on *Higher Education* under the UK heading.

451

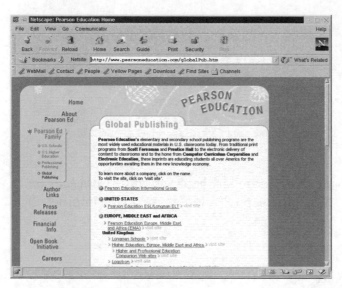

Now you can carry on searching for books.

Navigating websites

Would you like to return to one of the previous sites? There are various options.

1 Click on this button in the icon bar until the desired website is displayed again.

Do you wish to move forward again now?

2 Click on this
button on the icon bar.

Alternatively, you can jump back to one of the previously visited
websites.

1 Click directly on the desired
website in the *Go* menu, for example
Pearson Education Home.

Do you want to put aside a few addresses for future use? No need for
pen and paper – just use a browser function. Use the following
procedure to find your favourite sites.

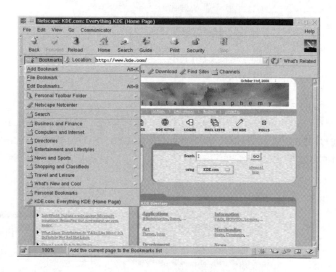

1 Click on the *Bookmarks* button and then on *Add Bookmark*.

2 Enter any new URL in the address field, such as *www.caldera.com*, and then press the ⏎ key.

3 Now click again on the *Bookmarks* button and then on the bookmark added last.

The website indicated with this bookmark is retrieved. You can re-access interesting websites at any time in this way.

You can organise your bookmarks using the *Edit Bookmarks* function, meaning you can move them into sub-folders, or delete or rename them.

Delete an added bookmark as follows:

1 Click on *Bookmarks*, then on *Edit Bookmarks*.

You will see all bookmarks you created listed below. The bookmarks already provided by Netscape in different folders are in the above list.

2 Click on the bookmark and then on *Edit* in the menu, and finally on *Delete*.

The bookmark is removed from the list.

455

3 Create a new folder for bookmarks with the help of the *File – New Folder* menu items.

Netscape: Bookmark Properties ✕

Name:	Travel Links
Location:	
Description:	
Last Visited:	
Added On:	Tue Oct 31 15:32:27 2000

Select Aliases

OK   Cancel

4 Call this directory *Travel Links*, for example.

5 Then click on *OK*.

Communicator Bookmarks for Jonathan

File   Edit   View   Communicator   Help

Name	Location	Last Visited	Created On
Bookmarks for	---	---	-
Travel Links	---	---	Tue Oct 31 15:32:27 2000
Personal Toolbar Folder	---	---	Tue Oct 31 15:24:58 2000
-----------------	---	---	Tue Oct 31 15:24:58 2000
Netscape Netcenter	http://home.netscape.../4_61/netcenter.htm	---	Tue Oct 31 15:24:58 2000
-----------------	---	---	Tue Oct 31 15:24:58 2000
Search	---	---	Tue Oct 31 15:24:58 2000
-----------------	---	---	Tue Oct 31 15:24:58 2000
Business and Finance	---	---	Tue Oct 31 15:24:58 2000
Computers and Internet	---	---	Tue Oct 31 15:24:58 2000
Directories	---	---	Tue Oct 31 15:24:58 2000
Entertainment and Lifestyles	---	---	Tue Oct 31 15:24:58 2000
News and Sports	---	---	Tue Oct 31 15:24:58 2000
Shopping and Classifieds	---	---	Tue Oct 31 15:24:58 2000
Travel and Leisure	---	---	Tue Oct 31 15:24:58 2000
What's New and Cool	---	---	Tue Oct 31 15:24:58 2000
-----------------	---	---	Tue Oct 31 15:24:58 2000
Personal Bookmarks	---	---	Tue Oct 31 15:24:58 2000
KDE.com: Eve... (Home Page)	http://www.kde.com/	Less th...our ago	Tue Oct 31 15:29:48 2000
KDE.com: Eve... (Home Page)	http://www.kde.com/	Less th...our ago	Tue Oct 31 15:30:34 2000

The appearance of the *Bookmark* window has changed accordingly.

You can move your bookmarks into any folder.

Would you like to move Pearson Education's website under *Computer &*
Internet, for example?

1 To do this, click on the
bookmark and hold down
the mouse button.

2 Drag the bookmark into the
Computer & Internet folder and then
release the mouse button.

The bookmark is now
in the desired folder.

Name	Location	Last Visited	Created On
⊟🗁 Bookmarks for	---	---	-
Travel Links	---	---	Tue Oct 31 15:32:27 2000
⊞🔖 Personal Toolbar Folder	---	---	Tue Oct 31 15:24:58 2000
------------------	---	---	Tue Oct 31 15:24:58 2000
Netscape Netcenter	http://home.netscape.../4_61/netcenter.html	---	Tue Oct 31 15:24:58 2000
------------------	---	---	Tue Oct 31 15:24:58 2000
⊞🗁 search	---	---	Tue Oct 31 15:24:58 2000
------------------	---	---	Tue Oct 31 16:24:50 2000
⊞🗁 Business and Finance	---	---	Tue Oct 31 15:24:58 2000
⊟🗁 Computers and Internet	---	---	Tue Oct 31 15:24:58 2000
Pearson Education Home	http://www.pearson-education.com	---	Tue Oct 31 15:36:08 2000
@vantage	http://home.netscape...artneratvantage.html	---	Tue Oct 31 15:24:58 2000
Computing Channel	http://home.netscape...omputingchannel.htm	---	Tue Oct 31 15:24:58 2000
Domain Name Registration	http://home.netscape...etworksolutions.html	---	Tue Oct 31 15:24:58 2000
eBay Computers	http://home.netscape...1/ebaycomputers.htm	---	Tue Oct 31 15:24:58 2000
Insight~Computing Product:	http://home.netscape...ark4_61/insight.htm	---	Tue Oct 31 15:24:58 2000
ONSALE Computer Auction:	http://home.netscape...onsalecomputer.htm	---	Tue Oct 31 15:24:58 2000
RealNetworks	http://home.netscape...61/realnetworks.html	---	Tue Oct 31 15:24:58 2000
TechSearch	http://home.netscape...4_61/techsearch.htm	---	Tue Oct 31 15:24:58 2000
Toshiba	http://home.netscape...rk4_61/toshiba.html	---	Tue Oct 31 15:24:58 2000
⊞🗁 Directories	---	---	Tue Oct 31 15:24:58 2000
⊞🗁 Entertainment and Lifestyles	---	---	Tue Oct 31 15:24:58 2000
⊞🗁 News and Sports	---	-	Tue Oct 31 15:24:58 2000
⊞🗁 Shopping and Classifieds	---	---	Tue Oct 31 15:24:58 2000
⊞🗁 Travel and Leisure	---	---	Tue Oct 31 15:24:58 2000
⊞🗁 What's New and Cool	---	---	Tue Oct 31 15:24:58 2000
------------------	---	---	Tue Oct 31 15:24:58 2000
⊞🗁 Personal Bookmarks	---	---	Tue Oct 31 15:24:58 2000
KDE.com: Ever...E (Home Page	http://www.kde.com/	Less th...our ago	Tue Oct 31 15:29:48 2000
KDE.com: Ever...E (Home Page	http://www.kde.com/	Less th...our ago	Tue Oct 31 15:30:34 2000

There are two other essential options in the Netscape browser.
Occasionally, it may happen that a website loads too slowly. This only
causes unnecessary costs, so you should interrupt the process.

Click on the traffic lights icon when red is displayed.

You may well regularly visit a website containing current information, such as weather details. You may notice from time to time that the contents have not been updated. This may well happen, as the browser remembers the contents of previously visited sites so it can load them directly from the PC itself rather than from the WWW. There is a simple solution for this:

Click on the *Reload* icon and the website is reloaded from the internet.

Do you wish to print the contents of a homepage? Not a problem.

Click on the printer icon in the icon bar.

A window opens. Click on *Print* to confirm the print job.

Of course, this only works if your printer is correctly installed (see chapter 7).

Sometimes printing simply does not work. Now and then you get an empty sheet or only the menu section of the website. Select a small text portion of the page to be printed with the mouse and try again. Some pages are simply divided up into several sub-pages and can only be printed after being activated with the mouse.

You can also specify a URL with which to start when surfing using Netscape. You can always return to this start page at any time.

1   Click on this icon in the icon bar.

You should define this entry page as follows:

1   Click on the *Edit* menu, then on *Preferences*.

2   Click on *Navigator*.

3   Enter your desired internet start page in the *Location* field.

459

TIP

If you prefer to start the browser with a blank page, click on the *Blank page* option.

4 Then click on *OK*.

Downloading pictures and texts from the web

WHAT'S THIS?

Most documents on the web are written in HTML format. This language defines how text and graphics of a website are displayed in the browser.

Not only can you print the contents of an internet page, you can also store them directly on your computer. However, text can only be saved in HTML format in this way.

Graphics must therefore be saved separately, though this is also fairly easy.

CAUTION

When downloading texts and graphics from the internet, you should always consider the copyright laws. Private use is not prohibited, but you are not authorised to continue to use, change or even distribute graphics and text from the WWW. Graphics from the internet are opened only when allowed on corresponding websites.

First you wish to save the text content of the www.linux.com website on your computer.

1 Enter the URL *www.linux.com*.

2 Confirm the entry with the ⏎ key.

3 Now click on *Save As* in the *File* menu.

Save the document in your work directory.

4 In the *Save As* window, name the HTML document to be saved *linux.html*.

461

In future you will also be able to call the document directly on this directory in the file manager.

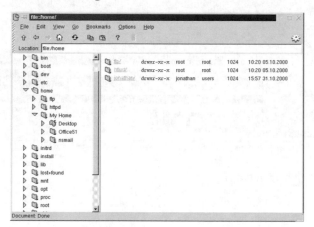

5 First open the file manager.

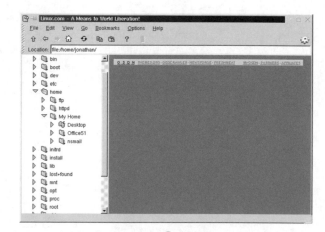

6 Simply click on the *linux.html* file to open it.

Would you like to copy a graphic from the internet onto your computer? As an example, take the logo from the *www.linux.com* website.

1 Click on the graphic.

Back	Alt+Left
Forward	Alt+Right
Reload	
Open Link in New Window	Button2
Open Link in Composer	
View Page Source	
View Page Info	
View Image (linux.com-shine.gif)	
Add Bookmark for Link	
Send Page	
Save Link As...	Shift+Button1
Save Image As...	
Copy Link Location	
Copy Image Location	

Save As...

Filter

/home/jonathan/*.gif

Directories   Files

..   snapshot01.gif
.kde
.kpackage
.netscape
.seyon
Desktop
Office51
nsmail

Format for Saved Document: Source

Selection

/home/jonathan/linux.com-shine.gif

OK   Filter   Cancel

2 Choose the *Save Image As* option in the context menu.

3 Indicate the directory and the name for the graphic to be saved.

In future you will also be able to open the graphic directly through the indicated directory in the file manager.

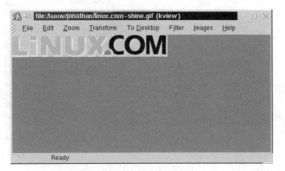

4 Simply click on the file.

Downloading a document from the internet means that you download the file from the internet computer onto your own PC, where you save and continue to use it.

Some websites offer you text documents or programs to be **downloaded** directly.

For example, you can download programs for the KDE graphic interface from the internet. The only costs which arise from it are the telephone costs, and the costs for your internet provider.

1 Enter the URL *www.kde.org*.

2 Confirm the entry with the ⏎ key.

3 Click on the *Download* hyperlink in the upper window area.

A new web page is retrieved.

4 Click again until the following website appears:
ftp://ftp.kde.org/pub/kde/stable/1.1.2/apps/games.

This is the download area for KDE interface games with the 1.1.2 version number, which are described as stable.

5 Click on a game of your choice, such as *Mahjongg*.

You are asked where on your computer and under which name you would like to save the file. Use the initial setting of your work directory and the name for the document to be saved.

6 Click on *OK*.

If it is a large file, the downloading takes longer, and you can observe the process in the window.

You can also interrupt the process if the downloading time appears too long. Click on the *Stop* button to do so.

Depending on the file format, you can open it directly by selecting it in the file manager. If the file has a format unknown to the KDE, you need to decide with which program you would like to open it. You can try it with the *kedit* editor, for example, but formatting problems may occur.

WHAT'S THIS?

Packed or **compressed** means that the size of the file was temporarily reduced with the help of a program. Using this, a download can be carried out faster. **Archive file** means that several files were combined in one.

The file downloaded in our example is a packed archive file, the format of which is recognised by Linux.

1 Open the *File Manager.*

2 Click on the file to unpack it.

The file reduction can be cancelled with a single click.

file:/home/OD/kmahjongg-0.4.0.tar.gz#tar:/

File Edit View Go Bookmarks Options Help

Location: file:/home/OD/kmahjongg-0.4.0.tar.gz

Root
  auto
  bin
  boot
  bru
  dev
  etc
  home
    OD
    UH
    ftp
    httpd
  initrd
  install
  lib
  lost+found
  mnt
  opt

kmahjongg-0.
4.0/

3 Now click on the unpacked file.

467

By the second step all files of the archive are listed individually again.

Searching on the internet

Until now you have used predefined URLs or put simple URLs together, such as *www.bbc.co.uk/weather*. What should you do if you do not know the URL but require specific information from the internet? This is what **search engines** are used for.

There are countless search engines on the internet, but at this point only two of the best known will be mentioned.

The first search engine that you visit has the international URL *www.altavista.com*, or the British URL *www.altavista.co.uk*.

1 Enter this internet address in the location field and press the ⏎ key.

2 Enter any search strings on the web page now displayed in the *Search for* entry field.

TIP

If you use more than one search string, you should separate the single strings with a blank space and type a plus sign in front of every search string. In this way the search engine knows that you would like to look for several strings simultaneously.

3 Then click on the *Search* button.

After a certain time the hits, or homepages, that contain search strings are shown as hyperlinks.

You can call the ones you wish to view by selecting them.

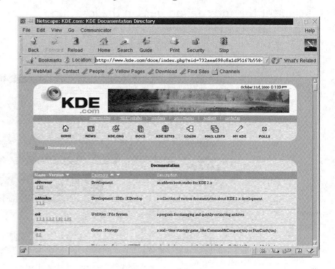

The second search engine mentioned here can also be started as an international (*www.yahoo.com*) or as an English search engine (*www.yahoo.co.uk*). Apart from a pure search, Yahoo! also offers a very good overview by category.

1 Enter *www.yahoo.co.uk* in the location field and press the ⏎ key.

2 Enter any search string on the web page now displayed in the *Search* entry field.

Separate them again with blank spaces if necessary, and add plus signs in front if more than one string is used.

3 Click then on the *Search* button.

Hyperlinks also have to be used here to reach the desired information.

Configuring e-mail

Several more configurations must be made before you can use electronic mail.

1 Open the *Preferences* option in the *Edit* menu.

2 Click on the *Mail & Newsgroups* option in the left half of the window.

3 Then click on the *Identity* option.

Netscape: Preferences

Category
▷ Appearance
▷ Navigator
▽ Mail & Newsgroups
Identity
Mail Servers
Newsgroups Servers
Addressing
Messages
Copies and Folders
Formatting
Return Receipts
Disk Space
▷ Roaming User
▷ Composer
▷ Advanced

Identity Set your name, email address, and signature file

The information below is needed before you can send mail. If you do not know the information requested, please contact your system administrator or Internet Service Provider.

Your name:

Jonathan

Email address:

jonathan@cybertechnics.co.uk

Reply-to address (only needed if different from email address):

Organization:

Cybertechnics

Signature File:

Choose...

☐ Attach my personal card to messages (as a vCard)   Edit Card...

OK   Cancel

4 Enter your name in the *Your name* field.

5 Type your electronic mail address in the *E-mail address* field.

Further entries are not necessary at this stage.

Now click on the *Mail Servers* option in the left-hand side of the window.

Netscape: Preferences

Category

- ▷ Appearance
- ▷ Navigator
- ▽ Mail & Newsgroups
  - Identity
  - Mail Servers
  - Newsgroups Servers
  - Addressing
  - Messages
  - Copies and Folders
  - Formatting
  - Return Receipts
  - Disk Space
- ▷ Roaming User
- ▷ Composer
- ▷ Advanced

Mail Servers Specify servers for mail

Incoming Mail Servers

192.1.1.70

Add...
Edit...
Delete

To set server properties (such as checking for new messages automatically), select a server and then click Edit.

Set as Default

Outgoing Mail Server

Outgoing mail (SMTP) server: localhost

Outgoing mail server user name:

Use Secure Socket Layer (SSL) or TLS for outgoing messages:
⬥ Never   ◇ If Possible   ◇ Always

Local mail directory

Directory: /home/jonathan/nsmail/   Choose...

OK   Cancel

Click on the *POP* entry in the Incoming *Mail Servers* window and then on the *Edit* button.

If you have used Force 9 as a provider, you can follow the instructions as shown in the diagram. Otherwise you must use the data of your own provider.

Netscape

General | POP

Server Name: 192.1.1.70

Server Type: POP

User Name:

☐ Remember password.

☐ Check for mail every 10 minutes.

☐ Automatically download any new messages.

OK   Cancel

3 Enter the *POP Server Name* of your provider in the *Server Name* field, for example *pop.btx.dtag.de* for T-Online.

4 Type the name of your provider's mail server in the *User Name* field, for example *mailto.btx.dtag.de* for T-Online.

Leave the remaining settings unchanged.

5 Click on *OK*.

Netscape: Preferences	

Category
- ▷ Appearance
- ▷ Navigator
- ▽ Mail & Newsgroups
  - Identity
  - Mail Servers
  - Newsgroups Servers
  - Addressing
  - Messages
  - Copies and Folders
  - Formatting
  - Return Receipts
  - Disk Space
- ▷ Roaming User
- ▷ Composer
- ▷ Advanced

Mail Servers   Specify servers for mail

Incoming Mail Servers

192.1.1.70

Add...
Edit...
Delete
Set as Default

To set server properties (such as checking for new messages automatically), select a server and then click Edit.

Outgoing Mail Server

Outgoing mail (SMTP) server: 192.1.1.70

Outgoing mail server user name:

Use Secure Socket Layer (SSL) or TLS for outgoing messages:
⬦ Never ✓ If Possible ✓ Always

Local mail directory

Directory: /home/jonathan/nsmail/   Choose...

OK   Cancel

1 Delete the *localhost* entry in the *Outgoing Mail (SMTP) Server* field.

2 Type in your provider's mail server, for example *mailto.btx.dtag.de* for T-Online.

The remaining settings do need to be changed, unless you do not wish to save your e-mails in the predefined folder of your work directory. You should then amend the corresponding entry under *Local mail directory*.

These are the required settings to receive and send e-mails with
Netscape Communicator.

3 Click on *OK*
to end.

There are countless services offering web-based e-mail addresses free of charge,
such as Yahoo! (*www.yahoo.co.uk*) or Hotmail (*www.hotmail.com*).

These providers run special links on their sites under which you can open a personal
e-mail account. This is not located on your PC like Netscape Communicator but
directly on the internet server.

Sending and receiving e-mails

Now we will finally send and receive e-mails.

Communicator	
Navigator	Alt+1
Messenger	Alt+2
Composer	Alt+3
Bookmarks	
Newsgroups	
Address Book	Alt+Shift+2
Tools	
Server Tools	
1. Netscape: Yahoo... results for linux	

1 Open the
Messenger option in
the *Communicator*
menu.

Now you are in
your *Inbox*
e-mailbox.

2 Click on the *Get Msg* button
to collect your latest e-mails.

The system asks you your
password.

3 Enter the password set by your
provider and then click on *OK*.

The electronic news is loaded on your computer by your provider's server and shown under *Inbox*. In the right-half window you can see all the e-mails that came in. If you click on one of the messages, the contents are displayed below the list.

In the right-hand side of the window you can see the different folders of the e-mail system. Netscape Communicator suggests that you use the Inbox as the standard folder for incoming e-mails and a *Sent* folder for sent e-mails. Deleted e-mails land in the recycle bin, until the *File – Empty Trash* menu items are enabled.

Now you would like to answer one of the incoming e-mails.

1 Click on the e-mail to be answered.

Reply

2 Click on *Reply*.

477

A window opens containing the sender of the incoming e-mail as the receiver. The subject is also automatically taken from the incoming e-mail. The text of the original e-mail is quoted in the text field.

3 Send the answered e-mail by clicking on the *Send* button.

Now you would like to write a new message.

1 Click on the *New Msg* button.

A window appears in which you can register your e-mail entries.

Compose: linux mail test

File Edit View Insert Format Tools Communicator   Help

Send   Quote Address Attach Options Spelling Save   Security   Stop   N

To: paul.watkinson@mailcity.com

▲ Subject: linux mail test   Priority: Normal

Normal   Variable Width   +0   A A A ℓ   ≔ ≔ ⫶ ⫶ ≡

Linux mail test

0%

TIP

Enter several e-mail addresses and separate them with commas.

2 Indicate one or more receivers in the *To* field.

TIP

Never forget the subject. It is easier for the receiver to know what the e-mail is regarding if the subject field is filled in.

3 Write down the subject in the *Subject* field.

Send

5 Send the e-mail by clicking the *Send* button.

4 Enter the desired text in the text area.

Finally, you would like to organise your e-mails into files. To do this you have to create new folders and then move the corresponding e-mails there.

1 Open the *New Folder* option in the *File* menu.

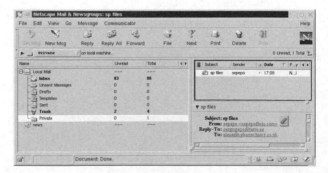

2 Enter a name for the folder, such as *Private*, and then click on *OK*.

The newly created folder is immediately displayed. It is still empty at the moment.

1 Click on the *Inbox* folder, then on one of the e-mails to be moved.

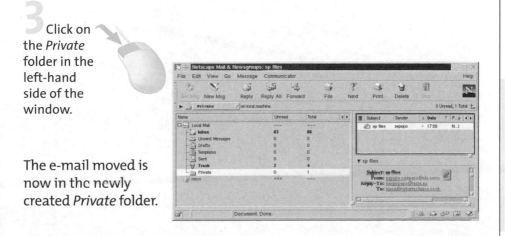

Click on *File*, then on *Private*.

The e-mail is no longer displayed in the *Inbox*.

3 Click on the *Private* folder in the left-hand side of the window.

The e-mail moved is now in the newly created *Private* folder.

What's in this chapter:

Linux is frequently used within an organisation to exchange data with other computers or share printers. Network computers often use a different operating system, such as Windows NT or Windows 98. In this chapter you will get to know the network functions of Linux supported by the Samba server. Then you will be able to access the drives and directories of a Windows computer from your Linux computer, and vice versa.

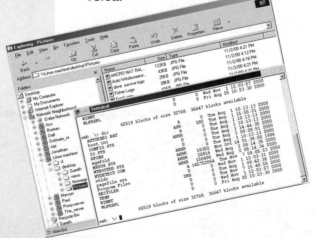

You already know about:

You are going to learn about:

Network basics

The concept of the **network** has already been explained briefly in chapter 1. It will be addressed here in greater detail.

A network quite simply indicates the connection between two or several computers. Several conditions are therefore required. The networked computers are connected by a network cable. This also needs a connection, or an interface for the computer.

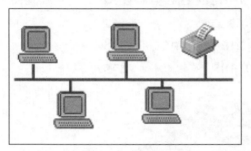

The computers are now connected – though a common language, or protocol, is still missing. TCP/IP is such a network protocol, recognised by both Linux and Windows. This protocol must be installed on the networked computers.

Several additional programs are still required to handle data transfer between computers running on different operating systems (such as Linux and Windows NT or 98). In the following section you will learn how to configure the Samba server in Linux.

What is a network used for? The most important reasons are the quick transfer of data between several computers, or the option of accessing files on other computers. Another reason is the lower administration overheads of system administrators: new users for a network are only created on one computer and not on each one individually. This is why a main computer, or **server**, is required.

Another essential reason is that all network users do not usually work on the local PC hard drive, but mainly on network hard drives. In this way, the system administrator can immediately secure all files.

A company should always network computers if employees are to share either printers or data. This happens quite frequently. Imagine a translation bureau, for example. The translator, Mr. Robertson, is assigned a large French translation project, which is too large to fit on a floppy disk. Mrs. Watkinson is to copy-edit the translation. If there were no network available, she would have to sit in front of Mr. Robertson's PC to check the file. Instead, Mr. Robertson simply puts the file on a network hard drive, which Mrs. Watkinson can also access. She opens the file and works on it. Finally, she would like to print the text on the fastest printer in the company. This printer is connected to Mr. Brown's PC. No problem – there is a network. Mrs. Watkinson can send the file to be printed on Mr. Brown's printer.

> TIP
>
> The concept of sharing resources is not only used for printers but also for files and directories in the network. Therefore, the same happens with data and devices which can be used by several computers.

Do you need a personal network? Not if you have only a single PC. However, you may now have a second PC because of the Linux installation. Are text documents and graphics you would like to use also on Linux on your first PC, the one that has Windows NT, 95 or 98 as an operating system? No problem – after the next section you will be able to configure a Samba server.

Starting network services

Before configuring the network card, check to see whether the *TCP/IP* network service has been started.

1 Click on the *COAS* button in the program bar.

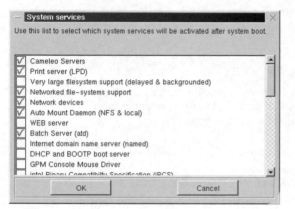

Date &Time ▶	Accounts
Network ▶	Daemons
Peripherals ▶	Filesystem
System ▶	Hostname
X-Server ▶	Resources
Kernel	Time

2 Click on the *System* menu, then on *Daemons*.

System services ✕

Use this list to select which system services will be activated after system boot.

- ☑ Cameleo Servers
- ☑ Print server (LPD)
- ☐ Very large filesystem support (delayed & backgrounded)
- ☑ Networked file-systems support
- ☑ Network devices
- ☑ Auto Mount Daemon (NFS & local)
- ☐ WEB server
- ☑ Batch Server (atd)
- ☐ Internet domain name server (named)
- ☐ DHCP and BOOTP boot server
- ☐ GPM Console Mouse Driver
- ☐ Intel Binary Compatibilty Specification (iBCS)

OK	Cancel

Now you need to check whether the required network services have been started. If so, both *BASIC IP services* and *Network Device* options are provided with a tester check. If this is not the case, simply start the services.

3 Click on *OK* in the *COAS* standard report.

4 Click on the check boxes of the two services so they are checked.

Once the settings are correct, you can end the program.

5 Click on *OK*.

Configuring network cards

1 Click on the *COAS* button in the program bar.

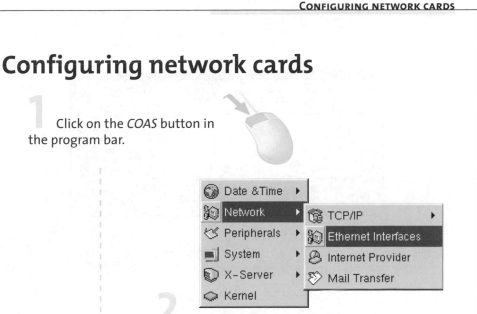

🌐 Date &Time ▸	
🦖 Network ▸	🖥 TCP/IP ▸
🐚 Peripherals ▸	🦖 Ethernet Interfaces
▪ System ▸	🐚 Internet Provider
🐚 X–Server ▸	🐚 Mail Transfer
🐚 Kernel	

2 Then click on *Network*, then on *Ethernet Interfaces*.

Enter your network card settings here.

If you only have one network card, the *Network Device* setting *eth0* is correct. Do not change the *PNP Configuration* either.

Ethernet Interface Configuration

Please select the network device and edit its configuration.

Network Device	eth0 ▾	New device
PNP Configuration	Disabled ▾	
Interface address	192.100.100.3	New alias
Network mask	255.255.255.0	
Broadcast address	192.100.100.255	Delete device
Default route	Enabled	
Default gateway	192.100.100.100	
Init at boot time	Enabled	

OK	Cancel

1 First click on the *New device* option to configure your network card.

```
─ Ethernet Cards                                              ✕

Please select your Ethernet card model. If your card is not listed here, click on the
Show Drivers button to select a network driver directly.

  3Com 3c501                                    ▲
  3Com 3c523                                    ▒       Show Models
  3Com 3c562                                    ▒
  3Com 3c579                                    ▒       Show Drivers
  3Com 3c589/3c589B                             ▒
  3Com 3c590/3c595                              ▒
  3Com 3c592/3c597                              ▼

                         Cancel
```

2 Select your network card
here.

Or click on *Show Drivers,* then select your network drivers from the list
displayed (use your network card manual if need be), such as *NE2000.*

3 Confirm that the new
settings are to be saved by
clicking on *Save.*

4 Enter an IP address at *Interface Address.*

The IP *address* is a number made up of a combination of four three-digit
numbers between 0 and 255. On the internet any attached server is
covered with a specific IP address, on which the other computers can
respond at any time.

You may assign separate IP addresses in an internal network. Ensure that each computer has its own individual IP address. In our example there are three computers in the network: the first IP address is 192.100.100.1 (Windows computer), the next one 192.100.100.2 (a UNIX computer) and the Linux PC is assigned 192.100.100.3. Note down the assigned IP addresses.

In a simple network the other settings in this window can be left to the system. Check that the *Default Route* is set on *Enabled*.

2 End the entries with *OK*.

You will be asked whether the modified information should be saved.

3 Click on *Save*.

Installing Samba servers

You can now begin configuring the Samba settings. The Samba server is only required if you wish to network two computers running on two different operating systems, such as your Linux computer with another computer running Windows NT, 95 or 98.

First of all check whether the necessary files are actually installed. This is usually the case for standard installation.

1 Click on the *File Manager* button on the program bar.

2 Open the */etc* directory and if available, the */etc/samba.d* directory.

Is it not available? No problem – simply install it as you learned in chapter 8.

1 Insert the Caldera OpenLinux installation CD into the CD-ROM drive.

2 Click on the *CD-ROM* button on the desktop.

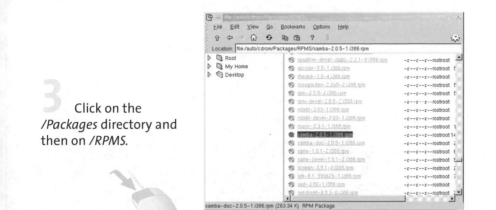

3 Click on the */Packages* directory and then on */RPMS*.

The concept of shared resources is not only used for printers but also for files and directories in the network. Therefore, the same happens with data and devices which can be used by several computers.

4 Look in this directory for the *smbfs r2.0.3-0b.i386.rpm* file using the scrollbar.

5 Click on the file.

The *kpackage* installation program is started.

491

6 Click on the *Install* button.

7 After installation, close the *kpackage* window.

Configuring Samba servers

The basic Samba package is now installed, and you can now configure the Samba server. There is currently no KDE program open for this. A terminal window therefore has to be opened in which the commands required are entered directly. However, working with a terminal window is quite simple.

1 Click on the *Terminal window* in the program bar.

An empty terminal window is opened. You can only see the cursor at present. This indicates the place in which Linux commands can be entered.

In this example, the cursor consists of the Caldera > signs. First, copy the sample configuration files so the correct Samba configuration file is available for editing.

TIP You can check to see if the *smb.conf* file is in the directory using the *ls* command

2 Type cp smb.conf.sample *smb.conf.*

3 Confirm the entry by pressing the ⏎ key.

TIP Samba server is a program to connect network PCs. Usernames and passwords should always be checked as there is always a danger of unauthorised persons logging in and destroying files.

In the next step a password file is created for Samba. This file is also copied using a normal password file.

```
Terminal
[root@jonathan samba.d]# cat /etc/passwd | mksmbpasswd > /etc/samba.d/smbpasswd
```

TIP The | character appears by holding down the Alt (Alt Gr) key, then pressing the keys with the >, < and | characters.

1 Now type: *cat /etc/passwd | mksmbpasswd > / etc/samba.d/smbpasswd*

2 Confirm the entry by pressing the ⏎ key.

Now create passwords for future network users. To do this, use the names of existing Linux users. Use your own username, and the root super user if need be.

```
[root@jonathan samba.d]# cat /etc/passwd | mksmbpasswd > /etc/samba.d/smbpasswd
[root@jonathan samba.d]# smbpasswd jonathan
New SMB password:
Retype new SMB password:
```

1 Type *smbpasswd* user name.

Replace *username* with one of your own user names.

2 Confirm the entry by pressing the ⏎ key.

You are now prompted for the new password of the future Samba user. You can enter the current password or use a new one. If you enter a new one, you should keep a note of it.

3 Enter the password twice.

4 Confirm the entries at any time by pressing the ⏎ key.

If the user and password were successfully created, this message appears. In case of an error you should repeat the entries.

```
Terminal                                                          □ ×
[root@jonathan samba.d]# cat /etc/passwd | mksmbpasswd > /etc/samba.d/smbpasswd
[root@jonathan samba.d]# smbpasswd jonathan
New SMB password:
Retype new SMB password:
Password changed for user jonathan.
[root@jonathan samba.d]# ▊
```

In this way a password is assigned to a current samba user. This current user was copied with the *cp* command into the password file in one of the previous steps. If you wish to create an additional Linux user and to configure it for use with Samba, you should proceed slightly differently.

You should enter the normal and Samba username.

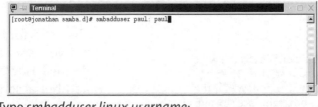

```
Terminal                                                          □ ×
[root@jonathan samba.d]# smbadduser paul: paul▊
```

1 Type *smbadduser linux username: samba username.*

TIP

If your Microsoft Windows PC requires a password in the network neighbourhood (see next section), use the following procedure: open a terminal window, delete the Samba password file using the command *rm/etc/samba.d/smbpasswd* and recreate ALL users requiring the Samba network service with the command *smbadduser.*

Replace *linux username* with the corresponding Linux username, and *samba username* with the Samba username. The usernames can be identical, as shown in the example.

2 Confirm the entries by pressing the ⏎ key.

You are now prompted for the new password for the new Samba user. You can either use the current password or enter a new one.

```
Terminal
[root@jonathan samba.d]# smbadduser paul: paul
Adding: paul to /etc/samba.d/smbpasswd
ERROR: paul: Already in smbpasswd database SKIPPING...
-------------------------------------------------------
ENTER password for paul
New SMB password:
Retype new SMB password:
Password changed for user paul.
[root@jonathan samba.d]#
[root@jonathan samba.d]#
```

3 Enter the password twice. - - - - - - - - - ➤ **4** Confirm the entries at any time by pressing the ⏎ key.

If the user and password were successfully created, a corresponding message appears. In case of an error you should repeat the entries.

The users for the Samba network service are now defined. However, several additional settings in the Samba configuration file are required.

1 Start the editor using the *Editors* menu entry, then click on *KEdit Editor*.

Now open the */etc/samba.d/samba.conf* configuration file.

2 Click on *File*, then *Open*. - - - ➤ **3** Return to the root directory. - - - ➤

4 Now open the *etc* directory, then the *samba.d* sub-directory.

```
Open                                                    ×
  ⇦  ⇨  ⬆  🏠  ⟳  ⋀  💡  🗋  ⚙   samba.d/              ▾
  🗋 ..
  🗁 codepages
  ⬦ lmhosts
  ⬦ smb.conf
  ⬦ smb.conf.sample
  ⬦ smbpasswd
  ⬦ smbpasswd~
  ⬦ smbusers
  ⬦ smbusers~

Location:  /etc/samba.d/smb.conf                           ▾
Filter:    *                               ▾  ☑ Show hidden
     Help              OK              Cancel
```

5 Click on the *smb.conf* file.

Now you can see a typical configuration file. It contains a lot of text. Most entries can be ignored. These are indicated by the # sign at the beginning of the line. An additional commentary character is the semi-colon(;).

```
🗋 /etc/samba.d/smb.conf                              ∧  □ ×
File  Edit  Options  Help
🗋 🗁 🗋  🗐 🗐 ✂  🖶 🗐  ?
# This is the main Samba configuration file. You should read the
# smb.conf (5) manual page in order to understand the options listed
# here. Samba has a huge number of configurable options (perhaps too
# many!) most of which are not shown in this example
#
# Any line which starts with a ; (semi-colon) or a # (hash)
# is a comment and is ignored. In this example we will use a #
# for commentry and a ; for parts of the config file that you
# may wish to enable
#
# NOTE: Whenever you modify this file you should run the command "testparm"
# to check that you have not many any basic syntactic errors.
#
#=========================== Global Settings =========================
[global]

# workgroup = NT-Domain-Name or Workgroup-Name
   workgroup = WORKGROUP

# server string is the equivalent of the NT Description field
   server string = Samba Server on Caldera OpenLinux

# This option is important for security. It allows you to restrict
# connections to machines which are on your local network. The
# following example restricts access to two C class networks and
# the "loopback" interface. For more examples of the syntax see
# the smb conf man page
                                           INS  Line: 1 Col: 1
```

Commentary characters have two meanings in configuration files. On the one hand, lines are not evaluated by the system if they include a commentary character. On the other hand, earlier or previously planned settings are mentioned, since they may be used again in the future. It is then easier to remove a commentary character instead of re-entering the command

One of the first settings you can make is the name of the workgroup on which the Windows computer runs. In this example the entry appears:

Workgroup = BORSIG16

1 Replace the word *BORSIG16* with the name of your Windows workgroup.

Remember to remove any commentary characters before the workgroup.

If you do not know the name of your Windows computer workgroup, then boot up the computer and open the *Start* menu. Click on *Control Panel,* then on the *Network* symbol. If you have installed Windows, you will see the *Computer name* and *Domain* entries on the first *Identification* tab. The domain name corresponds to the Workgroup entry in Samba. If you use Windows 95 or 98, you will find the *Computer name* and *Domain* entries on the second *Identification* tab.

You can also scroll down using the Pg⬇ key.

2 Further file entries can be seen by dragging the scrollbar with the mouse.

```
# Put a capping on the size of the log files (in Kb).
   max log size = 50

# Security mode. Most people will want user level security. See
# security_level.txt for details.
   security = user
# Use password server option only with security = server
;   password server = <NT-Server-Name>

# Password Level allows matching of _n_ characters of the password for
# all combinations of upper and lower case.
;   password level = 8
;   username level = 8

# You may wish to use password encryption. Please read
# ENCRYPTION.txt, Win95.txt and WinNT.txt in the Samba documentation.
# Do not enable this option unless you have read those documents
;   encrypt passwords = yes
;   smb passwd file = /etc/samba.d/smbpasswd

# The following are needed to allow password changing from Windows to
# update the Linux sytsem password also.
# NOTE: Use these with 'encrypt passwords' and 'smb passwd file' above.
# NOTE2: You do NOT need these to allow workstations to change only
#        the encrypted SMB passwords. They allow the Unix password
#        to be kept in sync with the SMB password
```

3 At *max log size*, enter the instruction *max log size = 50.*

Now look for a section containing the term *ENCRYPTION.txt*. This concerns the encoding of the data transfer between Linux and Windows computers. Two entries are required here.

4 Enter *encrypt passwords = yes*.

5 Type *smb passwd file = / etc/samba.d/smbpasswd*.

6 Drag the scroll box down to see further entries.

```
/etc/samba.d/smb.conf
File  Edit  Options  Help

# NOTE: Use these with 'encrypt passwords' and 'smb passwd file' above.
# NOTE2: You do NOT need these to allow workstations to change only
#        the encrypted SMB passwords. They allow the Unix password
#        to be kept in sync with the SMB password.
;  unix password sync = Yes
;  passwd program = /usr/bin/passwd %u
;  passwd chat = *New*UNIX*password* %n\n *ReType*new*UNIX*password* %n\n *passwd:*all*authen

# Unix users can map to different SMB User names
;  username map = /etc/samba.d/smbusers

# Using the following line enables you to customise your configuration
# on a per machine basis. The %m gets replaced with the netbios name
# of the machine that is connecting
;  include = /etc/samba.d/smb.conf.%m

# Most people will find that this option gives better performance.
# See speed.txt and the manual pages for details
   socket options = TCP_NODELAY

# Configure Samba to use multiple interfaces
# If you have multiple network interfaces then you must list them
# here. See the man page for details.
;  interfaces = 192.168.12.2/24 192.168.13.2/24

# Configure remote browse list synchronisation here
#  request announcement to, or browse list sync from:

INS  Line: 61 Col: 30
```

7 Now enter *username map = /etc/samba.d/smbusers* below the comment Unix users.

The concept of shared resources is not only used for printers but also for files and directories in the network. Therefore, the same happens with data and devices which can be used by several computers.

8 The term *socket options = TCP_NODELAY* should be displayed further down.

A further entry should be displayed below the *DNS Proxy* commentary.

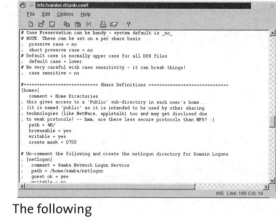

9 Enter *dnsproxy = no* if required.

The next essential comment block is entitled *Share Definitions*. There is an entry for the work directory of the users here. They are named [*homes*].

10 The following should be displayed here:
path = %H
browseable = yes
writable = yes
create mask = 0750

The user's work directory is made visible in the /home directory using this entry. If a user establishes a network connection from Windows to the Linux computer, he will then see his Linux work directory under the Windows network environment with the name *homes*. However, he must also be registered as a Samba user. In the following section you will learn how to establish a network connection from Windows.

There is a public general directory in Linux named */public*.

You still have to create the */home/public* directory. Use this menu sequence in the file manager: *File - New - Directory*. Give all users full access rights to the directory (cf chapter 5).

All Windows users can now see a directory named *public* in the network environment. It may be used by all users.

11 The following entries should be displayed here:
comment = Public Stuff
path = /home/public
browseable = yes
public = yes
writable = yes
printable = no
write list = @users

Access to other private directories is shared in the *private directories* section. Directories are indicated here which only a user defined under the *user* entry can access.

Such an entry can look like this:

[jonathan]
comment = Fred's Service
path = %H
valid users = jonathan
public = no
writable = yes
printable = no

Instead of *path = %H*, you could also write *path =/home/jonathan*, for example. The Windows *fred* user would then see a directory named *jonathan*, which actually corresponds to the work directory of the user *jonathan*.

The entry means that the Windows PC *Jonathan* user sees *Fred's Service* from one directory. The same applies to his work directory on the Linux computer. The reference is fixed in his work directory with the *% H* entry.

File changes now must be saved, and the file closed.

1 Click on *File*, then *Save*.

2 Click on *File*, then *Close*.

Starting Samba servers

You have done it! Everything is now configured. Samba services still have to be started.

Start the Samba service using a command line of the terminal window.

1 Type *samba start* in the terminal window.

2 Confirm the entry by pressing the ⏎ key.

Start the service in this way, but only for the current Linux session. As soon as you are registered under Linux, you will need to repeat this step next time. As this is too time-consuming, you can also configure services by making them start automatically at startup.

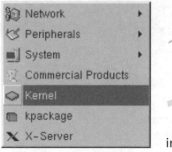

1 Click on the *COAS* button in the program bar, then on *Kernel*.

Look for an entry named *smbfs* in the left-hand side of the window.

2 Move the scroll box in the left-hand side of the window.

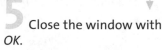

If the *smbf* service (Samba file server) is not automatically started up from the beginning, you should find a corresponding entry in the left-hand side of the window.

3 Click on the *smbfs* entry in the left-hand side of the window, then on *Load*.

In this way the service is loaded into the operating system core. It is now automatically started at startup.

You are now asked for further settings.

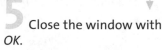

TIP

Should these configuration attributes be already provided, simply leave them unchanged.

4 Set the *Load at boot time* button on *Enabled*.

5 Close the window with *OK*.

You should now find the *smbfs* entry in the right-hand side of the window. In future, the Samba service will always be started at startup.

Kernel Modules

View Models

Please select a module to be loaded or unloaded. The list on the left shows all available modules, while the one on the right shows all modules currently loaded. You can restrict the display to certain categories of modules using the View menu.

3c501		slhc	
3c503	Load	slip	Unload
3c505		smbfs	
3c507	Info	soundcore	Info
3c509		soundlow	
3c515		sr_mod	
3c59x		st	
53c7,8xx		sunrpc	
8pack		umsdos	
82596		vfat	

OK

Accessing Windows files with Samba

It is now possible to access Windows files from Linux and vice versa. You can even test it.

However, several small changes still need to be made to your PC. First you must open the hard drive you would like to access from Linux. This means that you give the Linux computer permission to look at the Windows hard drive and to work on it.

You should proceed as follows using a computer running on Windows NT:

1 Open *Windows Explorer* on the Windows PC.

2 Click on the name of your hard drive, such as *C*.

3 Click on the *smbfs* entry in the left-hand side of the window, then on *Load*.

Presumably a standard release has already been typed in the *Open as* section.

4 If so, click on *New release* and enter the new release name.

Do you have a Windows 95 or 98 computer and cannot find the *Open* entry in the context menu? Don't worry – this is easily rectified.

1 Open the Control Panel via the *Start* menu.

2 Click on the *Network* icon.

3 Click on the *File and printer* release button in the first *Configuration* tab.

4 Activate the *File access available for other users* option.

Now execute the release of the hard drive as described above for Windows NT.

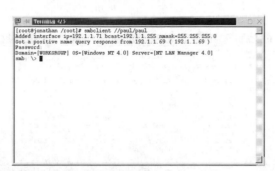

1 Type *sbmclient // windows computer name/release name* in the terminal window.

Replace *Windows computer name* with the name of your Windows computer (in the above example, the Windows PC is called *pc_k233nt*) and *release name* with the name you have set for the release of your Windows hard drive (*vol_o* in the example).

Do you not know the name of your Windows computer? No problem, start the Windows PC and open the *Start* menu. Click on *Control Panel,* then on the *Network* icon. On the *Identification* tab you will see the *Computer name* and *Domain* entries or *Workgroup*. You will find the computer name here.

You are asked for the password again. Enter the one you assigned to your current username as the Samba password.

2 Confirm the entry by pressing the ⏎ key.

3 Enter the password and press the ⏎ key.

```
[root@jonathan /root]# smbclient //paul/paul
Added interface ip=192.1.1.71 bcast=192.1.1.255 nmask=255.255.255.0
Got a positive name query response from 192.1.1.69 ( 192.1.1.69 )
Password:
Domain=[WORKGROUP] OS=[Windows NT 4.0] Server=[NT LAN Manager 4.0]
smb: \>
```

Following successful connection configuration you are given another *smb* prompt: \>. You now have access to the released hard drive of your Windows computer. Use the Samba program commands.

507

```
Terminal                                                                    □ ×
[root@jonathan /root]# smbclient //paul/paul
Added interface ip=192.1.1.71 bcast=192.1.1.255 nmask=255.255.255.0
Got a positive name query response from 192.1.1.69 ( 192.1.1.69 )
Password:
Domain=[WORKGROUP] OS=[Windows NT 4.0] Server=[NT LAN Manager 4.0]
smb: \> help
ls           dir          du           lcd          cd
pwd          get          mget         put          mput
rename       more         mask         del          open
rm           mkdir        md           rmdir        rd
prompt       recurse      translate    lowercase    print
printmode    queue        cancel       quit         q
exit         newer        archive      tar          blocksize
tarmode      setmode      help         ?            !
smb: \> ls
  AUTOEXEC.BAT                  A        0  Tue Aug  1 10:13:13 2000
  boot.ini                    ASR      285  Tue Aug  1 15:55:21 2000
  CONFIG.SYS                    A        0  Tue Aug  1 10:13:13 2000
  IO.SYS                     AHSR        0  Tue Aug  1 10:13:13 2000
  KPCMS                         D        0  Tue Aug  1 14:44:35 2000
  mgafold                       D        0  Tue Aug  1 09:28:51 2000
  MSDOS.SYS                  AHSR        0  Tue Aug  1 10:13:13 2000
  NTBOOTDD.SYS               AHSR    18352  Mon Oct 14 01:38:00 1996
  NTDETECT.COM               AHSR    26816  Wed Aug  2 08:14:35 2000
```

4 Enter *help* and then press
the ⏎ key.

The Samba server commands are listed. The command is a mixture of
DOS and Linux commands. For example, you can display the contents of
the hard drive under Windows either with the *dir* DOS command or with
the *ls* Linux one. The result will be identical.

```
Terminal                                                                    □ ×
  WINNT                         D        0  Wed Nov  1 12:03:57 2000
  WLPRSPL                       D        0  Fri Aug 25 10:23:30 2000

           65519 blocks of size 32768. 36647 blocks available
smb: \> dir
  AUTOEXEC.BAT                  A        0  Tue Aug  1 10:13:13 2000
  boot.ini                    ASR      285  Tue Aug  1 15:55:21 2000
  CONFIG.SYS                    A        0  Tue Aug  1 10:13:13 2000
  IO.SYS                     AHSR        0  Tue Aug  1 10:13:13 2000
  KPCMS                         D        0  Tue Aug  1 14:44:35 2000
  mgafold                       D        0  Tue Aug  1 09:28:51 2000
  MSDOS.SYS                  AHSR        0  Tue Aug  1 10:13:13 2000
  NTBOOTDD.SYS               AHSR    18352  Mon Oct 14 01:38:00 1996
  NTDETECT.COM               AHSR    26816  Wed Aug  2 08:14:35 2000
  ntldr                      AHSR   156496  Wed Aug  2 08:14:34 2000
  pagefile.sys                  A 145752064  Tue Nov  7 09:05:53 2000
  Program Files                 D        0  Wed Nov  1 12:03:31 2000
  RECYCLER                    DHS        0  Tue Aug  1 09:42:38 2000
  TEMP                          D        0  Tue Nov  7 15:48:55 2000
  WINNT                         D        0  Wed Nov  1 12:03:57 2000
  WLPRSPL                       D        0  Fri Aug 25 10:23:30 2000

           65519 blocks of size 32768. 36647 blocks available
smb: \> █
```

5 Enter the *ls (*or *dir)* command and then press the ⏎ key.

The contents of the Windows hard drive are displayed.

Would you like to transfer a file from your Linux work directory to the Windows hard drive now? Simply use the *put* command.

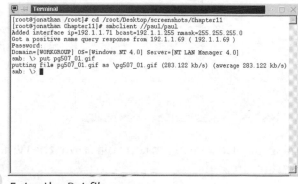

6 Enter the *Put file name* command and then press the ⏎ key.

Replace *Filename* with a filename of your choice. In our example the file assigned was *pg507_01.gif*.

7 Leave the Windows hard drive contents displayed with the *ls* (or *dir*) command again.

A copy of the *pg507_01.gif* file is now on the Windows hard drive.

Alternatively, you can of course see the directory contents with Windows Explorer on your Windows PC. The file is also displayed here and can now continue to be used in Windows.

Samba can also be used to copy files from the Windows computer using the *get* command.

```
AUTOEXEC.BAT          A          0  Tue Aug  1 10:13:13 2000
boot.ini            ASR        285  Tue Aug  1 15:55:21 2000
Chapter_01.doc        A     100352  Tue Sep 19 09:11:45 2000
CONFIG.SYS            A          0  Tue Aug  1 10:13:13 2000
IO.SYS             AHSR          0  Tue Aug  1 10:13:13 2000
KPCMS                 D          0  Tue Aug  1 14:44:35 2000
mgafold               D          0  Tue Aug  1 09:28:51 2000
MSDOS.SYS          AHSR          0  Tue Aug  1 10:13:13 2000
NTBOOTDD.SYS       AHSR      18352  Mon Oct 14 01:38:00 1996
NTDETECT.COM       AHSR      26816  Wed Aug  2 08:14:35 2000
ntldr              AHSR     156496  Wed Aug  2 08:14:34 2000
pagefile.sys          A  145752064  Tue Nov  7 09:05:53 2000
pg507_01.gif          A      52185  Tue Nov  7 17:27:22 2000
Program Files         D          0  Wed Nov  1 12:03:31 2000
RECYCLER            DHS          0  Tue Aug  1 09:42:38 2000
TEMP                  D          0  Tue Nov  7 17:31:34 2000
WINNT                 D          0  Wed Nov  1 12:03:57 2000
WLPRSPL               D          0  Fri Aug 25 10:23:30 2000

            65519 blocks of size 32768. 36604 blocks available
smb: \> get Chapter_01.doc
getting file Chapter_01.doc of size 100352 as Chapter_01.doc (882.882 kb/s) (ave
rage 882.883 kb/s)
smb: \> █
```

8   Enter *get filename*, then press the ⏎ key.

Replace *filename* with a filename of your choice. In this example *Chapter_01.doc* was assigned to the file. You must either open a file manager or end Samba in order to check whether the transfer was successful. In this case, end the Samba program.

```
╔═ Terminal                                                  ╳ □ ╳
 lioot.ini                    ASR      285  Tue Aug  1 15:55:21 2000   ▲
 Chapter_01.doc               A     100352  Tue Sep 19 09:11:45 2000
 CONFIG.SYS                   A          0  Tue Aug  1 10:13:13 2000
 IO.SYS                    AHSR          0  Tue Aug  1 10:13:13 2000
 KPCMS                        D          0  Tue Aug  1 14:44:35 2000
 mgafold                      D          0  Tue Aug  1 09:28:51 2000
 MSDOS.SYS                 AHSR          0  Tue Aug  1 10:13:13 2000
 NTBOOTDD.SYS              AHSR      18352  Mon Oct 14 01:38:00 1996
 NTDETECT.COM              AHSR      26816  Wed Aug  2 00:14:35 2000
 ntldr                     AHSR     156496  Wed Aug  2 08:14:34 2000
 pagefile.sys                 A  145752064  Tue Nov  7 09:05:53 2000
 pg507_01.gif                 A      52185  Tue Nov  7 17:27:22 2000
 Program Files                D          0  Wed Nov  1 12:03:31 2000
 RECYCLER                   DHS          0  Tue Aug  1 09:42:38 2000
 TEMP                         D          0  Tue Nov  7 17:31:34 2000
 WINNT                        D          0  Wed Nov  1 12:03:57 2000
 WLPRSPL                      D          0  Fri Aug 25 10:23:30 2000

           65519 blocks of size 32768. 36604 blocks available
 smb: \> get Chapter_01.doc
 getting file Chapter_01.doc of size 100352 as Chapter_01.doc (882.882 kb/s) (ave
 rage 882.883 kb/s)
 smb: \> exit
 [root@jonathan Chapter11]# █                                      ▼
```

9 Enter the *exit* command and
then press the ⏎ key.

The usual prompt character is now displayed again. As the terminal
window is still open, you should not use the file manager for the
contents display of the work directory. Instead, get to know a Linux
command for this.

```
╔═ Terminal                                                  ╳ □ ╳
           65519 blocks of size 32768. 36604 blocks available  ▲
 smb: \> get Chapter_01.doc
 getting file Chapter_01.doc of size 100352 as Chapter_01.doc (882.882 kb/s) (ave
 rage 882.883 kb/s)
 smb: \> exit
 [root@jonathan Chapter11]# ls -1
 Chapter_01.doc
 pg507_01.gif
 pg507_02
 pg508_01
 pg509_01
 pg509_02
 pg510_01
 pg511_01
 pg511_02
 pg512_01
 pg513_01
 pg514_01
 pg514_02
 pg515_01
 pg516_01
 pg517_01
 pg521_01                                                         ▼
```

10 Enter the *ls -l* command
and then press the ⏎ key.

A list of all files and sub-folders of your work directory is now displayed.
The file recently copied by the Windows PC (*Chapter_01.doc* in this case)
is displayed here as well.

Accessing Linux files from Windows

Working with the Samba program in Linux is very time-consuming. You will now learn how to access a Linux computer from a Windows PC, which is far easier.

1 Open Windows Explorer via the Windows PC start menu.

2 Scroll down using the scrollbar until you see *Network Neighborhood* on the left-hand side.

3 Open *Network Neighborhood* by clicking on the plus symbol.

Your Linux computer will now be listed in the *Network Neighborhood*. In this example it is called Caldera. The current user on the Windows PC is called *freds*. This user also exists on the Linux computer with the same username. Both the *freds* work directory and the *public* directory may be seen on the Linux computer. The *jonathan* directory can also be used from Windows via the *smb.conf* file. The *freds* work directory is again located in the *home* directory.

Now display the contents of your work directory.

Click on the name of your work directory in the left-hand side of the window.

You can also exchange files via your Linux-Windows network using the Samba server.

A general piece of advice for all problems: you should create system settings as the *root* user, such as installing a printer or running system tools. Otherwise you will not be authorised, or the settings will not be applied to all users.

Installation problems

The boot program does not start

Have you inserted the boot disk but the boot program has not started? Check whether you have inserted the right disk. It should be labelled 'Open Linux 2.4 Boot/Install Disk'. Be sure you are using the correct CD-ROM: 'Open Linux 2.4 Installation CD'.

Have you used the correct disk and CD-ROM? Then check whether the boot sequence is correctly set in the BIOS. Go into the BIOS by following the *Press DEL to enter setup* command at startup (it may be *F2* on some computers). You will find the *Boot Sequence* setting in the *BIOS Feature Setup*, which should read *A,C* or *CDROM,C*.

Mouse installation does not work

During installation you are prompted to move the mouse so the system can recognise the type of mouse and the connection used.

But the mouse does not react. You may have moved it too fast or too late so that the system now no longer recognises it. Simply reboot the computer and start the installation process again. Take care to move the mouse slowly in this installation phase so that it can be recognised.

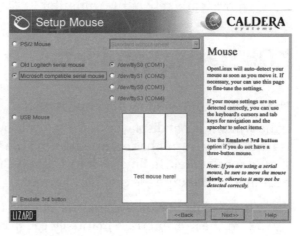

Startup problems

Nothing happens after switching on

In this case you should check the following:

- Is the monitor switched on?
- Are all main plugs connected to electrical sockets?
- Are all cables attached to the PC and monitor correctly and in the right place?

The 'Keyboard Error' message appears

In this case you should check the following:

- Is the keyboard connection cable attached to the PC correctly?
- Have you put something on the keyboard?
- Is a button of the keyboard stuck down?

The 'No system or drive error' message appears

In this case you should check the following:

➡ Is a disk still in the floppy drive?

If so, remove it and reboot the computer.

KDE startup problems

The graphic login window does not appear

If the window is not displayed automatically by Caldera OpenLinux at startup, then an error has occurred during the installation process. You should consider reinstalling, as it can be very difficult for a Linux beginner to configure the graphic interface.

If a text-based login window appears labelled *Login*, you can log in and try to start the KDE interface manually. Log in as the *root* user and press the ⏎ key. Then enter the password and press ⏎ again.

At this point the "Welcome to your OpenLinux system!" message should appear. The graphic interface can now be started using the *init 5* command. This instructs the system to use the fifth operating level which uses a graphic interface.

Did your graphic interface 'crash' when logging on? This means that only a grey screen can be seen. Press Ctrl + Alt + ⌫ to return to the command interface. Then restart the entire operating system using the *reboot* command.

The 'Logon not allowed' message appears

You can see the graphic logon window, yet the 'Logon not allowed' message appears in the lower left-hand corner of the window after the username and password have been entered.

➡ Check the username displayed – is it correct? If not, re-enter it.

➡ Enter the password again slowly – and pay attention to lower and upper case letters.

➡ Is perhaps the ⬇ (caps lock) key engaged? You can check this with the control light on the upper right-hand side of the keyboard. If the middle light shines, then the caps lock key is engaged. Press it again to release it – the light will go out.

➡ Does your password contain numbers, and do you use the number block for input? Then check whether the (Num) button is depressed. If so, the left control light shines up on the right above the keyboard.

Problems after KDE startup

Icons are missing in KDE windows and on the KDE interface

If your KDE interface does not contain specific icons described in this book, then you may have omitted a stage. Chapter 4 outlines configuration setup in detail – you should read this chapter again.

If the *Fastened* and *Close* symbols are missing from the title bar after logon, then you have not yet defined the title bar lay-out for this particular user accordingly. This setting must be carried out for every user as soon as he is registered. This same procedure is also outlined in chapter 4 in the section about the KDE control centre.

The window title bar is no longer accessible

If a program window was inadvertently moved under the taskbar, then the buttons to close or move the window, or alter its size, will no longer be visible. Simply press the Alt button and click somewhere in the 'inaccessible' window. The window can then be moved to an arbitrary position by pressing the Alt key and the mouse button.

Should this not work, right-click in the program bar on the lower margin and select *Configure*. In the *Control bar* tab, click on the *Taskbar – not displayed* option, then on *Apply*. The taskbar disappears and you can move the incorrectly positioned window into the free screen area by clicking and dragging the title bar. Click on the *Taskbar – Above* option, then on OK to display the taskbar again.

A program window is too large for the screen area

When opening the KDE control centre, it may happen that a window is larger than the screen area. The program bar can be reduced by clicking on either of the two small black arrows on the left- or right-hand side. The area is still not usually large enough, as you will not be able to see the *Apply* or *Cancel* buttons.

Click once with the left mouse button on the program icon in the upper left-hand corner next to the title bar. Click on *Size change* in the menu. The mouse pointer immediately places itself on the lower right-hand corner. Simply drag this up until you can see the entire window. Then click once with the left mouse button to save the setting.

The KDE interface has 'frozen'

Whilst working in KDE the screen suddenly freezes and the system will not react to any keyboard action or mouse movement. Try the Ctrl + Alt + ⇦ key combination to return to the command interface. You may well need to change console: use the Alt + ⇩ 1 or Alt + ⇩ 2 etc. key combination to get a login request. Then register as *root* (as described in the 'KDE startup problems' section) and try to start the graphic interface with the *init 5* command. If problems arise you should reboot. Alternatively, you can use the Ctrl + Alt + Del key combination which corresponds to the *reboot* command.

Under no circumstances should you end Linux by pressing the *Reset* button or by simply turning off the machine, as doing this could destroy the system. First, try to get a character-based login request, such as the change between the consoles described above. Then, if you have registered as *root*, you can stop the system properly with the *stop* command and then switch off as soon as the *System stopped* report appears. Otherwise, restart with the *reboot* command.

A KDE application has 'crashed'

You will frequently work with several KDE program windows opened at once. Assume you are working with StarOffice, when it suddenly crashes and will not react to any entry. However, you can still move to other windows on the taskbar and start the process manager on the main menu.

1 Click on *System*, then *Task Manager*.

2 Open the *Process tree* tab in the Task Manager and switch the sorting over to *Sort by name*.

519

KDE Task Manager

File Refresh Rate Process Help

Processes List | Performance Meter

Running Processes

Name	PID	User ID	CPU	Time	Nice	Status	Memory	Resident	Shared	Comm
init	1 root	0.00%	0:04	0 Sleep	1092	448	1012 init [5]
nmbd	1152 root	0.00%	0:00	0 Sleep	1508	820	1040 nmbd
smbd	1150 root	0.00%	0:00	0 Sleep	2108	908	1188 smbd
kdm	723 root	0.00%	0:00	0 Sleep	5416	2276	4448 /opt/kd
kdm	1469 root	0.00%	0:00	0 Sleep	6324	4032	4736 -:0
kwm	1482 root	0.00%	0:00	0 Sleep	6156	4100	4708 kwm
kpanel	1527 root	0.00%	0:00	0 Sleep	6356	4376	4708 kpane
krootwm	1526 root	0.00%	0:00	0 Sleep	5684	3504	4708 kroot
kwmsound	1525 root	0.00%	0:00	0 Zombie	0	12	0
kfm	1523 root	0.00%	0:01	0 Sleep	8596	5992	6056 kfm
ksnapshot	2264 root	0.14%	0:00	0 Sleep	9272	7020	5132 ksnap:
ktop	2259 root	2.66%	0:12	0 Run	6084	4224	4820 ktop
kbgndwm	1503 root	0.00%	0:00	0 Sleep	6124	3616	5132 /opt/kd
X	725 root	1.96%	1:38	0 Sleep	18700	8336	1132 /usr/X
getty	722 root	0.00%	0:00	0 Sleep	1096	440	1012 /sbin/g
getty	721 root	0.00%	0:00	0 Sleep	1096	440	1012 /sbin/g
getty	720 root	0.00%	0:00	0 Sleep	1096	440	1012 /sbin/g
getty	719 root	0.00%	0:00	0 Sleep	1096	440	1012 /sbin/g
getty	718 root	0.00%	0:00	0 Sleep	1096	440	1012 /sbin/g

☑ Show Tree   [All processes ▼]   [Refresh Now]   [Kill task]

42 Processes   Memory: 109336 kB used, 18716 kB free   Swap: 0 kB used, 0 kB free

3 Drag the scroll box down until you see the crashed application (on the uppermost level of the process), *Kwm sound* is our example.

4 Click on the crashed application, then on *Launch*.

The system prompts you to confirm your decision (you may have selected the wrong item by mistake).

Task Manager

⚠ Send signal SIGKILL to process 1525?
(Process name: kwmsound Owner: root)

[Continue]   [Abort]

5 Click on *Continue.*

You will see the crashed program temporarily in the program manager as it has already disappeared from the taskbar.

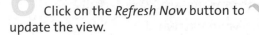

6 Click on the *Refresh Now* button to update the view.

The application is now no longer displayed, so the system closes it down.

How do I change my password?

You wish to modify your password as a normal user or *root*. Open a terminal window (using the program bar) and type in the *passwd* command.

As a normal user you will be asked for the current password, which you should enter and confirm using the ⏎ key. You will not be asked as a super user. The new password then must always be entered twice and confirmed. As the password is not displayed for security reasons, you might have made a mistake the first time. If so, the following error message appears:

Sorry, passwords do not match

Password modification can be cancelled using the Ctrl + C key combination. The following message then appears:

Passwd: Authentication token manipulation error

The password entered can be rejected with error messages for several

521

reasons:

If you enter the previous password as a new password, it is rejected with the **Password unchanged** report.

If you enter a password with less than six characters, you receive the following report: **BAD PASSWORD: it's WAY too short**. Increase the number of characters in the password.

If you enter a password which only consists of letters, you receive the following report: **BAD PASSWORD: it's too simple**. The system requires a combination of letters and numbers, or special characters.

A successful password change ends with this report:

Passwd: all authentication tokens updated successfully

From then on, this is the only valid password.

Printer installation problems

Printer installation does not work

Do you have problems installing a printer? Repeat the instructions in chapter 7. Does your printer appear in the printer list offered by the COAS system program? If not, it is not guaranteed that your printer is Linux compatible. Check this again with the printer list in the Appendix. You can usually find a fairly current list of Linux-compatible printers at *http://www.picante.com/~gtaylor/pht*.

Do you have a laser printer which is not on the list? You should consult the printer manual to check whether it is compatible with an HP LaserJet or PCL compatible. In this case, try to install it with an HP LaserJet printer driver.

Printer problems in StarOffice

Your printer works perfectly when you print a short text from the editor. Yet you are experiencing problems printing in StarOffice (such as the print view), even after proceeding with the installation as described in chapter 8.

This can be solved by installing an additional printer driver in StarOffice. The StarOffice printer driver list shows more models than COAS.

First you need to define an additional printer type with the COAS support.

1 Open the *Peripherals* menu and then *Printer* with the *COAS* button in the program bar.

Select printer model

Select your printer, or a model close to it.

Epson Stylus Color II
Epson Stylus Color 400
Epson Stylus Color
Epson Stylus Color 600
Epson Stylus Color 800
Generic remote printer
Generic postscript printer

Cancel

2 Look for *Generic postscript printer* in the lower half of the window using the scrollbar.

3 Click on *Generic postscript printer*.

Printer name

Please enter the logical name for the new printer, e.g. lp1, ps1 etc.

Name   Generic Printer

OK   Cancel

4 Enter an arbitrary printer name (such as *Generic Printer*) and click on *OK*.

523

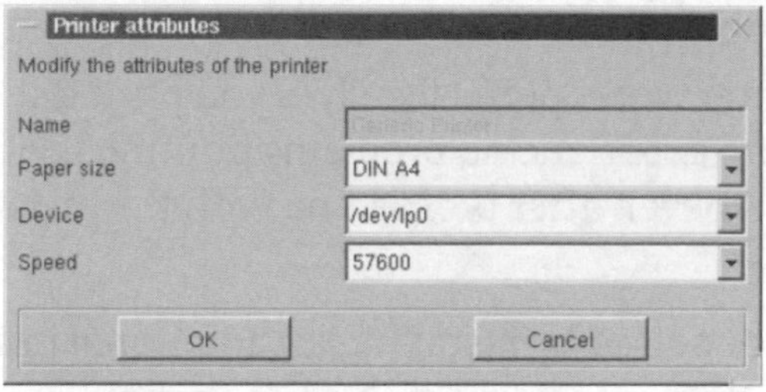

Printer attributes

Modify the attributes of the printer

Name	
Paper size	DIN A4
Device	/dev/lp0
Speed	57600

OK   Cancel

Choose *DIN A4* in the *Paper size* field
and click on *OK*.

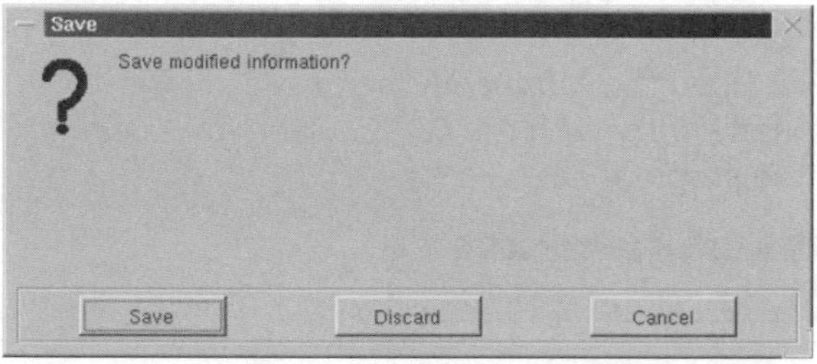

Save

? Save modified information?

Save   Discard   Cancel

Click on *Save* to confirm
your settings.

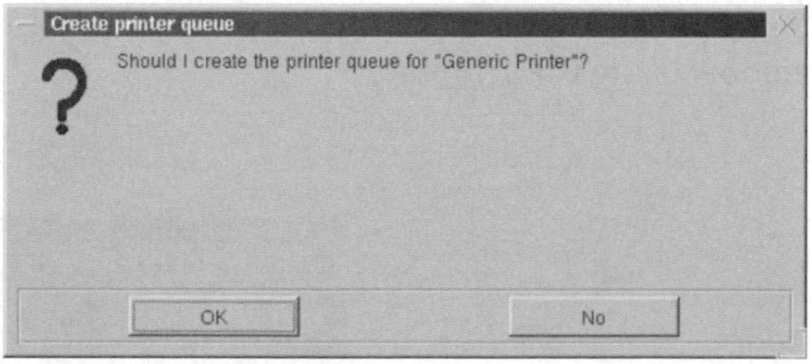

Create printer queue

? Should I create the printer queue for "Generic Printer"?

OK   No

Click on *OK* so that the system
establishes a print queue for the
newly configured printer.

Two established printers can now be seen in the COAS printer menu.

Printer configuration ✕

Printer Daemon

Configure the printers connected to your computer or network.

Name	Description
hplaser5l	HP DeskJet 500
Generic l	Generic postscript prin

| OK | Cancel |

Start the StarOffice program to configure the printer there.

1 Click on the *Configure printer* icon in the StarOffice program window.

Printer Installation · □ ✕

Default printer
Generic Printer
n queue default_queue=lpr

Installed printers
Generic Printeron queue default_queue (lpr)

Default Printer

Existing printer drivers
Adobe LaserJet II Cartridge
Agfa–Compugraphic 9400P
Agfa Matrix ChromaScript
Agfa TabScript C500 PostScript Printer
Apple LaserWriter
Apple LaserWriter IIf
Apple LaserWriter IIg
Apple LaserWriter II NT
Apple LaserWriter II NTX

Add new printer

Install new driver...   Deinstall driver...

File: /home/jonathan/Office51/xp3/Xpdefaults

Close
Connect...
Configure...
Remove...
Rename...
Test Page
Edit Font Attributes...
Add Fonts...
Store Settings Locally

2 Look for the name of your printer in the lower half of the window using the scroll box.

3 Click on the corresponding printer type and then on *Add new printer*.

In the upper half, the new printer driver is added with a blue background.

4 Click on *Connect*.

5 Click on *Generic Printer = lp-d Generic Printer*.

Replace the Generic Printer name with the one which you have assigned to your installed printer.

As the last step you still need to establish the recently configured printer as the default printer in StarOffice.

A **standard printer** is the printer which the system automatically selects for printing among several available printers. However, this setting can be avoided by instructing the system to use another printer.

6 Mark the newly configured printer and then click on the *Default printer* button.

7 Click on the *Close* button in order to complete printer configuration.

Problems with files/directories

Problems with reading files/directories

Try as a normal user to read, change or delete a file or directory of another user.

You are given the following error message: **You have no reading rights for the file**. You should now check two things:

┅► Does the corresponding file or directory belong to you, or do you have any rights to it?

┅► Check the same for the primary directory in which the file or directory in question is located.

1 Open the file manager and look for the file or directory.

2 Open the context menu and select *Properties*.

You should check in the *Permissions* tab whether you are the *Owner* of the file or directory, or whether the *Group* or *Others* also have read and writing rights.

In this example, the current user is *doo*, but the owner is Jonathan – and *doo* has no rights either as a group member or as *Others*.

If you are not the owner and you do not even have the rights mentioned as a group member or as *Others*, then you must ask the owner to give you the corresponding file rights. Alternatively, you can change the rights as a *root* user. To do so, register as *root* and make the corresponding settings.

Problems in finding files/directories

You can look for a specific file or directory with the *Looking for files* option in the main menu. As a result, you only receive the **File not found** report, although you are sure that the file exists. Check the type of file: Linux **always** distinguishes between lower and upper case letters!

Problems in reading a floppy disk or CD-ROM

Problems in mounting the floppy disk or the CD-ROM

You would like to look at the contents of a floppy disk using the *Floppy Disk* icon you have created on the desktop using the KDE Configuration Wizard.

This error message appears:

This error message can have three causes:

- There is no disk in the floppy disk drive.
- The floppy disk is not formatted in Linux and cannot be read.
- As normal user, you do not have the right to mount the floppy disk.

The second point is explained in the following, 'Problems with DOS floppy disks'. As a rule, Linux can read disks formatted in DOS in the KDE.

You should therefore check the first fault possibility immediately. You should also check that there is a disk inserted. Then check whether you may put a disk in the file tree (the mounting) as a normal user or not.

1 Open the file manager and go into the */etc* directory.

2 Open the *fstab* file.

Read the */dev/fdo /mnt/floppy* entry. Does the *defaults* term follow this? This is not always correct as a normal user does not always have the rights to mount a floppy disk.

```
/etc/fstab
File    Edit    Options    Help

/dev/hda3 / ext2 defaults  1  1
devpts /dev/pts devpts gid=5,mode=620 0 0
/proc /proc proc defaults 0 0
/dev/fd0 /mnt/floppy auto defaults,user,noauto 0 0
/dev/hdc /mnt/cdrom iso9660 ro,user,noauto 0 0

                                          INS  Line: 1 Col: 1
```

3 Click on *Close*.

As a normal user, you should not change the file. You must therefore cancel the KDE and register again as the *root* super user.

1 Now open the *Kedit* editor window.

2 Then, open the */etc/fstab* file.

```
/etc/fstab                                                    _ □ ×
File   Edit   Options   Help
 ▯ ☞ ▯   ▯ ▯ ✂   ▯ ▯   ?
/dev/hda3 / ext2 defaults  1  1
devpts /dev/pts devpts gid=5,mode=620 0 0
/proc /proc proc defaults 0 0
/dev/fd0 /mnt/floppy auto user,user,noauto 0 0
/dev/hdc /mnt/cdrom iso9660 ro,user,noauto 0 0



                                          INS  Line: 5 Col: 47
```

3 Change the *dev/fdo* line as follows:
replace the word *defaults* with *user*
behind the */mnt/floppy* entry.

In this way, the normal user is also allowed to mount floppy disks.

> If you have the same problem with CD-ROMs, you should also check the
> entry for the CD-ROM mounting. In this case the */dev/hdd* line is used for
> this purpose. If you are not allowed to read a CD-ROM as a normal user,
> you should then amend the line for the CD-ROM entry in the same way as
> for the floppy disk.

4 Save and close the
modified file.

If you register as a normal user again, you should be able to mount the
floppy disk.

Problems with DOS floppy disks

Linux has a different file system from DOS. Therefore, Linux cannot
usually read any DOS formatted floppy disks and vice versa. However,
there are help tools in Linux: the **mtools**. With these, DOS commands can
be executed in Linux, simply by placing the letter *m* before the
corresponding DOS command. The commands are entered in a terminal
window.

Here are some **mtools** commands and their meanings:

Command	Meaning
mcopy * a:	Copying everything from the current list on the DOS floppy disk
mformat a:	Initialising a floppy disk with the DOS file system
mdir a:	Listing the contents of the DOS floppy disk
mdel a:*.txt	Deleting all files with the *.txt* extension on the DOS floppy disk

Problems shutting down

You are registered as a normal user and would like to shut down the system in order to end working with the Linux computer.

You wish to use the *reboot, halt* or *shutdown* command in a terminal window. You are given the 'Command not found' report. This means that only *root* is authorised to execute this command for security reasons. Now you can sign off from KDE and re-register as *root*, and then shut down the system. However, this is far too time-consuming.

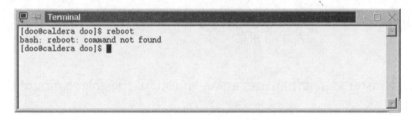

As the *root*, you need only grant all users the right to shut down the system once. Open the KDE Control Centre on the program bar.

Open the *Applications* sub-folder by clicking on the plus symbol, then click on the *Login Manager* function. Go to the *Sessions* tab and change the *Allow to shutdown* option to *All*.

In future, sign off as a normal user on the *Sign off* symbol in the program bar. You are now in the login window, where you can click on the *Finish* button. Select the *Finish* option and press on *OK*. In this way you can shut down the system as normal user.

Alternatively, you can register as super user within your normal session for a short time. Enter the *su-* command in a terminal window. The system asks you to enter and confirm the super user password. Now, as super user, you can execute the *shutdown*, *reboot* or *halt* command.

533

A brief history of Linux

Despite common opinion, Linux is not the same as UNIX. It is merely an operating system similar to UNIX.

The first UNIX system was developed in 1969 by an employee of the AT&T company. In 1973, it was transcribed into the C programming language so it could be used on different computer hardware. Until then, operating systems were only developed by manufacturers for specific hardware.

As UNIX was distributed to third parties at a low cost, including its complete program code, academic facilities soon began to show interest, including Berkeley University in California. As many large hardware manufacturers also showed interest, there were many variations on the market before long, such as Solaris by Sun Microsystems, HP/UX by Hewlett-Packard, AIX of IBM, etc.

Unfortunately the different versions were not very compatible, meaning that the system administrators constantly had to adapt them. Due to its lack of uniformity, the market interest in UNIX was not as common amongst smaller firms as in Microsoft Windows, for instance, which only came onto the market at the end of the 1980s.

In 1996, the 'Open Group' association finally succeeded in defining standards for UNIX through marketing and uniform development, after which acceptance became more widespread.

At the beginning of the 1990s, a Finnish student named Linus Torvalds developed the Linux operating system. But, instead of using the licensed UNIX program codes, he programmed the new operating system in form and function. He also published the source code on the internet. Anyone interested can therefore acquire Linux free of charge, and even carry on developing it.

A couple of years before the appearance of Linux, a project arose with the aim of creating a licence-free operating system similar to UNIX. It was called GNU ('GNU is not UNIX'). The basic idea is the development and distribution of free software that can be altered in order to guarantee the freedom of the user. Before Linux, there were already many free software tools, such as the X-Window graphic system, editors such as Emacs and the C compiler and so on. The Linux kernel developed by Linus Torvalds therefore completed the GNU project very well.

Perhaps you wonder why Linux is available free of charge, whereas in certain stores Linux software packages cost between £20 and £40. In these cases you are not paying for the Linux operating system but for additional tools, such as the CD-ROMs and the manuals provided by the manufacturer. And compared with the prices of other operating systems, the initial costs are very low. You can also download Linux without a manual from the internet, allthough this can be fairly time-consuming.

In case of problems, you can consult the manufacturer from whom you purchased the product. There are also many Linux internet sites aimed at troubleshooting. The Newsgroups are highly recommended, where problems can be discussed and solved by e-mail. As a Linux user, you will never be left completely in the dark...

Hardware recommendations

You will probably have heard that Linux does not require a high hardware specification. This statement is fundamentally correct, but it refers to the original Linux system without graphic interface such as the KDE. Graphic applications always require more memory.

The Linux operating system without KDE will therefore easily run on an old computer with a 80386s or 80486s processor. An 8 or 16 MB main memory would be sufficient. At least 300 MB of hard drive space is required. A floppy disk and CD-ROM drive are also required.

Of course you could always play around with Linux on an old clapped-out computer. However, you will have little joy with the graphic interface if you use such a computer as a basis for your Linux system. You will then have to adjust to long waiting periods when working with the KDE. This would not work in Microsoft Windows – a graphic system nowadays requires a fair amount of memory space.

Are you genuinely interested in working with the Linux operating system in future? Then use a modern computer. The minimum requirements are an INTEL compatible processor of at least 133 MHz, about 32-64 MB of main memory and a hard drive of at least 800 MB. You would be unable to install all Linux applications with a smaller hard drive.

It is essential that when purchasing a printer, you ensure it is Linux compatible. Unfortunately, some printers cannot be used with Linux, such as the special GDI or Windows printer. It is impossible, for example, to operate one of the cheap Lexmark ink-jet printers in Linux. You can find information on Linux-compatible GDI printers on the internet at *http://www.httptech.com/ppa.*

The following printers should all be compatible with Caldera OpenLinux:

Apple Dot Matrix Printer

Apple Image Writer hi-res

Apple Image Writer low-res

Apple Image Writer LQ

Brother HL-660

Brother HL-760

Canon Bubble Jet BJ10e

Canon Bubble Jet BJ20

Canon Bubble Jet BJC-70 (B/W only)

Canon Bubble Jet BJ200

Canon Bubble Jet BJC-210 (B/W only)

Canon Bubble Jet BJC-240 (B/W only)

Canon Bubble Jet BJC-250 (B/W only)

Canon Bubble Jet BJC-600

Canon Bubble Jet BJC-610 (360dpi only)

Canon Bubble Jet BJC-4000

Canon Bubble Jet BJC-4100 (B/W only)

Canon Bubble Jet BJC-4200

Canon Bubble Jet BJC-4300

Canon Bubble Jet BJC-4550

Canon Bubble Jet BJC-210 (Colour)

Canon Bubble Jet BJC-240 (Colour)

Canon Bubble Jet BJC-70 (Colour)

Canon Bubble Jet BJC-800

Canon Bubble Jet BJC-6999 (Colour)

Canon LPB-8II

DEC LA 50

DEC LA 70

DEC LA 75

DEC LA 75 plus

DEC LJ 250

DEC LN 03

Epson Stylus 800

Epson Stylus Colour

Epson Stylus Colour II

Epson Stylus Colour 400

Epson Stylus Colour 600

Epson Stylus Colour 800

Epson compatible (9-pin)

Epson compatible (9-pin) high quality

Epson compatible (9-pin) average quality

HP Deskjet

HP Deskjet Plus

HP Deskjet 500

HP Deskjet Portable

HP Deskjet 400 (with exchengeable cartridge for colour print)

HP Deskjet 500C

HP Deskjet 500C (3 bit/pixel)

HP Deskjet 500C (B/W only)

HP Deskjet 510 (B/W only)

HP Deskjet 520 (B/W only)

HP Deskjet 540C (B/W only)

HP Deskjet 693C (B/W only)

HP Deskjet 540C

HP Deskjet 550C

HP Deskjet 560C

HP Deskjet 600 (B/W or 32 bit/pixel)

HP Deskjet 660C

HP Deskjet 670C

HP Deskjet 672C

HP Deskjet 680C

HP Deskjet 682C

HP Deskjet 683C

HP Deskjet 690C

HP Deskjet 693C

HP Deskjet 694C

HP Deskjet 850C

HP Deskjet 855C

HP Deskjet 850

HP Deskjet 855

HP Deskjet 890

HP Deskjet 1100C

HP Deskjet 1200C

HP Deskjet 1600C

HP DesignJet 650c

HP LaserJet 2p / 2d

HP LaserJet 3

HP LaserJet 3p

HP LaserJet 3si

HP LaserJet 3d

HP LaserJet Plus

HP LaserJet 5

HP LaserJet 5L

HP LaserJet 6L

HP 2536B line printer

HP PaintJet (alternate)

HP PaintJet

HP PaintJet XL

HP PaintJet XL 300

IBM Pro compatible (9-pin)

IBM 3852 Jet Printer

ImPress Images

Lexmark Optra E+

Mitsubishi CP 50 (Colour)

NEC SuperScript 860

OCE 9050

Oki OL410ex LED printer E+

OkiPage ew/ew+ LED printer

Ricoh 4081 Laser printer

Ricoh 6000 Laser printer

StarJet SJ 48 printer

It may also be possible to use another printer without problems, though this cannot be guaranteed.

Useful Linux internet sites

Usergroups and links

German Linux Usergroup and information   http://www.linux.com

Links grouped according to category	http://www.linuxstart.com
Links grouped according to category	http://www.webwatcher.org
American Usergroup and Information	http://www.linux.org
Links grouped according to category	http://www.linux.com
Links grouped according to category	http://www.linuxlinks.com

Linux distributors

Caldera OpenLinux	http://www.caldera.com
RedHat	http://www.redhat.com
Slackware	http://www.slackware.com
Debian, Germany	http://www.debian.de
MkLinux (Apple Linux)	http://www.mklinux.com

Application and free software

K Desktop Environment	http://www.kde.org
Linux applications	http://www.linuxnow.com/library.shtml
Tools, programming languages etc. for Linux	http://www.freshmeat.net
Tools for Linux developers	http://www.linuxprogramming.com
Links to applications	http://www.free-soft.org
StarOffice by Sun Micro-systems	http://www.sun.com/dot-com/staroffice.html
GNU-Project	http://www.fsf.org
Information for the Gimp graphic program	http://www.gimp.org
Linux games	http://www.linuxgames.com

Support and information

Linux resource on the Web	http://www.linuxresources.com
List of companies offering commercial support	http://linux-biz.com

Search engine and information	http://www.searchlinux.com
American magazine	http://www.linuxworld.com
American magazine	http://www.linuxgazette.com

Hardware information

Search engine for hardware information	http://www.linuxhardware.net
XFee86-Project (development of the X-Window-Systems)	http://www.xfree86.org
Linux kernel downloads	http://www.kernelnotes.org

A

Access right

These decide which users may read, change or delete files.

Account (or user account)

Entitlement to log on to a computer. It describes the user data (usernames and password) and the field of work assigned to the user on a hard drive.

Application (or application program)

A program used for working on the computer, such as StarWriter, StarCalc, Editor, etc.

Archive

A file archive (or archive file) usually includes several other files. These files are generally summarised for use with data backup or data transfer.

B

Backup (or data backup)

Files and directories are copied on another data carrier (such as a floppy disk or tape) and can be backed up again if the original is damaged or deleted.

Bit

The smallest unit of information possible, referring to the memory capacity of a PC. It has either a value of 0 or 1.

Boot

Booting the system means switching the computer on and starting the operating system.

Browser (or internet browser)

A browser such as Netscape Communicator is used to display the contents of web pages on the internet.

Byte

A byte is a unit for calculating memory capacity. A byte consists of 8 bits.

C

Chat

A chat is a 'written conversation' held between two or more people using specific programs on the internet.

Command line (or prompt)

A user can type a Linux command here. The system then executes this command once and confirms it with the *Return* button.

Context menu

A menu usually opened by the right mouse button. It offers support and detailed functions to the object located under the mouse pointer.

CPU (or processor or central processing unit)

The CPU is the main item of the computer. It controls all input-output and arithmetic processes of the PC. The CPU processes the programs which are in the working memory.

Cursor

The cursor describes the position on the screen where the user can enter data. It can assume different forms: a vertical line, an arrow, a hand, etc.

D

Data base

A data base is a collection of equal-type data helped by a special program which supports data management, memory and query of data.

Data carrier

A means of saving data, such as a floppy disk, hard drive or CD-ROM.

Demon (or daemon or system process)

A demon processes specific tasks in the operating system, such as supervising the print service.

Directory

A directory combines files. A user can organise structured files using directories and sub-directories so as to be able to find them more quickly at a later date.

Distribution

Linux is developed worldwide. The different programs are summarised and sold on CD-ROMs by companies such as Caldera. Such a composition is described as distribution.

Download

The downloading of files from the internet on the same computer using a modem or ISDN connection.

E

Editor

A program for creating and editing simple texts.

E-mail (or electronic mail)

News sent via electronic paths.

Ext2fs

The file system usually used by the Linux operating system (see file system).

F

File

A file is a collection of data, such as a report or a drawing.

File system

This regulates the physical memory of data on the data carrier, which means how, where and what is saved on the hard drive.

Floppy disk

Floppy disks can save small amounts of data.

Font

Another name for script. Every font has its own appearance.

Popular scripts are Arial or Times New Roman, for example.

Freeware

Software available free of charge.

FTP (or file transfer protocol)

A protocol used for the transfer of files between several computers connected to each other in a network.

G

GB (or gigabyte)

A name used for calculating memory capacity. A GB corresponds to 1024 MB. 1 MB corresponds to one million bytes. The capacity of hard drives is indicated in GB nowadays.

Graphics card

The interface between computer and monitor. The PC controls the monitor via the graphics card.

H

Hard drive

A data carrier permanently installed in the PC. All programs and data of the system and user are saved on a hard drive. It is loaded into the working memory in order to execute a program.

Hardware

All component parts of a computer, such as the processor, hard drive or printer.

Homepage

The main site of internet entry of a person or enterprise, containing hyperlinks to further websites.

HTML (or Hypertext Markup Language)

The page description language used as the format for documents in the World Wide Web. The language defines how texts and graphics of a website are displayed.

Hyperlink

A cross-reference in a document from which another document can be called.

I

Installation

The setting-up of an operating system or application program on a computer.

Internet

A worldwide network of computers that offers many free information sites (websites).

K

Kbyte (or kilobyte)

A name for calculating memory capacity. 1 KB corresponds to 1024 bytes.

KDE (or kwm)

One of the graphic user interfaces used in Linux. The KDE makes working with the operating system easier using windows and menus.

L

Linux

A multi-user, multi-task capable operating system which also has extensive network functions. Linux is developed worldwide and sold for a token price.

M

Mailbox

Name for the electronic mailbox containing e-mails.

MB

A name for calculating storage capacity. 1 MB corresponds to 1024 KB. The capacity of the working memory is indicated in MB.

Modem

A device with which data can be transferred from one computer through a telephone line (for example, data from or to other computers on the internet).

Mounting

The input of data carriers (for example hard drives, diskettes or CD-ROMs) in the Linux file tree. A mounted device can be quired about a directory name.

MS DOS

An older operating system developed by Microsoft, formerly quite common on a PC.

MS Windows

The graphic user interface for the DOS operating system, developed by Microsoft.

Multi-user mode

Efficient computer systems are displayed from the start so that several users can work (perhaps on a network) at the same time.

N

Network

A connection between several computers in order to facilitate data interchange.

Newsgroups

Discussion forums on the internet organised according to category.

O

Online service

A company such as Force 9 or AOL which enables internet access to users.

Operating system

The operating system is the interface between the hardware and the user. It translates and carries the user commands (such as the print file) to the system (such as the printer).

Output devices

Parts of the computer which distribute data for the user in any form, such as the monitor or printer.

P

Partitioning

The division of a hard drive into different areas in order to enable the installation of various operating systems.

Password

The password a user must enter when logging on to identify himself.

Path

The path consists of all directory names which indicate the memory location of a file (for example */home/otto/bericht.txt*).

Peripheral (device)

Hardware component outside the computer, such as the printer or modem, etc.

Print queue

A print job sent to the printer is placed in a print queue. From here the print jobs are passed on to the printer in a specific order.

Processor

See CPU.

Prompt (character)

A character in a terminal window which displays whether the system is ready to operate. Commands can only be entered in the terminal level after a prompt. The most common prompt character for normal users in Linux is the $ (dollar) character, and the # (gate) sign for the super user.

R

RAM

See working memory.

Restart (reboot)

On restarting, a computer is shut down properly and then restarted.

Root (or super user)

The user of a Linux system with access rights to everything. They create, change and delete files in any place in the system.

S

Screen saver

A program which prevents screen contents from being left visible on-screen when the system is unattended

Server

The (or one of the several) host computer(s) in a network offering services to other computers (called clients), such as storage, printer or internet access.

Shareware

Software passed on free of charge. If the software meets with the user's approval and they continue to use it, they are then to obliged to pay the authormorally a small fee.

Shell (or command interpreter)

The shell contains a set of commands with which the user can give instructions to the operating system. The commands must be entered with a prompt.

Shutdown

The stopping of all operating system processes, in order to be able to turn off the computer safely.

Software

A primary concept for all kinds of program. Operating systems, and system and application programs, are part of it.

Spreadsheet analysis

A program with which calculations are carried out in tabular form.

U

UNIX

A multi-user, multi-task capable operating system which also has extensive network functions. It acted as a blueprint for Linux.

URL (or uniform resource locator)

Name for the address of a website or a computer on the internet.

User interface

This offers the user graphic support when working with a system. Instead of the direct command entry, the user can start programs using buttons and menus.

V

VGA (Virtual Graphic Adapter)

Name for a graphics standard containing 16 colours and 640 x 480 microdots. Today's standard Super VGA is a further development and essentially uses more colours and microdots.

Viruses

Programs that develop by attaching themselves to other programs. They often cause great damage to computers as they can change and destroy data.

W

Website

A name for documents in HTML format which display information on the internet.

Window

Component of the graphic interface which is usually strung together with the execution of a program. For example, the editor displays text in its window.

Word processing

A program for creating and editing simple and complex texts, such as letters, books, etc.

Working memory (or RAM or main memory)

Every PC needs a working memory to read and execute the hard drive programs. The memory size is indicated in MB.

WWW (World Wide Web)

The service on the internet mostly used by companies and individuals. The WWW contains websites of businesses, organisations and people.

X

X Window Manager

This offers a choice between the different graphic interfaces in Linux, such as *fwm*, *olwm*, *kwm* and so on.

It also provides sets of menus, desktops and graphic operating items. There are various X Window managers which differ in appearance and function. KDE is a very popular X Window Manager.

X Window System

A standard for how programs can control and change the contents and display of your window.

561